Becoming a Music Teacher

Becoming
a Music Teacher
From Student to Practitioner

Donald L. Hamann and Shelly C. Cooper

OXFORD
UNIVERSITY PRESS

OXFORD

UNIVERSITY PRESS

Oxford University Press is a department of the University of
Oxford. It furthers the University's objective of excellence in research,
scholarship, and education by publishing worldwide.

Oxford   New York
Auckland   Cape Town   Dar es Salaam   Hong Kong   Karachi
Kuala Lumpur   Madrid   Melbourne   Mexico City   Nairobi
New Delhi   Shanghai   Taipei   Toronto

With offices in
Argentina   Austria   Brazil   Chile   Czech Republic   France   Greece
Guatemala   Hungary   Italy   Japan   Poland   Portugal   Singapore
South Korea   Switzerland   Thailand   Turkey   Ukraine   Vietnam

Oxford is a registered trademark of Oxford University Press
in the UK and certain other countries.

Published in the United States of America by
Oxford University Press
198 Madison Avenue, New York, NY 10016

Library of Congress Cataloging-in-Publication Data
Hamann, Donald L.
Becoming a music teacher: from student to practitioner / Donald L. Hamann and Shelly C. Cooper.
   pages cm
Includes bibliographical references and index.
ISBN 978-0-19-024507-8 (hardcover: alk. paper)—ISBN 978-0-19-024508-5 (pbk.: alk. paper)
1. Music teachers-Training of.   2. Music-Instruction and study.   I. Cooper, Shelly.   II. Title.
MT1.H1358 2016
780.71—dc23
2015014194

CONTENTS

WHAT'S IN THIS BOOK?

Using a topic-centered approach, *Becoming a Music Teacher: From Student to Practitioner* focuses on developing personal teaching awareness skills, personal musicianship skills, pre-conducting skills, and professional knowledge. *Becoming a Music Teacher* distinguishes itself by its highly interactive and personal student-development approach, and it is the only introductory music education text based on a flexible delivery model.

HOW IS THIS BOOK ORGANIZED?

Each of the book's 40 modules contains four components: personal awareness, personal musicianship, pre-conducting, and professional knowledge. Music professors may use all materials, they may pick and choose modules, and/or they may select components from various modules to create a personalized and stylized Introduction to Music Education curriculum. The flexible delivery model meets the needs of colleges and universities with various class sizes and class sessions within a structurally sequenced foundation for effective instructional delivery.

The rationale for the 40 modules was conceptualized based on a 16-week semester system, with three class meetings, of 45 to 50 minutes each, per week. Should you have fewer class meetings, you are encouraged to choose those modules and/or particular components that best address your students' needs. Following a topic-centered approach, this text can be used for classes with smaller enrollments while still accommodating typical class sizes at larger universities. However you use this book, your students will benefit from the content.

WHY SHOULD I READ AND USE THIS BOOK?

Introduction to Music Education is one of the first classes that music education students complete during their journey from student to practitioner. During an introductory course, students begin developing the necessary skills to become effective, dynamic classroom music teachers and immerse themselves in the craft of teaching. Yet, students often complain that the learning content in an Introduction to Music Education class is too far removed from the "real classroom," is not practical, or is too theoretical in nature. *Becoming a Music Teacher* has been designed to be an interactive, hands-on text, focused on developing individual skills—skills that all music educators need to function effectively in today's music classrooms.

Becoming a Music Teacher focuses on making direct connections between the college classroom and the school classroom transparent, visible, and relevant. If students view the classroom as disconnected (not "real life"), they cannot visualize how the transfer of knowledge and activities in the college classroom manifests itself in the public school classroom. *Becoming a Music Teacher,* through the in-class activities within the various components, demonstrates "real life" transfers. As prospective teachers, all students need to develop body-awareness skills, conducting skills, and singing skills. No other Introduction to Music Education text includes student self-development skills in the areas of body awareness, public-speaking refinement, pre-conducting exercises, and personal-musicianship acquisition. Rather than simply presenting materials in a discourse fashion, *Becoming a Music Teacher* directly engages students through hands-on self-development awareness, conducting, singing activities, and vocal exercises. Component activities focus on developing effective classroom delivery, classroom and self/teacher-awareness skills, conducting techniques, singing aids, music-reading fluency, solfège training, and creating vocal and/or instrumental accompaniments. *Becoming a Music Teacher* guides students to become professional music teachers, taking them from individual discovery to discovering their ability to be classroom leaders.

HOW CAN I USE THIS BOOK?

The book can be used as a stand-alone text for an Introduction to Music Education course or can serve as a supplementary source for an introductory course or other courses that focus on music-teacher skill development. However the book is used, students will benefit from its content. It is unique in that each interactive module is devised to enhance individual skill sets while providing an overview of professional topics relevant to developing teachers. Designed according to the concept of student activity-based skill acquisition, *Becoming a Music Teacher* is intended to inspire young aspiring professionals and enhance their personal, musical, and professional skills in their journey toward becoming outstanding music teachers. The content of this text will serve as a springboard for students' educational foundation through their undergraduate years and professional preparation as they progress from music *students* to music *practitioners*.

In addition to using it as an Introduction to Music Education text, teachers of conducting and teachers of choral, band, string, elementary, and secondary methods will find this book—with its unique content—a welcome addition as a supplemental text. Containing an in-depth focus on self-development resources not found in other Introduction to Music Education texts, this book's versatility and distinctiveness greatly enlarge its applicability to any course designed to enhance music students' teacher-preparation skills.

ACKNOWLEDGMENTS

We would like to thank all of those individuals, too numerous to list, who have contributed to this book. We would especially like to thank Oxford University Press for their support of *Becoming a Music Teacher: From Student to Practitioner,* with very special thanks to Norman "Norm" Hirschy, OUP Senior editor, Academic and Trade. We would also like to thank Deepti Agarwal, Project manager at Newgen North America and Simon Benjamin, Production manager at OUP, Lisbeth Redfield, Assistant editor at OUP, and Wendy Keebler, copyeditor.

Becoming a Music Teacher

AN INTRODUCTION TO THE MODULES

In all 40 modules, four components are presented, the order of components is as follows:

1. Personal awareness
2. Personal musicianship
3. Pre-conducting
4. Professional knowledge

Each component addresses a particular aspect of teacher skill development. Each module can be completed within a 45- to 50-minute class period, with individual components lasting 10 to 15 minutes.

Components are successive, in that one component generally builds on skills learned in a previous component. The personal awareness, personal musicianship, and pre-conducting components directly involve students in hands-on, interactive activities through sequential exercises designed to develop the individual skills needed in the music classroom. The professional knowledge components are designed to provide overviews of topics and issues important to future music educators.

The personal awareness components begin by enhancing awareness of yourself and your body gestures. Building on this foundational awareness, each successive component introduces new exercises that enable you to expand your awareness from self to others. As future teachers and/or directors, you will be guided through awareness of skill elements within music settings (band, orchestra, choir, and general music) and will increase your success in detecting foundational issues for excellent musical performances. Finally, you will develop effective and lasting vocal-delivery skills that will inspire students in your classrooms and assist in clarifying and elucidating presentations in meetings and conferences with parents, colleagues, and administrators.

The personal musicianship components begin by helping you develop a system to (1) enhance your singing quality, (2) further your sight-singing skills, and (3) foster your accompaniment and voice-leading skills. As a musician, you need to continue developing and refining your singing skills in order to be a successful vocal model in the classroom, be able to sight-sing individual lines of a score, and use your voice correctly during everyday teaching activities. The personal musicianship components are designed to progressively and sequentially advance your current vocal production, sight-singing, and arranging levels.

All music educators, regardless of the age level they teach or their teaching situation (classrooms or ensembles), must be effective conductors. The pre-conducting components help you develop skills as you prepare to become a successful musical leader in the classroom. The pre-conducting components will assist you in developing the physical and mental skills needed to develop right and left arm and hand independence. From this foundational framework, you will continue to develop additional conducting skills to become a successful leader. You will be guided in various conducting patterns, cues on various beats, cutoffs on various beats, and so on, through a systematic and progressive approach.

The professional knowledge components present thought-provoking topics relevant to the aspiring successful music practitioner. Whether discussing legal and ethical and moral issues, the importance of collegiality, working with diverse learners, or the applicability of learning theories in the classroom, these components will help you understand the "real world" issues you will encounter as a professional practitioner.

The book contains 40 modules. Each interactive module is devised to enhance your individual skill sets while providing an overview of topics relevant to you as a developing teacher. The components are interactive. When you enhance awareness of yourself and your surroundings, you will become a better conductor; once you are a better conductor, you will become a stronger leader and potential teacher. When you refine your singing skills, you will be a stronger leader, able to model for your future students and sight-sing scores, whether choral or instrumental. When you understand and reflect on the issues you will encounter as a music practitioner, you will be a knowledgeable and beneficial member of the profession you are entering. The content of this text is intended to serve as a springboard for your next few years of study and professional preparation as you are *Becoming a Music Teacher* and progressing *From Student to Practitioner.*

Posture—Kodály—Conducting Posture and Rebound—Our Profession and Decision-Making

In this module, as in all future modules, there are four components, in order as follows:

1. Personal awareness
2. Personal musicianship
3. Pre-conducting
4. Professional knowledge

In this module, you will be introduced to:

- Personal awareness: The elevated posture, in which you will become more aware of your body stance and balance.
- Personal musicianship: Zoltán Kodály and his system of notation and hand signs.
- Pre-conducting: The conducting posture and the conducting rebound.
- Professional knowledge: How we define our profession and the use of decision-making in the classroom.

PERSONAL AWARENESS: BODY STANCE AND BALANCE

The message you send by the way you hold and carry yourself transmits a wealth of information to others. Strong, positive stance and posture convey a message that exudes confidence, self-assuredness, and leadership qualities. That stance is known as the *elevated posture.*

An elevated posture allows for a relaxed stance while communicating poise, confidence, and leadership. The exercises that follow will help you find your elevated posture.

Classroom Setup

To complete the following exercise, the classroom should be arranged to allow room between individuals. No particular chair configuration is necessary other than allowing adequate room. All class members can complete this exercise simultaneously.

Exercise

1. During this exercise, do not hold your breath at any point; breathe normally.
2. Stand and place your feet shoulders' width apart, making sure your feet are pointed forward.
3. Relax your shoulders, and make sure your knees are not locked.
4. Imagine you are being pulled up from the top of your head, perhaps by a string.
5. As you feel yourself being elevated, notice that your shoulders remain relaxed, your knees remain unlocked, and your body is balanced evenly over your feet, which remain shoulders' width apart.
6. Gently shift your weight from one leg to the other, and then return to your center. Move your weight forward and back, and then return to your center. You should begin to feel a core balance from which movement can be made without moving your feet.
7. Have one individual from the group walk around the room and gently nudge each person. As individuals are nudged, they may move forward, backward, or sideways, but you will notice that when they are centered in the elevated posture, the nudge will not move their feet.

Assignment

Practice using the elevated posture daily. Observe your posture in different situations, and if it's not elevated, make the needed adjustments.

Observation

Notice the posture of individuals around you, in the classroom, at rehearsals, and so forth. Do you receive different messages from individuals based on their posture?

PERSONAL MUSICIANSHIP: INTRODUCTION TO PERSONAL MUSICIANSHIP AND USING KODÁLY NOTATION

Zoltán Kodály (1882–1967) dedicated much of his career to preserving Hungarian folk songs and providing and refining strategies for teaching music literacy. True literacy in a language gives an individual the ability to read, write, and think in the language. Similarly, music literacy is the ability to read, write, and think in music. Kodály believed that singing and movement were inseparable; therefore, the use of hand signs provides a kinesthetic tool that assists in training the eye and ear with intervalic pitch relationships.

The personal musicianship components of this text provide you with opportunities to practice singing in traditional notation and stick notation. All music examples are illustrated with both systems. Stick notation, commonly used with the Kodály method, does not use a traditional staff system but rather has all pitches placed on a single linear plane. See figures 1.1 and 1.2 for a comparison of the notation styles.

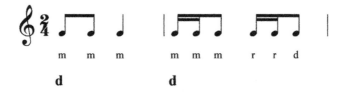

Figure 1.1 Stick notation.

Figure 1.2 Traditional notation.

Stick notation provides the pitch syllables—written in lower-case letters—and allows for practice with "movable *do*." As you proceed through the exercises in this book, both traditional and stick notations provide opportunities for adding vocal accompaniments, either single tone or triad. Traditional notation incorporates Roman numeral representation for chords, whereas stick notation provides the pitch syllable representing the tone or chord. The use of Roman numerals also offers practice opportunities to accompany with piano, guitar, ukulele, and so on.

Practice Skill

For this module, the focus is on the ability to outline and sing major triads with various pitches functioning as tonic. You will also practice the hand signs of *do, mi,* and *so.*

Practice the following steps for outlining the tonic on various pitches (suggested pitches for tonic: F, D, G, C, Eb). See figure 1.3 for a notated example.

1. Sing tonic or *do*
2. Outline the triad (d-m-s-m-d)
3. Sing tonic or *do*
4. Sing cadence (d-s,-d)

Figure 1.3 Outlining the tonic.

PRE-CONDUCTING: ELEVATED POSTURE
AND REBOUND

As music teachers and directors, we will all be conducting. Whether leading a class in song, a band or orchestra or choir in concert, or a group
of individuals in a sing-along, musicians are expected to lead people
"in song." While you may already have some conducting experience,
you will undoubtedly receive additional conducting training in formal
classes, experiential situations in which feedback is given, and other such
opportunities.

The purpose of these exercises is to prepare you for conducting experiences. These pre-conducting exercises are intended to help cultivate basic
movement skills, advance hand/arm independence, and provide further
coordination skills required in the art of conducting.

It should be noted that modifications of conducting techniques are not
unusual as you progress through your studies. As with the acquisition
of any skill, you should remain open to new ideas and approaches when
attempting to master a task. Certain approaches or techniques will resonate more with some than with others. As a student of the arts, your goal
is to determine which approaches work best for you.

Classroom Setup

All class members can complete this exercise simultaneously. Students
should stand and allow about one arm's length of space around them.

Exercise
Phase 1

The first phase of this exercise will establish a basic conducting posture.

1. Starting in an elevated standing posture, with your hands/arms resting naturally at your sides, raise your arms in front of you. Your elbows
   will be above your waist, and your upper arms and forearms form a
   45-degree angle. Your wrists become an extension of the forearms.
   Note that your right hand will be in front of your right thigh, and your
   left hand will be in front of your left thigh. The shoulders should remain
   relaxed.
2. Relax, and let your arms again fall naturally to your sides. Repeat the
   process above several times. Turn toward classmates on either side or

in back of you, and have them observe you completing the exercise and then provide comments on your posture, poise, and position.

3. Once all class members can perform this exercise with ease, move to the next phase.

Phase 2

The second phase of this exercise involves the rebound of the hand in conducting.

1. Having established your conducting posture and the resultant height of your hands/arms, imagine a horizontal line about one or two inches below your hands. The line represents the plane from which your pre-conducting beat will rebound, whether it occurs on beat one, two, three, or four.
2. While holding both hands one or two inches above your imagined horizontal line, drop your right hand and forearm (one or two inches) until your right hand contacts the horizontal line, at which point it will rebound upward to about the height of your chest but not higher than your chin. Note that during this movement, your shoulder and upper forearm will also move in sympathetic motion with your forearm and hand.
3. Once your right hand reaches chest height, but not higher than your chin, let both arms relax to your sides, and return to an elevated posture.
4. Repeat the exercise, beginning with the establishment of your conducting posture. It is often helpful if some independent practice or individual exploration time is provided during the session. However, when the class is ready, an instructor can signal the beginning steps of the exercise by saying:
   a. "Posture" (adopt the conducting pose).
   b. "Ready rebound" (drop your right hand and forearm one or two inches, and rebound upward until your right hand is at about the height of your chest but not higher than your chin).
   c. "Relax" (drop both arms to the sides).
5. The exercise should be repeated until all class members are performing it with ease using the right hand. Again, class members can check and assess other class members' performance.
6. The exercise should now be performed using the left hand, repeating the steps outlined above. The idea of using the left hand is to facilitate dexterity and independence in both hands (not to foster left-hand conducting devotees).

Assignment

Most likely, each individual will find that either the right or the left hand/ arm can perform the exercise more fluidly or with less concentration or effort than the other side. The goal is to be able to perform the task equally with either hand. Continue to perform this exercise until you reach that goal.

Observation

During your rehearsals and while observing other rehearsals, watch the rebound movements of various directors.

PROFESSIONAL KNOWLEDGE: THE MUSIC EDUCATION PROFESSION

For this component, the focus is to:

- Define *profession*.
- Discuss decision-making in the music classroom.

A profession is "a paid occupation, especially one that involves prolonged training and a formal qualification" (*New Oxford American Dictionary*). By definition, *profession* designates a paid position. It is important to consider that a profession also includes factors such as extensive education and preparation, responsibility for making decisions, commitment to the work, and an organization established to ensure the profession's advancement.

In preparation for moving along the continuum from personal musician to professional teacher, your coursework will include a variety of classes. Music classes typically include music theory, music history, applied lessons, ensembles, technique classes (learning various instruments), methods classes (learning how to teach others), voice class, piano class, and so on. Classes you will take outside of music typically include math, English, science, psychology, learning theories, child development, and others. It is definitely a given that your profession requires extensive education and training.

How do we ensure that music learning will occur in the classroom? A teacher standing in front of the class to deliver a lecture or conduct the ensemble does not guarantee the transfer of knowledge. You will be responsible for making decisions in your classroom that promote personal and music growth. When you select repertoire, what do you want your students to learn? What are the "teachable moments" within the music that justify its use in your classroom? Yes, music can be "fun," but to be included in your classroom, the music—at its core—must have "fun"-damental purposes for promoting student growth.

Let's use learning a song as an example. Can the students identify the musical form? How does the text enhance the melody or provide insight regarding a social setting? How will you encourage your students to engage in musician-like thinking—thinking that requires analysis and reflection? How will you incorporate creative thinking and personal decision-making?

Skills and *activities* are not synonymous. Skills are the physical activities, such as vibrato or instrument fingerings, while activities are those actions or engagements that promote learning, such as singing, playing, moving, and so on. Activities are not a substitute for subject matter content. A teacher's responsibility is to strike a balance that provides students opportunities to participate, understand, and value music.

Another factor of a profession is commitment to the work. This commitment involves promoting student learning and your personal growth. Teachers who continue to seek learning opportunities that enhance their personal musicianship and professional leadership find the greatest rewards within their vocation. Commitment also involves advocating for the profession. When we advocate for music education, we are educating others about its values and purposes.

Discussion

1. Whom do we need to educate about the importance of music education?
2. How can you ensure that an activity or an experience supports or transfers to music outcomes or goals?
3. How can you promote lifelong learning in music for the students in your classroom?
4. How will your friends and colleagues know that you are a professional?
5. What will be some of your guidelines for selecting repertoire?

Eye Contact—Sight-Singing Steps—Conducting Rebound and Hand/Arm Independence—School Community

In this module, you will focus on:

- Personal awareness: Establishing eye contact and developing awareness of proximity within various settings.
- Personal musicianship: Learning to establish steps to sight-singing a melody.
- Pre-conducting: Further developing rebound and additional right and left hand/arm independence skills.
- Professional knowledge: Becoming aware of your school community and the levels of involvement in which you will engage in the school community as a teacher.

PERSONAL AWARENESS: EYE TO EYE

Establishing eye contact and feeling comfortable with that contact are a valuable skill set for teachers to acquire. While other exercises in this book will help you become aware of establishing eye contact in a group situation, such as a classroom, this exercise will help develop comfort and awareness when establishing eye contact in close proximity.

While we all experience situations in which close proximity is required in communication, teachers in such situations must maintain a level of comfort to function at optimal levels. Edward T. Hall (1990), an anthropologist, defined four levels of proximity:

- *Intimate distance.* This is the distance (6 to 18 inches) that can generally be maintained with comfort between individuals who know each other. Intimate distance is often initiated when engaging in contact such as hugging, whispering, or touching.
- *Personal distance.* An interval of 1.5 to 4 feet is usually maintained between people for personal distance. Personal distance is often initiated among those who are family members or close friends.
- *Social distance.* Individuals who are acquaintances, such as coworkers, often use social distance, which is an interval of 4 to 12 feet, when communicating.
- *Public distance.* An interval of 12 to 25 feet denotes public distance. This distance is maintained in public-speaking situations such as talking in front of a large class or giving a presentation.

Individuals' comfort levels with various distances differ among cultures and individuals. People from different cultures or backgrounds may feel more comfortable standing closer to one another during interactions, while others need more distance.

Classroom Setup

You will be working in pairs. The classroom should be set up to accommodate this arrangement.

Exercise

This exercise will help you become aware of your comfort level when establishing eye contact and being in close proximity with another individual. With continued practice and exposure, you may begin to feel more at ease in these types of situations.

1. Pair off.
2. Using an elevated posture, stand face to face, and extend your arms so your fingertips touch each other's. You will most likely be at the outermost extremes of personal distance or even at the beginning of social distance interval.

3. Establish eye contact. Do not look away from your partner; maintain eye contact for 10 seconds. (Someone, most likely the instructor, will indicate when to begin the eye contact and then count out loud the number of seconds remaining.) It is important that no talking or laughing occurs during this process. Such actions mask the exercise's intent.

4. Once each set of partners has successfully completed this task, each pair should move half a step closer to each other. Where you were approximately 4 to 4.5 feet apart previously, you will now be about 2 feet apart. This interval is considered personal distance. You may feel less comfortable at this distance. Maintaining your elevated posture and silence, repeat the 10-second eye-contact exercise. Remember to breathe normally and stay relaxed and focused on your partner's eyes.

5. Finally, take another small step forward. You will now be extremely close to each other, almost touching. This is intimate distance. Repeat the 10-second eye-contact exercise.

At this juncture, you can discuss the comfort level felt by each individual. If desired, make a list of feelings imparted during the process. The idea of this exercise, however, is to begin to feel comfortable in any situation you may encounter, to feel comfortable with yourself in these situations, and to focus on the interaction rather than feelings of comfort or discomfort.

Assignment

Practice speaking to individuals at the various distances outlined above. How do people respond when conversing with you at various distances? Do they respond differently physically?

Observation

Note the distances people maintain in one-to-one conversations with you or with others. You will notice that distances vary among individuals. Some individuals feel very comfortable being close to another, while others like to maintain significantly greater distances.

PERSONAL MUSICIANSHIP: STEPS
TO SIGHT-SINGING A MELODY

For this component, the focus is to:

- Review the steps for outlining the tonic.
- Transfer those steps to sight-reading a song.
- Sing a melody with limited pitches (d-r-m).
- Add single-note accompaniments to a melody.

In the personal musicianship component of module 1, you practiced outlining the tonic. Notice how the steps for outlining the tonic form the foundation for the steps to sight-singing a melody. This process works for both vocal and instrumental sight-reading practice.

1. Sing tonic or *do.*
2. Outline the triad (d-m-s-m-d).
3. Sing tonic or *do.*
4. Sing cadence (d-s-d).
5. Determine what syllable the song begins with. (It is not always the tonic or *do.*)
6. Look for familiar patterns (scale-wise movement, triad outline, *so-do* cadence, repeated patterns).
7. Sing through "in your head" (auditation).
8. Sing tonic or *do.*
9. Perform using solfège.
10. In a group setting, divide the class into two sections, with half singing the melody and the other half singing the accompaniment; then switch roles.

Sing the melody "Closet Key," which is a song written in stick notation (figure 2.1). Once you have successful performed the melody, add the single-note accompaniment, which is notated with solfège syllables below the melody. Find a partner or a small group for performing the combined melody and single-note accompaniment.

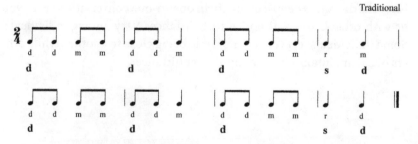

Figure 2.1 "Closet Key," stick notation.

PRE-CONDUCTING: INDEPENDENCE EXERCISE

In the pre-conducting component of module 1, conducting posture, hand/arm positioning, and the rebound were introduced. In this exercise, the rebound will continue to be practiced, along with the introduction of additional right and left hand/arm independence training.

Outstanding conductors appear to move seamlessly and effortlessly between right and left hand/arm movements and gestures. This ability is, for most individuals, a learned skill. The following exercise is one of many that will help you develop independence between right and left hand/arm movements.

Classrooom Setup

All class members can complete this exercise simultaneously. Students should stand and allow about one arm's length of space around them.

Exercise
Phase 1

1. Establish your conducting posture, remembering to maintain an elevated standing position. Your hands/arms should be slightly above your waist.
2. Having established your conducting posture and the resultant hand/arm height, complete one rebound with your right hand/arm, and return to your conducting position (both hands/arms should be slightly above your waist, and so forth). Check to make sure:
   a. Your hand dropped one or two inches from your conducting position.
   b. The hand rebounded to the height of the chest but not higher than the chin.
   c. Your shoulders remained relaxed.
3. After you have paused and evaluated the points above, complete the same procedure for a rebound with your left hand/arm.

Phase 2

1. Once all class members can perform the first phase of this exercise, making sure that both right and left rebounds are of equal quality, continue the exercise by removing the pause between right and left rebounds.

2. Using a tempo of about mm = 66 and commencing with the right hand/arm, begin this exercise when instructed. (See http://www.metronomeonline.com for a metronome that can be used and heard in a classroom situation.)

3. While some independent practice or individual exploration time may be provided at this point, it may also be helpful to perform this portion of the exercise as a group. When the class is ready, the instructor may indicate when to begin. Starting at a tempo of mm = 66, all students should begin by saying and performing the following:
   a. "Rebound" (the right hand/arm begins and completes the rebound movement during one beat at mm = 66).
   b. "Down" (the right hand/arm returns to the conducting position during one beat at mm = 66).
   c. "Rebound."
   d. "Down."
   e. Continue to perform the exercise until students complete this phase successfully.

Phase 3

1. Incorporate the return to the conducting position as part of the rebound. The rebound should be performed by alternating the right and left hands. It is suggested that a slower tempo be used when initiating this exercise (mm = 46). Follow this sequence:
   a. "Rebound" (the right hand begins and completes the rebound movement, moving into the conducting position during one beat at mm = 46).
   b. "Rebound" (the left hand begins and rebounds while the right hand remains in conduction position).
   c. "Rebound" (right hand).
   d. "Rebound" (left hand).
   e. And so forth. As one hand/arm completes a rebound, the other is preparing and begins its rebound movement.

2. Again, some independent practice or individual exploration time may be provided at the beginning of this exercise phase, but when members are ready, the class should perform the task as a unit. An instructor should indicate the tempo (mm = 46, initially) and begin the exercise. While students may say "Rebound," it may be easier for them not to do so at this point. This should be left to the individual's preference.

3. When performing this phase, be attentive to the following:

  a. The rebound begins as a drop from the conducting position without any movement upward prior to that drop.

  b. The drop is one or two inches and rebounds to chest height but not higher than the chin.

  c. The rebounding hand returns to the original conducting position.

  d. Maintain an elevated posture throughout the exercise.

  e. Have classmates help assess your progress, or check your own progress in a mirror.

4. As students improve, the tempo can be increased. You may notice that as the tempo increases, the height of the rebound may decrease. Even though the rebound height may decrease, it should still be approximately at the level of the chest and below the chin.

Assignment

Most likely, individuals will find during any of these exercise phases that either their right or left hand/arm can perform the exercise more fluidly or with less concentration or effort than the other side. With practice, this difference will diminish. It is also important that you do not exceed a tempo at which you can successfully perform each exercise phase. Slow and careful practice will allow your body and mind to develop the independence and muscle memory required in this exercise.

Observation

During your rehearsals and in observing other rehearsals, watch the various ways directors use their right and left hands.

PROFESSIONAL KNOWLEDGE: PROFESSIONAL EDUCATOR—CANINE OR FELINE: YOU AND YOUR SCHOOL COMMUNITY

For this component, the focus is to:

- Identify the members of your school community.
- Discuss levels of involvement.

As the footsteps approach the front door, there is a mad scramble inside the house. The door swings open, and the family dog leaps joyously and excitedly toward you, happy to have you home again. Dogs are loyal and social—one call from you, any time of day, and they are ready to go. Cats, on the other hand, tend to be more aloof. Yes, they love to luxuriate in your attention, but it is often on their own terms. They come to you when it suits them and are not as dependable to come when called.

Now, you are surely thinking of all the exceptions to the rule regarding the behaviors of cats and dogs, but putting that aside, let's consider you and your future school community. Your school community has many different levels—the students, the teachers in your building, the music teachers in the district, and so on. Each level has different needs and expectations for you to meet. Will you always be available for assistance? Will you seek out friendly conversations? Offer to help at school events? Or will you be like the cats described above and only seek out the members in your community when you need something or when it suits your agenda?

What does it mean to be part of the community? "At the heart of a high-community school is an inclusive web of respectful, supportive relationships among and between students, teachers and parents. We learn best from, and with, those to whom we relate well" (Schaps, 2008). This inclusive web, in order to remain intact, needs the support of all involved.

It is important to remember that your school community extends far beyond the walls of your classroom and even beyond the school campus. Parents and community members play an important role, and, as stakeholders, they need to be included in communications and activities. T. J. Sergiovanni, author of *Building Community in Schools*, reminds readers that "we become connected for reason of commitment rather than compliance" (1999, p. 58). He urges readers to remember that strong relationships build community. Students are more likely to be academically motivated when they attend schools that they perceive to have a "strong sense of community" (Solomon, Battistich, Watson, Schaps, & Lewis, 2000).

The need for community is a universal phenomenon. "Community is the tie that binds students and teachers together in special ways, to something more significant than themselves: shared values and ideals. It lifts both teachers and students to higher levels of self-understanding, commitment, and performance—beyond the reaches of the shortcomings and difficulties they face in their everyday lives." Community can provide teachers and students with a "unique and enduring sense of identity, belonging, and place" (Sergiovanni, 1999, p. xiii).

Schools are social settings. Collegiality originates from mutual respect, interests, and a passion for teaching, not from being structured, organized, or forced. It is up to you to want—and seek out—cooperative relationships with your colleagues. When future colleagues are asked to evaluate your sense of collegiality, how will they respond?

Discussion

1. Think of the high school you attended. Do you feel there was a strong sense of community among the staff? Why or why not?
2. How can we build strong school communities?
3. Describe a time when you felt disconnected from a community.

MODULE 2 REFERENCES

Hall, Edward T. (1990). *The hidden dimension*. New York: Anchor.

Schaps, E. (2008). Creating caring school communities. http://www.acsa.org/FunctionalMenuCategories/AboutACSA/CommitteesGroups/EAD-for-Success/Creating-caring.aspx

Sergiovanni, T. J. (1999). *Building community in schools*. San Francisco, CA: Jossey-Bass.

Solomon, D., Battistich, V., Watson, M., Schaps, E., & Lewis, C. (2000). A six-district study of educational change: Direct and mediated effects of the Child Development Project. *Social Psychology of Education*, 4(1), 3–51.

Establishing Carriage—Rhythmic Duration Syllable Systems—Hand/ Arm Independence—Classroom Word Choice

I n this module, you will focus on:

- Personal awareness: The establishment of appropriate carriage and gait.
- Personal musicianship: Rhythmic duration syllable systems.
- Pre-conducting: Further development of hand/arm independence skills.
- Professional knowledge: The development of word choices and the promotion of constructive class discussions.

PERSONAL AWARENESS: WALK THE WALK

Have you ever noticed how some individuals capture your attention, respect, and interest when they walk into a room? There is just something about the way they carry themselves and the way they enter. You sense that they are in control and are leaders, yet they haven't said a word.

As a teacher, regardless of the length of time you've been teaching, that initial entrance into a classroom is often frightening. We want to exude confidence, poise, and security to convey leadership, experience, and knowledge. We want students to know we feel comfortable in our roles as teachers, leaders, and directors. The initial entrance can set the tone for a class for the remainder of the year.

Great teachers walk the walk. They are confident in what they do and what they have to offer, and this is conveyed immediately with their entrance. However, such an entrance does not necessarily come naturally, and for many it is a practiced skill.

Classroom Setup

The classroom should be cleared of as many desks and chairs as possible to create an open space in which class members can walk freely and in a straight line. Desks and chairs should be moved to the side or the back of the room to make such a space available.

Practice the exercise first in groups of not more than 10 individuals. Depending on the size of the class, all members can practice the exercise simultaneously, or you can divide into appropriate-size groups. Once you've practiced as a group, have individuals practice in front of the class until all have had a chance to do so. Positive and corrective instructor feedback will help establish a healthy protocol which all should be encouraged to follow.

Exercise

This is an exercise in walking the walk. It details the steps needed to help you create and practice your own leadership entrance into a room.

1. Begin by establishing an elevated posture.
2. Once you have an elevated posture, lean slightly forward to the point where you must then take a step. Maintain your elevated posture.
3. As you begin your walk, let your arms move or swing naturally so that your right foot moves forward as your left arm naturally follows, and vice versa. (Often, when we are nervous, we lock our arms or seem to forget how to move our legs and arms in a natural motion.)
4. Imagine that your class is to your left. You will be turning toward the class at the end of your walk.
5. Establish your ending point, the place where you will end your walk. That point should be within the parameters of the group. You should be close enough to the group that you can easily see everyone in the class but not so far away as to distance yourself from them. (Remember, you are a member of this class, albeit the leader.) Upon reaching your ending point, turn purposefully toward the class. Do not turn too quickly, as if you were marching and doing a turn, but rather turn slowly and purposefully. Maintain an elevated posture.

6. Stand and scan the entire class for two or three seconds. Make brief eye contact with members of the class.
7. Now introduce yourself. "Hello, I am Mr./Mrs./Ms. X. I will be your teacher/director." For this exercise, focus on speaking loudly enough for all to easily hear you and slow enough to be understood. We will talk more about vocal inflection, speech rate, articulation, and so on, in future exercises.
8. Again, positive and corrective instructor feedback will help establish a healthy feedback protocol, which all should follow when they are asked to comment.

Assignment

Practice using the "walk the walk" exercise upon entering classrooms and rehearsals. How do you feel when you are aware of your walking?

Observation

Observe others as they enter a room or a rehearsal. What do they transmit by the way they walk?

PERSONAL MUSICIANSHIP: RHYTHM DURATION SYLLABLES

For this component, the focus is to:

- Review the "Steps to Sight-Reading a Song."
- Practice reading rhythms using a preferred rhythm system.
- Sing a melody with limited pitches (d-r-m) in standard notation.
- Add single-note accompaniments to a melody using Roman numerals.

There are various rhythm systems associated with music (see figure 3.1). The number system is designed to designate duration of note values and how they function within the meter. A commonality among all systems is that they are usually referred to as rhythm duration syllables, meaning syllables that represent the duration of a note. When you speak "ta" or "du," the one-syllable text matches the duration of a quarter note. When speaking the word "quarter," one hears two syllables, yet there is only one sound heard in performing.

ta	ti	ti	tick - a	tick - a	ta
1	2	&	3	e & a	4
Du	Du	De	Du Ta De Ta		Du

Figure 3.1 Sample rhythm systems.

You will again be singing the song "Closet Key," but this time, the example is written with standard notation (figure 3.2). Clap rhythms within the melody using your preferred rhythm duration system (numbers, Kodály rhythm duration syllables, Gordon, etc.). Sing the melody with pitch syllables and hand signs, and then practice the single-note accompaniment represented by Roman numerals rather than solfège syllables. Find a partner or a small group for performing the combined melody and single-note accompaniment for the song "Closet Key."

Traditional

Figure 3.2 "Closet Key," standard notation.

PRE-CONDUCTING: INDEPENDENCE EXERCISES
USING RIGHT- AND LEFT-HAND REBOUNDS

In the pre-conducting component of module 2, the independence exercise used a continuous, fluid motion with both right and left hand/arm, introduced as a means to develop further your rebound skill and to enhance hand/arm independence. In this exercise, we will continue to develop hand/arm independence skills. We will revisit the conducting rebound in future pre-conducting exercises, and you are encouraged to continue practicing the exercises in earlier modules.

In the following independence exercises, it is important to monitor carefully each suggested movement. Observe yourself in a mirror or with an electronic feedback system, such as those found on most computers (e.g., Photo Booth on MacBook Pro).

Whether you find these exercises easy, challenging, or somewhere in between, each exercise should be mastered to continue your trajectory toward hand/arm independence. These motions will be combined with the rebound motion in an upcoming pre-conducting exercise, so you will want to be secure in the performance of these movements before proceeding.

Classroom Setup

All class members can complete any of the following three exercises simultaneously. Students should stand and allow about one arm's length of space around them. An instructor should initiate each exercise and each step of any given exercise so the class practices as a unit.

Exercises
Exercise 1

1. Establish your conducting posture, remembering to maintain an elevated standing position. Your hands and arms should be slightly above your waist.
2. Having established your conducting posture and the resultant hand/arm height, complete the following task:
   a. Simultaneously move both hands/arms vertically (up and down), and then move one hand up while the other is going down. The movement should be fluid in both hands/arms. (See figure 3.3.)

Figure 3.3 Vertical movement pattern.

b. Next, simultaneously move both hands/arms horizontally (sideways), then reverse direction. Again, the movement should be fluid in both hands/arms. (See figure 3.4.)

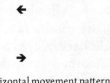

Figure 3.4 Horizontal movement pattern.

c. Now, move your right hand/arm in a horizontal motion while moving the left hand/arm in a vertical motion. Try to make the movements independent so that each side is moving at a different rate/tempo (i.e., there is no ordered pattern to the movements, you are not changing patterns of the vertical motion at the same time you are changing the motion of the horizontal, and one hand is changing faster than the other). (See figure 3.5.)

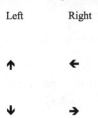

Figure 3.5 Vertical and horizontal movement patterns.

d. Next, switch movements in the hands/arms. Again, try to make the movements independent so that each side is moving at a different rate/tempo and there is no ordered pattern to the movements. (See figure 3.6.)

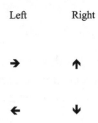

Figure 3.6 Horizontal and vertical movement patterns.

Exercise 2

1. Once all class members can perform the first exercise, check your conducting posture and the resultant hand/arm height, and then complete the following task:
   a. Simultaneously move both hands/arms in a circle, one going clockwise and the other counterclockwise.
      i. Reverse that motion.
      ii. Next, move both hands/arms in a clockwise motion.
      iii. Finally, move both hands/arms in a counterclockwise motion.
   b. Now, move your left hand/arm in a clockwise circular motion while moving the right hand/arm in a horizontal motion. Try to make the movements independent so that each side is moving at a different rate/tempo (i.e., there is no ordered pattern to the movements, you are not changing patterns of the horizontal motion at the same point as during your circular motion). (See figure 3.7.)

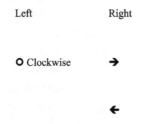

Figure 3.7 Clockwise circular and horizontal movement patterns.

      i. Now, move the left hand/arm in a counterclockwise circular motion, and continue the horizontal motion with the right hand/arm. (See figure 3.8)

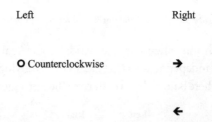

Figure 3.8 Counterclockwise circular and horizontal movement patterns.

      ii. Next, move the left hand/arm in a horizontal motion and the right hand/arm in a clockwise motion and then in a counterclockwise circular motion. See figure 3.9.

Left   Right

→   O Clockwise and Counterclockwise

←

Figure 3.9 Horizontal and clockwise and counterclockwise circular movement patterns.

2. Now, move your left hand/arm first in a clockwise and then in a counter-clockwise circular motion while moving the right hand/arm in a vertical motion. Again, try to make the movements independent so that each side moves at a different rate/tempo (i.e., there is no ordered pattern to the movements, and you are not changing patterns of the horizontal motion at the same point as during your circular motion). (See figure 3.10.) Next, move the left hand/arm in a vertical motion, and move the right hand/arm in a clockwise and then a counterclockwise circular motion. (See figure 3.11.)

Left   Right

O Clockwise and Counterclockwise ↑

↓

Figure 3.10 Clockwise and counterclockwise circular and vertical movement patterns.

Left   Right

↑   O Clockwise and Counterclockwise

↓

Figure 3.11 Vertical and clockwise and counterclockwise circular movement patterns.

Exercise 3

1. Once these tasks have been satisfactorily completed, check your con-ducting posture and the resultant hand/arm height, and complete the following task:

a. Simultaneously move both hands/arms in a sideways figure-eight pattern (∞), one going in one direction and the other in the opposite direction, and then move both hands/arms in the same direction.

b. Now, move your left hand/arm in a sideways figure-eight pattern while moving the right hand/arm in a horizontal motion. Try to make the movements independent so that each side is moving at a different rate/tempo and there is no ordered pattern to the movements. (See figure 3.12.) Next, move the left hand/arm in a horizontal motion while moving the right hand/arm in a figure-eight pattern. (See figure 3.13.)

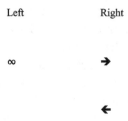

Figure 3.12 Figure-eight and horizontal movement patterns.

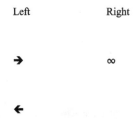

Figure 3.13 Horizontal and figure-eight movement patterns.

2. Now, move your left hand/arm in the figure-eight motion while moving the right hand/arm in a vertical motion. (See figure 3.14.) Next, move the left hand/arm in a vertical motion and the right hand/arm in a figure-eight pattern. (See Figure 3.15.)

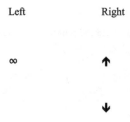

Figure 3.14 Figure-eight and vertical movement patterns.

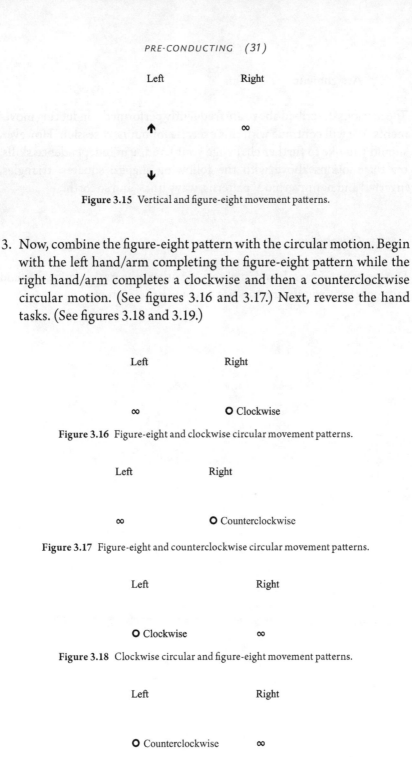

Left   Right

Figure 3.15 Vertical and figure-eight movement patterns.

3. Now, combine the figure-eight pattern with the circular motion. Begin with the left hand/arm completing the figure-eight pattern while the right hand/arm completes a clockwise and then a counterclockwise circular motion. (See figures 3.16 and 3.17.) Next, reverse the hand tasks. (See figures 3.18 and 3.19.)

Left   Right

∞   O Clockwise

Figure 3.16 Figure-eight and clockwise circular movement patterns.

Left   Right

∞   O Counterclockwise

Figure 3.17 Figure-eight and counterclockwise circular movement patterns.

Left   Right

O Clockwise   ∞

Figure 3.18 Clockwise circular and figure-eight movement patterns.

Left   Right

O Counterclockwise   ∞

Figure 3.19 Counterclockwise circular and figure-eight movement patterns.

Assignment

The motions described above are frequently performed conducting movements. We will continue with this exercise for our next session. However, should you like to further challenge your hand/arm independence skills, try the motions above with the following shapes: squares, triangles, inverted and noninverted V patterns, wavy lines, and so forth.

Observation

During your rehearsals and in observing other rehearsals, notice the fluid motions that various directors use to convey their intent.

PROFESSIONAL KNOWLEDGE:
THE POWER OF WORDS

For this component, the focus is to:

- Identify how teachers' word choices affect student learners.
- Determine how to promote constructive class discussions.

"As teachers, we choose our words and, in the process, construct the class-room worlds for our students and ourselves. The worlds we construct offer opportunities and constraints" (Johnston, 2012, p. 1). The language you use in your classroom—positive and negative—can profoundly affect students. How you respond to student achievements and mistakes is important. How you respond to your own mistakes can provide learning opportunities for your students. When you make a mistake, don't try to cover it up. You might hear some teachers say, "I did that on purpose to see if you were paying attention." Students are perceptive and will often see through that type of charade. When you make an error—and, yes, be assured that you *will* make them—model for students how you can fix it and, more important, learn from it. This creates an environment where mistakes happen for students and teachers, and it is OK to make them.

"Errors usually happen at the edge of what we can do, when we are stretching into new territory—when we are learning" (Johnston, 2012, p. 3). Advancing our knowledge and skill sets and traveling into new territories are the aims of education. If your students are easily mastering the musical and theoretical concepts, then you are ready to challenge them with more complex content.

Imagine a large canvas on the wall in front of you. One of your class-mates is given a large tube of toothpaste and instructed to make a mark on the canvas with the toothpaste. Each person in class then has the oppor-tunity to add to the design to make a "toothpaste masterpiece." When all have added their artistic flair, the student who made the first mark is then told, "Now it is your job to put all the toothpaste back in the tube."

If you've ever attempted to put toothpaste back into a tube, you know that it is indeed a futile effort. Now, think of the toothpaste as the words you speak in your classroom—conversations with students, other teach-ers, administrators, support staff, and others. Just like the toothpaste, once your words are spoken, they cannot be put back. They linger and "mark" the minds of those who heard you. And, like paint on an artist's canvas that accidentally runs and affects the colors surrounding it, your words can move beyond the walls of your classroom and "run" into other spaces.

Others may repeat your words or use them as models—either positive or negative—during their future interactions.

During teaching, we verbally respond to students' actions and responses. Our words can motivate, inhibit, or extinguish student learning and enthusiasm for the class. "Teaching requires constant improvisation and our responses can be thought of as 'conversational jazz'" (Johnston, 2012, p. 4). In jazz, the key we choose for each selection is important; therefore, in classroom conversational jazz, it is also important to choose a productive key in which to improvise.

Discussion

1. Think of a time when a teacher's words inspired you. Reflect on why.
2. Think of a time when a teacher's words embarrassed you. Determine an alternative approach that would result in a different outcome.
3. How can you promote productive and constructive classroom conversations?
4. Think of various ways to respond to student errors that result in learning rather than frustration or humiliation.

MODULE 3 REFERENCE

Johnston, P. H. (2012). *Opening minds: Using language to change lives*. Portland, ME: Stenhouse.

Facial Expression—Sight-Singing—Hand/ Arm Conducting Independence—Ethics in Teaching

I n this module, you will focus on:

- Personal awareness: Facial expression.
- Personal musicianship: Additional sight-singing practice.
- Pre-conducting: Continuation of the pre-conducting hand/arm independence exercises in module 3.
- Professional knowledge: The concepts of trustworthiness, ethics, and moral decision-making.

PERSONAL AWARENESS: FACIAL EXPRESSION— WHAT DO I LOOK LIKE?

According to Paul Ekman, Wallace V. Friesen, and Maureen O'Sullivan (1987), facial expressions universally convey emotional and expressive information and are important in conveying nonverbal communication. Facial gestures are often used in conjunction with body gestures, proximity, and postures to help convey specific messages.

Have you ever noticed that some people's neutral facial expressions convey happiness while those of others seem to convey sullenness? In a neutral position—when someone's mouth naturally curves downward at the sides—one's expression may be perceived as sadness, discontent, or anger. Someone who has naturally upturned mouth corners when in a neutral position may be perceived as being happy, contented, or cheerful.

When you stand in front of a group, even before speaking or doing anything, you are sending some type of message. You need to identify that message. In this exercise, you will explore your classmates' interpretation of your so-called neutral facial expression.

Classroom Setup

The class will work in pairs. The classroom should be set up to facilitate this arrangement.

Exercise

One individual in each pair should have a laptop, iPad, cell phone, or other device to take photographs that can be viewed immediately. Each person should take a photograph of his or her partner's neutral facial expression and then discuss what expression he or she perceives the partner conveys. Once a pair has completed the task, each individual should pair with another person and repeat the process. Do not share your former partner's perception of your neutral facial expression. Allow each partner to give you his or her impression of your neutral facial expression. The exercise can continue as long as time allows, but a minimum of four or five pairings should be completed. Here is a list of possible facial expressions, but your interpretation is not limited to these. This list is provided only to help stimulate your thought process:

Amused
Angry
Anxious
Bored
Cheerful
Concerned
Contemptuous
Coy
Disgusted
Disturbed/troubled
Engaged

Fearful
Happy
Impish/mischievous
Inattentive
Sad
Seductive
Surprised
Thoughtful
Uninterested
Worried

Once this exercise is completed, you should note what your partners have told you. Knowing how others perceive you when you're displaying your neutral facial expression can help you interpret future reactions during communications.

Assignment

Continue to ask others how they perceive your neutral facial expression.

Observation

Observe the facial expressions of others, and note the variety that exists among individuals' neutral facial expressions.

PERSONAL MUSICIANSHIP: ADDITIONAL SIGHT-SINGING PRACTICE

For this component, the focus is to:

- List the steps to sight-reading a melody.
- Practice reading rhythms using a preferred rhythm system.
- Sing a melody with limited pitches (d-r-m) in stick notation.
- Add single-note accompaniments to a melody using solfège syllables.

With a partner or a small group, write down and review the sequence of steps to sight-reading a melody and the purpose of rhythm duration syllables. Following the review, apply the sequence to the folk song "Hop, Old Squirrel" (figure 4.1). Practice performing the song with various pitches serving as *do*.

Figure 4.1 "Hop, Old Squirrel," stick notation.

PRE-CONDUCTING: INDEPENDENCE EXERCISES USING RIGHT- AND LEFT-HAND REBOUNDS

In the pre-conducting independence exercises in module 3, the use of a continuous, fluid motion with both right and left hand/arm was introduced as a means to further develop your rebound skill and to enhance hand/arm independence. In this exercise, you will continue to develop hand/arm independence skills. You will revisit the conducting rebound in future pre-conducting exercises, and you are encouraged to continue practicing the exercises.

In the following independence exercises, it is important that you carefully monitor each of the movements suggested. Observe yourself in a mirror or with an electronic feedback system, such as those found on most computers (e.g., Photo Booth on MacBook Pro).

Whether you find these exercises easy, challenging, or somewhere in between, each exercise should be mastered to continue your trajectory toward hand/arm independence. These motions will be combined with the rebound motion in an upcoming pre-conducting exercise, so you will want to be secure in performing these movements before proceeding.

Classroom Setup

All class members can complete any of these exercises simultaneously. Students should stand and allow about one arm's length of space around them. An instructor should initiate each exercise and each step of any given exercise so the class practices as a unit.

Exercises
Exercise 1

1. Establish your conducting posture, remembering to maintain an elevated standing position. Your hands and arms should be slightly above your waist.
2. Having established your conducting posture and the resultant hand/arm height, complete the following task:
   a. Simultaneously move both hands/arms vertically (up and down), and then move one hand up while the other is going down. The movement should be fluid in both hands/arms. (See figure 4.2.)

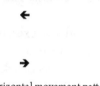

Figure 4.2 Vertical movement pattern.

b. Next, simultaneously move both hands/arms horizontally (sideways), then reverse direction. Again, the movement should be fluid in both hands/arms. (See figure 4.3.)

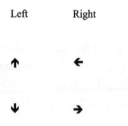

Figure 4.3 Horizontal movement pattern.

c. Now, move your right hand/arm in a horizontal motion while moving the left hand/arm in a vertical motion. Try to make the movements independent so that each side moves at a different rate/tempo (i.e., there is no ordered pattern to the movements, you are not changing patterns of the vertical motion at the same time you are changing the motion of the horizontal, and one hand is changing faster than the other). (See figure 4.4.)

Left   Right

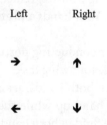

Figure 4.4 Vertical and horizontal movement patterns.

d. Next, switch movements in the hands/arms. Again, try to make the movements independent so that each side is moving at a different rate/tempo and there is no ordered pattern to the movements. (See figure 4.5.)

Left   Right

Figure 4.5 Horizontal and vertical movement patterns.

Exercise 2

1. Once all class members can perform the first exercise, check your conducting posture and the resultant hand/arm height, and then complete
   the following task:
   a. Simultaneously move both hands/arms in a circle, one going clock-
      wise and the other counterclockwise.
      i. Reverse that motion.
      ii. Next, move both hands/arms in a clockwise motion.
      iii. Finally, move both hands/arms in a counter clockwise motion.
   b. Now, move your left hand/arm in a clockwise circular motion
      while moving the right hand/arm in a horizontal motion. Try
      to make the movements independent so that each side moves
      at a different rate/tempo (i.e., there is no ordered pattern to the
      movements, and you are not changing patterns of the horizon-
      tal motion at the same point as during your circular motion).
      (See figure 4.6.)

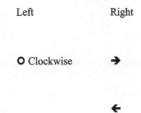

Figure 4.6 Clockwise circular and horizontal movement patterns.

      i. Now, move the left hand/arm in a counterclockwise circular
         motion, and continue the horizontal motion with the right
         hand/arm. (See figure 4.7.)

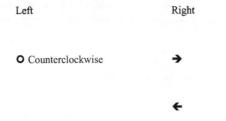

Figure 4.7 Counterclockwise circular and horizontal movement patterns.

      ii. Next, move the left hand/arm in a horizontal motion and the
          right hand/arm in a clockwise motion and then in a counter-
          clockwise circular motion. (See figure 4.8.)

Left   Right

→   O Clockwise and Counterclockwise

←

Figure 4.8 Horizontal and clockwise and counterclockwise circular movement patterns.

2. Now, move your left hand/arm first in a clockwise and then in a counter-clockwise circular motion while moving the right hand/arm in a vertical motion. Again, try to make the movements independent so that each side is moving at a different rate/tempo (i.e., there is no ordered pattern to the movements, and you are not changing patterns of the horizontal motion at the same point as during your circular motion). (See figure 4.9.) Next, move the left hand/arm in a vertical motion, and move the right hand/arm in a clockwise and then a counterclockwise circular motion. (See figure 4.10.)

Left   Right

O Clockwise and Counterclockwise ↑

↓

Figure 4.9 Clockwise and counterclockwise circular and vertical movement patterns.

Left   Right

↑   O Clockwise and Counterclockwise

↓

Figure 4.10 Vertical and clockwise and counterclockwise circular movement patterns.

Exercise 3

1. Once these tasks have been satisfactorily completed, check your con-ducting posture and the resultant hand/arm height, and complete the following task:

a. Simultaneously move both hands/arms in a sideways figure-eight pattern (∞), one going in one direction and the other in the opposite direction, and then move both hands/arms in the same direction.

b. Now, move your left hand/arm in a sideways figure-eight pattern while moving the right hand/arm in a horizontal motion. Try to make the movements independent so that each side is moving at a different rate/tempo and there is no ordered pattern to the movements. (See figure 4.11.) Next, move the left hand/arm in a horizontal motion, and move the right hand/arm in a figure-eight pattern. (See figure 4.12.)

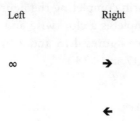

Figure 4.11 Figure-eight and horizontal movement patterns.

Figure 4.12 Horizontal and figure-eight movement patterns.

2. Now, move your left hand/arm in the figure-eight motion while moving the right hand/arm in a vertical motion. (See figure 4.13.) Next, move the left hand/arm in a vertical motion and the right hand/arm in a figure-eight pattern. (See figure 4.14.)

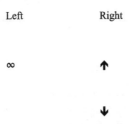

Figure 4.13 Figure-eight and vertical movement patterns.

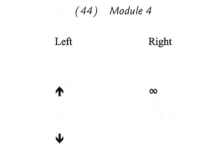

Figure 4.14 Vertical and figure-eight movement patterns.

3. Now, combine the figure-eight pattern with the circular motion. Begin with the left hand/arm completing the figure-eight pattern while the right hand/arm completes a clockwise and then a counterclockwise circular motion. (See figures 4.15 and 4.16. Next, reverse the hand tasks. (See figures 4.17 and 4.18.)

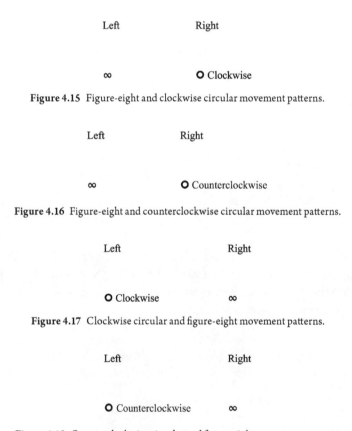

Figure 4.15 Figure-eight and clockwise circular movement patterns.

Figure 4.16 Figure-eight and counterclockwise circular movement patterns.

Figure 4.17 Clockwise circular and figure-eight movement patterns.

Figure 4.18 Counterclockwise circular and figure-eight movement patterns.

Assignment

The motions described above are frequently performed conducting movements. We will continue with this exercise in the next module. However, should you like to further challenge your hand/arm independence skills, try the motions above with the following shapes: squares, triangles, inverted and noninverted V patterns, wavy lines, and so forth.

Observation

During your rehearsals and in observing other rehearsals, notice the fluid motions that various directors use to convey their intent.

PROFESSIONAL KNOWLEDGE: ARE YOU TRUSTWORTHY? ETHICAL AND MORAL DECISIONS IN TEACHING

For this component, the focus is to:

• Define ethics and morals.
• Stress the importance of ethics and morals in daily life.

"The professional educator acts with conscientious effort to exemplify the highest ethical standards" (Association of American Educators). Teachers hold a position of public trust. Accompanying that trust are expected standards of high moral and ethical decision-making. The Association of American Educators provides teachers with guidelines for ethical behaviors and identifies four categories: ethical conduct toward students, ethical conduct toward practices and performance, ethical conduct toward professional colleagues, and ethical conduct toward parents and the community.

Ethics are the standards governing an individual's conduct or the conduct of members of a profession. Ethics can be divided into two main categories: morals and conduct. Morals are what we value or believe, while conduct involves how we act on those beliefs. Ethics are "the continuous effort of studying our own moral beliefs and our moral conduct, and striving to ensure that we, and the institutions we help to shape, live up to standards that are reasonable and solidly-based" (Velasquez, Andre, Shanks, Meyer, & Meyer, 2010). Therefore, ethics and morals are intimately and permanently connected.

As future educators, you likely understand the basic tenets of being honest, protecting students, protecting confidential information, respecting the law, and so on. Yet have you participated in class discussions or personal conversations with fellow students regarding ethics and morals? Although you are expected to be ethical, responsible, and moral, opportunities to discuss these topics are not always included in your coursework.

Will you be an ethical model for your students? Will you discuss ethics in your classrooms? Teaching ethics is only part of the process; the need remains for context and definitions. "Telling right from wrong in everyday life is not that hard; the hard part is overcoming laziness and cowardice to do what one perfectly well knows one should" (Solomon, 1992, p. 5). As a music educator, you will encounter numerous moral and ethical decisions regarding the use and sharing of music. "The nature of music-making is being revised via an internet-based democracy" (Draper, 2009, p. 1). Yet what do you know of copyright law, use of graphics in presentations and printed materials, YouTube downloads, fair use, recording performances, or music sharing?

Teachers assume responsibility for student learning and course content. They are also expected to follow all school policies and be law-abiding citizens. It is important to remember that it will also be your responsibility—whether intentional or unintentional—to teach your students about morals and ethics. Your words, actions, and decisions will influence the moral and ethical decisions of every student in your classroom.

Discussion

1. List personal characteristics or traits that you believe are associated with moral and ethical behavior.
2. A music-store owner offers to repair your instruments for free if you will send all your band students to the shop for their repairs, music, and accessories. How do you respond?
3. You have been appointed to organize a mass concert of all the choirs in your school district. A teacher at one school has already spent her entire music budget and can't purchase the music. What will you suggest she do?
4. Is it OK to copy or reproduce music (CDs, sound files, sheet music) for any educational purpose?

MODULE 4 REFERENCES

Association of American Educators. http://aaeteachers.org/index.php/about-us/aae-code-of-ethics

Draper, P. A. (2009). How online social networks are redefining knowledge, power, 21st century music-making and higher education. *Journal of Music Research Online.* http://hdl.handle.net/10072/30354

Ekman, P., Friesen, W. V., & O'Sullivan, M. (1987). Universals and cultural differences in the judgments of facial expressions of emotion. *Journal of Personality and Social Psychology, 53*(4), 712–717.

Solomon, R. C. (1992). *Ethics and excellence: Cooperation and integrity in business.* New York: Oxford University Press.

Velasquez, M., Andre, C., Shanks, T., Meyer, M., & Meyer, M. (2010). What is ethics? http://www.scu.edu/ethics/practicing/decision/whatisethics.html

SUGGESTED READING

Dunbar, L., & Cooper, S. (2015). Balancing convenience and ethics in higher education: Refining and reconfiguring the music classroom technology culture. In S. O'Neill (Ed.), *Music and media infused lives: Music education in a digital age*. Waterloo, ON: Canadian Music Educator's Association. pp. 225-238.

Receiving Facial Expression Messages—Body Posture and Singing—Conducting Independence and Rebounds—Diverse Learners

In this module. you will focus on:

- Personal awareness: Sending and receiving different messages through facial expressions.
- Personal musicianship: Body posture and its relation to successful singing.
- Pre-conducting: Combining independence exercises with the conducting rebound motion.
- Professional knowledge: Diverse learners.

PERSONAL AWARENESS: FACIAL EXPRESSION— SENDING AND RECEIVING DIFFERENT MESSAGES

If you completed the personal awareness component in module 4, then you will have an idea of the emotional range you have at your command through facial expressions. As teachers and directors, we want to be certain that the message we send is the one being received by those attending our rehearsals and classroom sessions.

Certainly, when facial expressions are combined with other nonverbal information—such as gestures, body proximity, and so forth—the observer receives more contextual information to better determine how another person feels, but facial expressions are an important component in this assessment (Carroll & Russell, 1996). Additional nonverbal information will be explored in later modules.

In this exercise, you will explore the variety of expressions you can send through manipulation of your forehead and eyebrows, eyes and eyelids, nose, and mouth and lips. Before we begin, a brief explanation of the various manipulations of these facial components will be presented so you may experiment with them as you explore this facet of nonverbal communication.

Forehead and Eyebrows

While the forehead has its place in nonverbal communication, it is often connected with the movement of the eyebrows.

- Lowering the eyebrows conceals the eyes to a degree. When the eyebrows are lowered and the forehead is kept relatively smooth, this can be an indication of annoyance, displeasure, or intense mistrust or questioning.
- Raised eyebrows and a wrinkled forehead indicate surprise and openness or, in some cases, disbelief, cynicism, or questioning, as in "Are you sure?"
- When the eyebrows are pulled together, thereby pulling up the forehead, the eyebrows generally slope outward and can indicate relief ("Whew!") or anxiety ("Oh, no!").
- When the eyebrows are pulled down, sloping inward, and the forehead is kept smooth, this often conveys anger or frustration. It can also signal intense concentration.
- Eyebrows that are pulled together can signal confusion or an attempt to understand, as if you were asking, "What's that?"
- Quickly moving the eyebrows up and then down is a signal of recognition or greeting or, at times, mild disbelief.

Eyes and Eyelids

Often called the windows of the soul, the eyes can send many different messages. Below are descriptions of eye movements and possible interpretations of those actions. However, such interpretations should be combined with other information to provide a more reliable interpretation of the message being sent.

- Gazing at someone shows interest, and, depending on our focus, the nature of our interest is revealed. Prolonged eye contact can feel threatening, but an individual who frequently breaks eye contact or looks away may appear to be distracted, found out, threatened, uncomfortable, or trying to conceal feelings.
- Glancing at something is usually an indication that we have a desire for that thing. For example, glancing at a door indicates a desire to leave; glancing at a person may indicate a desire to meet or talk with him or her. Glancing can also indicate disapproval, especially if the glance is sideways, without raised eyebrows.
- Blinking tends to increase when we feel discomfort or stress and is associated with lying. Infrequent blinking may be a sign that a person is intentionally controlling eye movements, as if his or her picture is being taken or he or she is trying to hide or focus something. Rapid blinking or fluttering of the eyelashes can signal a romantic invitation, or it can suggest arrogance.
- Staring can indicate shock, disbelief, or interest when the eyes are focused, lack of interest if the eyes are not focused. A stare when squinting signals aggression, whereas it implies surprise when the eyes are open.
- Squinting is a natural reaction to harsh light or an indicator of tiredness. As already noted, squinting can indicate aggression when combined with a stare. It can also suggest uncertainty or evaluation, as if thinking about something being said.
- Winking can be a somewhat familiar greeting or can be used as a conspiratorial gesture, as when two individuals are in agreement but others are not involved.
- Closing one's eyes is equivalent to turning away and signals a desire to avoid or ignore. Some individuals close their eyes to better visualize or focus without external distraction.
- Tears and/or damp eyes can indicate sadness, joy, anxiety, tiredness, frustration, fear, and, at times, anger.
- "Following eyes" suggest interest, either positive, as when you are looking at something about which you desire more information, or negative, as when you fear something or someone.
- Looking up is generally associated with thinking, visualizing pictures, or recalling thoughts or words. Looking up can signal boredom or disbelief. If the head is lowered and one looks up at a person, this can indicate a coy or suggestive action or perhaps a judgmental act. Looking upward and to the left is often associated with memory recall, while looking upward and to the right can indicate imaginative construction of a picture.

- Looking down can express submission or guilt, but if a person tilts his or her head back and then looks down at a person, this is an indication of power or dominance. Looking down and to the left is often associated with inner dialogue (talking to oneself) while looking down and to the right often signals attention to internal emotions.
- Looking sideways is perhaps the most common of all visual actions. Sideways movements are indicators of looking away from what is in front of someone or looking toward something of interest. Quick sideways glances can be a check on the source of a distraction, such as a potential threat or other interest. It can also be a sign of irritation. Sideways motion to the left is associated with sound recall, and movement to the right is correlated with imagining a sound. Again, as with other visual movements, these can be reversed in different individuals. Lateral movement of the eyes is often linked with shiftiness and lying and can also happen when a person is being conspiratorial.
- Lowering eyelids can signal tiredness or be part of a romantic and suggestive message when looking at another person.

Nose

Our noses can also change with emotional messages. The nostrils can be flared, indicating anger or disgust, or we can "twist or turn" our noses, as in a sneer, when envious or disgusted.

Mouth and Lips

Our mouths and lips can be finely controlled and shaped to convey many types of nonverbal information. While not definitively relegated to specific emotions, the following are often perceived to convey emotive qualities.

- Parted lips and a slightly open mouth are generally signs of attentiveness and, when combined with licking the lips, can indicate flirting or desire. When the lips are parted, it can also be an indication that a person wants to talk or to share something.
- Pursed lips, pulled inward from all directions, and a closed mouth typically indicate tension, frustration, or perhaps disapproval. This is a classic sign of suppressed anger.

- Puckered lips and a closed mouth in the classic kiss shape characteristically indicate desire but can also indicate uncertainty, mild concern, or confusion.
- Lips in a flat, tight line and a closed mouth can indicate disapproval, displeasure, frustration, and determined refusal. If the mouth is slightly open, it can indicate strong anger or rage.
- A closed mouth with lips turned up at the corners can be a sign of disgust (a grimace), especially if the lips are tense. Less tense lips can be a signal of pleasure (a smile). When the mouth is open and the lips are turned up at the corners, pleasure or approval is indicated. In a fully engaged smile, the teeth are often showing.
- Down-turned lips with the mouth closed generally signify sadness, but when the mouth is slightly open, this can imply disgust or displeasure.
- Retracted lips, pulled back to expose the teeth, can suggest a broad smile or may signal aggression or angst. One must also scan the person's eyes to fully interpret this facial pose.
- A single rapid twitch at the corner of the mouth may signal cynicism or disbelief.
- Protruding lips, when one lip covers another, can indicate guilt, uncertainty, or petulance (especially when the lower lip protrudes). If both lips protrude and are pressed out, this can suggest uncertainty or doubt. If a protruding lip is combined with biting, it is a sign of stress, nervousness, or anxiety.

Emotions and Facial Signals

According to David Straker (2010), some of the emotions conveyed through facial expressions are signaled as follows:

- Anger: Eyes wide and staring; eyebrows pulled down (especially in middle); wrinkled forehead; flared nostrils; mouth flattened or clenched teeth bared; jutting chin.
- Anxiety: Eyebrows slightly pushed together; trembling lower lip; chin possibly wrinkled; head slightly tilted down.
- Boredom: Eyes looking away or not focused; face generally immobile; corners of mouth turned down or lips pulled to the side; head propped up with hand.
- Calm: Relaxed facial muscles and steady gaze with eyes; mouth perhaps turned up slightly at sides in a gentle smile.

- Desire: Eyes wide open with dilated pupils; slightly raised eyebrows; lips slightly parted or puckered or smiling; head tilted forward.
- Disgust: Eyes squinted slightly; eyebrows flat and pulled inward slightly; head turned away; nostrils flared; nose twisted in sneer; mouth closed, possibly with tongue protruding; chin jutting.
- Envy: Eyes staring; mouth corners turned down; nose turned in sneer; chin jutting.
- Fear: Eyes wide, closed, or pointing down; raised eyebrows; mouth open or corners turned down; chin pulled in; head down.
- Happiness: Mouth smiling (open or closed); possible laughter; crow's-feet wrinkles at sides of sparkling eyes; slightly raised eyebrows; head held level.
- Interest: Steady gaze of eyes at item of interest (may be squinting); slightly raised eyebrows; lips slightly pressed together; head erect or pushed forward.
- Pity: Eyes in extended gaze and possibly damp; eyebrows slightly pulled together in middle or downward at edges; mouth turned down at corners; head tilted to the side.
- Relief: Eyes relaxed but open, eyebrows tilted outward (lowered outer edges); mouth perhaps slightly open as if making a "Whew" sound and/or either tilted down or smiling; head tilted.
- Sadness: Eyes cast down and possibly damp or tearful; head down; lips pinched; head down or to the side.
- Shame: Eyes and head turned down; eyebrows held low.
- Surprise: Eyes wide open; eyebrows raised high; mouth dropped wide open with consequent lowered chin; head held back or tilted to the side.

Classroom Setup

The class will work in pairs. The classroom should be set up to facilitate this arrangement.

Exercise

There is a lot of information to assimilate in this module. The purpose of this exercise is not to make you an expert at reading facial expressions but rather to make you aware of the many ways you can understand and read the messages you send and the messages others are sending. It is difficult to control individual facial muscles when attempting an expression; therefore, it is suggested that you incorporate all facial muscles (forehead, eyebrow, eyes, etc.) in each action.

In pairs, attempt to display at least four or five of the emotions listed below. You will find that some emotions, such as anger or happiness, are easier to convey than others. It is suggested that you not tell your partner the emotion you are trying to convey. Have your partner guess the emotion being attempted, and if it's not correctly guessed, attempt the emotion again, modifying your eyes, eyelids, forehead, mouth, and so on, to communicate that emotion more effectively, or try another emotion. After each person has attempted four or five emotions, and as time allows, move to another partner.

These are the facial expressions detailed by Straker. You may wish to begin with these emotions:

Anger
Anxiety
Boredom
Calm
Desire
Disgust
Envy
Fear
Happiness
Interest
Pity
Relief
Sadness
Shame
Surprise

Because of the volume of information presented, this exercise may be repeated as needed.

Assignment

Practice displaying the various emotions suggested in this component along with others you may want to convey in a classroom or rehearsal setting. Think about your role as a teacher and director. What types of emotional messages will you be sending? Can you convey those messages convincingly?

Observation

Note the facial expressions of individuals with whom you talk daily. What kinds of changes do you notice? Do you feel more confident about interpreting the emotional messages being sent?

PERSONAL MUSICIANSHIP: BODY POSTURE AND SUCCESSFUL SINGING

For this component, the focus is to:

- Discuss posture and body alignment that promotes successful singing.
- Sing a melody with limited pitches (d-r-m) in standard notation.
- Add single-note accompaniments to a melody using Roman numerals.

At one time or another during your childhood, it is likely that an adult said to you the following phrases: "stand up straight," "sit up straight," "don't slouch," "get your shoulders back," and others. Unfortunately, years of sitting in classrooms in a chair at a desk or table—often uncomfortable and/or the wrong height for your body—have promoted the tendency to slouch. Most singers know the importance of proper posture, but it is easy to slip into the slouch if one doesn't make a focused effort to maintain proper posture during singing. Proper posture helps release tension, allows the diaphragm to function at full capacity, and allows air to flow more freely through your vocal folds. How are you sitting (or standing) as you read this text? Take a moment to evaluate your posture and review the elevated posture in the personal awareness component of module 1.

There are many resources for proper body alignment for singing, but they share commonalities. Let's start with your feet. They should be equal in bearing the weight of your body with your hips aligned. Shoulders should be square with your hips, your head centered on your shoulders, and your chin approximately parallel to the floor.

Before singing the melody in figure 5.1, utilizing the sequential steps from previous modules, focus on alignment of your body. With a partner or a small group, provide feedback on others' ability to align their bodies in a position that will be conducive for singing.

Figure 5.1 "Hop, Old Squirrel," standard notation.

PRE-CONDUCTING: INDEPENDENCE
EXERCISES—REBOUNDS AND MOTIONS

In the pre-conducting component of module 4, developing independence through the use of right- and left-hand/arm coordination exercises was introduced. Now you will combine the movements presented in those exercises and associate them with the conducting rebound, while further developing independence and the conducting rebound.

In the following exercises, it is important to monitor carefully each of the movements suggested. Observe yourself in a mirror or with an electronic feedback device.

Classroom Setup

All class members can complete any of these exercises simultaneously. Students should stand and allow about one arm's length of space around them. An instructor should initiate each exercise and each step of any given exercise so the class practices as a unit.

Exercises
Exercise 1

1. Establish your conducting posture, remembering to maintain an elevated standing position. Your hands and arms should be slightly above your waist.
2. Having established your conducting posture and the resultant hand/ arm height, complete the following task:
   a. Using a tempo of mm = 66, practice rebounds with your right hand/arm, making sure that your rebound begins with a fall of one or two inches and rebounds at about chest height and below your chin. The rebound should begin and end at the same point or location. That location should be approximately in line with your right hip. (See figure 5.2.)

Figure 5.2 Initial drop, rebound, and resultant drop.

b. The left hand/arm should now be moved in a vertical motion. Be sure the movement is fluid. (See figure 5.3.)

Figure 5.3 Left-hand vertical motion indication.

c. Your right hand/arm is "tapping" out rebounds, while the left is moving vertically. Try to make the movements independent so that each side moves at a different rate/tempo (i.e., there is no ordered pattern to the movements, you are not consistently changing your vertical pattern on a particular beat, etc.). (See figure 5.4.)

Left (Vertical Motion)   Right (Drops and Rebounds)

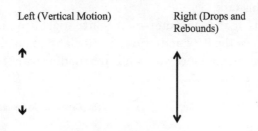

Figure 5.4 Left-hand (vertical) and right-hand activity indicators.

Exercise 2

1. Once all class members can perform the first exercise, begin this one.
2. Having checked your conducting posture and the resultant hand/arm height, complete the following task:

a. Again, using a tempo of mm = 66, begin the right-hand/arm rebounds.
b. Now move the left hand/arm in a horizontal motion. (See figure 5.5.)

Left

Figure 5.5 Left-hand horizontal motion indicator.

c. Your right hand/arm is "tapping" out rebounds, while the left hand/arm is moving horizontally. Again, try to make the movements as independent as possible. (See figure 5.6.)

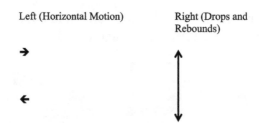

Figure 5.6 Left- (horizontal) and right-hand activity indicators.

Exercise 3

1. Once all class members can perform the first two exercises, check your conducting posture and the resultant hand/arm height, and complete the following task:
   a. Again, using a tempo of mm = 66, begin the right-hand/arm rebounds.
   b. Now move the left hand/arm in a circular motion, first clockwise and then counterclockwise, while rebounding with the right hand/arm. (See figure 5.7.)

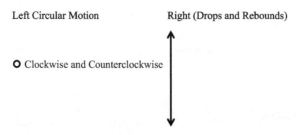

Figure 5.7 Left- (circular) and right-hand activity indicators.

Exercise 4

1. Once exercise 3 has been satisfactorily performed, complete the following task:
   a. With the right hand/arm rebounding, have the left hand/arm move in a sideways figure-eight pattern (∞). (See figure 5.8.)

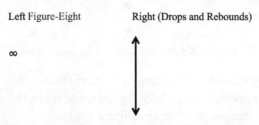

Figure 5.8 Left- (figure-eight) and right-hand activity indicators.

b. Continue this task until you can perform it successfully.

Exercise 5

1. Once all of the four exercises above have been satisfactorily completed, try reversing hands. Thus, the left hand/arm completes the rebounds, and the right hand/arm performs the other motions.

Assignment

Should you want to further challenge your hand/arm independence skills, try the suggested exercises with the following shapes: squares, triangles, inverted and noninverted V patterns, wavy lines, and so forth.

Observation

As you complete these exercises, do you notice a change? Do you feel development of right- and left-hand/arm independence? Notice your directors' and conductors' right- and left-hand/arm independence skills.

PROFESSIONAL KNOWLEDGE:
DIVERSE LEARNERS

For this component, the focus is to:

- Discuss various types of student learners.
- Provide an overview of Bloom's taxonomy.

"The Animal School" is a fable written by George Reavis (see Reavis, 1999). It was his response to dissatisfaction with then-current school-reform policies. Many different versions of this tale exist since its creation in the 1940s, but the premise remains the same. The animals form a school so they can meet the problems of the "new world." The curriculum includes running, climbing, swimming, and flying. It was determined that the easiest way to assess all the animals would be to require everyone to satisfactorily complete all classes. You, of course, are already thinking the obvious: not all animals *can* realistically run, climb, swim, and fly. The duck, although a great swimmer, had to stop swimming in order to spend time after school practicing running. The rabbit excelled at running but struggled in swimming class. (You'll need to read a version of the story to find out which animal earned the title of valedictorian.)

One version of the fable is dedicated "to those children and adults who have unjustly suffered the fate of standardized tests and inappropriate curriculum standards." It is unrealistic for us to think that all students in our classrooms will be able to reach the same skill or performance level and meet or master all curriculum standards. It is equally unrealistic for us to think that a uniform lesson-delivery system will accommodate all learners in the classroom. Teachers must consider how each student learns.

Benjamin Bloom (1913–1999), an American educational psychologist, developed a taxonomy, or system, that is widely used by educators (see Bloom, 1984). He divided learning into three domains—or overlapping categories—that outline an individual's preferred learning style: cognitive, affective, and psychomotor. Cognitive learning involves knowledge acquisition, understanding, or comprehension. The affective domain involves emotions or responses. Bloom categorized learning that involves the mental processes that control movements as psychomotor.

How do we assess the three types of learning? How do we assess diverse learners? It's likely that the most common assessments you've experienced during your education have been written tests. These have assessed your cognitive domain. Written tests require students to recall or recognize terminology and information. Keywords commonly used in these exams include *define, list, describe, discuss,* and *label,* to name a few.

Within the music classroom, assessments can easily address the needs of psychomotor learners. Skills tests and performances serve as the most authentic form of assessment but can be time-consuming for classes with large enrollments. Keywords commonly associated with psychomotor assessment include *copy, perform, demonstrate,* and *show.*

The affective domain is more difficult to assess, as feelings and emotions are subjective; therefore, there likely isn't a right or wrong answer in the response. We can evaluate students' responses to music through reflective writings and observing use of expression and dynamics to meet the musical style or genre during performances. Typically, these types of assessments are evaluated and recorded but not necessarily assigned a grade designation. Keywords commonly used in these types of assessments include *respond, react, interpret,* and *justify.*

Effective teachers recognize that presenting material in multiple domains assists in improving student mastery levels. Bloom's taxonomy can serve as a framework for creating lesson plans and instructional materials to meet the individual needs of students. In a classroom of diverse learners, it is important that instructional delivery and assessments be equally diverse.

Discussion

1. How can you relate "The Animal School" to music education?
2. What would you identify as your preferred learning domain? How did you come to that decision?
3. How will this information affect your lesson planning?
4. How will this information affect your teaching philosophy?

MODULE 5 REFERENCES

Bloom, B.S. (1984). Taxonomy of educational objectives book 1: Cognitive domain. Addison Wesley Publishing Company, 2nd edition.

Carroll, J. M., & Russell, J. A. (1996). Do facial expressions signal specific emotions? Judging emotion from the face in context. *Journal of Personality and Social Psychology, 70,* 205–218.

Reavis, G. H. (1999.) *The animal school: The administration of the school curriculum with references to individual differences.* Peterborough, NH: Crystal Springs.

Straker, D. (2010). *Changing minds* (2nd ed.). syque.com/bookstore/changingminds.htm

Facial Gestures with Hands—Breathing and Singing—Conductor Cueing—Classroom Modeling

In this module, you will focus on:

- Personal awareness: Embellishing facial gestures with your hands.
- Personal musicianship: Connecting breathing to singing.
- Pre-conducting: Cueing.
- Professional knowledge: Modeling in the music classroom.

PERSONAL AWARENESS: FACIAL EXPRESSIONS— HANDS WITH FACIAL GESTURES

One's hands often embellish and clarify the emotions being conveyed through facial gestures. We use our hands and fingers in various poses, either touching or in close proximity; similarly, we touch our faces to support facial messages we hope to convey. Placing one's hands on the side of one's face; touching or tapping one's chin, nose, forehead, or lips with the fingers; stroking one's chin, cheek, or forehead with the hands; or simply having one's hands near one's face all support different facial messages.

As teachers and directors, we need to be able to interpret these messages (Pease & Pease, 2006). Often, because students are seated, other helpful body gestures are not available to us for interpretive assistance. Thus, facial gestures, along with hand gestures, may be the primary means of interpreting emotional messages (Mahmoud & Robinson, 2013). Additionally, when we interact as teachers and directors, we also use hand-to-face gestures. Therefore, an understanding of the interpretive nature of such gestures is important. As you can see in figure 6.1, placement of the hands and fingers can enhance or change the interpretation of the facial message sent.

| Thinking | Choosing | Suspicious |

| Evaluating | Bored | Frustrated |

Figure 6.1 Facial expressions using the hands.

Holding the chin or forehead with a closed hand can suggest interest, thinking, or being unsure. An open hand in the same pose may suggest happiness or boredom, while using both hands can indicate thinking, uncertainty, interest, or frustration.

Touching any part of the face with a closed hand can imply being lost in thought, unsure, concerned, fatigued, or frustrated. An open hand touching the face often sends a message of uncertainty, while placing an index finger or several fingers on the face conveys thinking, concentration, or uncertainty.

Someone leaning on a closed hand may be unsure, thinking, happy, interested, or bored, depending on other facial gestures. An open hand in the same pose can suggest happiness, boredom, worry, passive interest, or frustration and anxiety, while leaning on both hands generally indicates thinking.

Stroking or tapping with an open hand can signal thinking, uncertainty, creativity, coyness, or recollection, depending on facial placement of the tapping, the number of fingers used, and other facial gestures.

At times, people use their hands to enhance an emotion without touching the face. For example, holding the hands in front of the face, palms facing outward, indicates "stop" or "I've had enough." Holding the hands parallel to the sides of the head with eyes wide and mouth in an O shape may signal surprise. Holding cupped hands underneath the chin with palms facing up can convey confusion ("What?"), inquiry ("What do you mean by that?"), or disbelief ("You've got to be kidding me!" or "I don't believe you just said that!").

Classroom Setup

The class will work in groups of three to five individuals. The classroom should be set up to facilitate this arrangement.

Exercise

For this exercise, form groups of three to five individuals. Ideally, each individual will have access to a computer, iPad, cell phone, or other device from which to obtain pictures of facial expressions and hand/finger placements.

Think of an emotion in which you either (1) hold your chin or forehead, (2) touch a part of your face with your hand or fingers, (3) stroke or tap with one or more fingers, or (4) hold your hands close to your face without touching it.

You can select an emotion from the list below or think of one not listed. Remaining within your group, practice that emotion while others in your group practice their gestures. Then, after no more than 10 seconds of practice, share your gesture with others in the group, and have them identify the emotion. Continue this until each group member has tried all four hand/finger enhancement techniques.

If time allows, move to another group, or try permutations of the four hand/finger enhancement techniques using a closed or open hand, one finger or more, and so on.

Possible Facial Expressions

Amused
Angry
Anxious
Bored
Calm
Concerned
Contemptuous
Coy
Desire
Disgust
Disturbed/troubled
Engaged
Envy
Fearful
Happy
Impish/mischievous
Inattentive
Interest
Pity
Relief
Sadness
Seductive
Shame
Surprise
Thoughtful
Uninterest
Worried

Assignment

Practice the various emotions suggested, along with others you may want to convey. Think about your role as a teacher and/or director. What types of emotional messages will you be sending through your hand and finger gestures? Can you accurately read the emotional messages sent by others? Can you more accurately interpret those expressions when fingers or hands are added to support those messages?

Observation

Note the facial expressions of individuals, and observe how they do or don't use their fingers and hands to support those expressions.

PERSONAL MUSICIANSHIP: CONNECTING BREATHING AND SINGING

For this component, the focus is to:

- Review the posture and body alignment that promote successful singing.
- Discuss breathing that promotes successful singing.
- Sing a melody with limited pitches (d-r-m-s) in stick notation.
- Perform single-note accompaniments added to a melody using solfège syllables.

Your voice is your first instrument and will be used in every music classroom regardless of specialty (e.g., band, choir, general music, strings); therefore, it is important to maintain vocal health. Proper body alignment promotes healthy singing. Let's review alignment for singing. Are your feet bearing your weight equally? Are your hips aligned with your feet? Have you squared your shoulders with your hips? Is your head centered on your shoulders?

Star athletes recognize the importance of training and body health. Musicians also have an obligation to promote body health. Breathing involves the coordinated efforts of mental processing and physical response.

> *Chi sa respirare, sa cantare.* "He who knows how to breathe knows how to sing."
> (Italian proverb)

Place one hand on your rib cage and the other on your back. Inhale silently through your nose, and imagine filling up a balloon inside you. Then exhale using the consonant *s*. During exhalation, imagine the balloon deflating. Sustain the "sss" sound as long as possible. Using a watch or stopwatch, record how long you can maintain the "sss" sound during exhalation. Monitor your progress and ability to lengthen your vocal exhalations throughout the semester.

Before singing the melody in figure 6.2—utilizing the sequential steps from previous modules—align your body, and focus on starting the exercise with a supported breath.

Figure 6.2 "Dinah," stick notation.

PRE-CONDUCTING: PRECURSOR TO CUEING

In this exercise, we will use the conducting rebound in both hands/arms. This will further develop left/right hand/arm independence along with the conducting rebound. This exercise will also prepare you for cueing.

In the exercise, it is important to monitor carefully each of the suggested movements. Observe yourself in a mirror or with an electronic feedback device.

Classroom Setup

All members of the class can complete this exercise simultaneously. Students should stand and allow about one arm's length of space around them. An instructor should initiate each exercise and each step of any given exercise, allowing the class to practice as a unit.

Exercise

1. Establish your conducting posture, and complete the following task:
   a. Using a tempo of mm = 66, the right hand/arm will be performing a conducting rebound.
   b. The left hand/arm will also be doing a rebound, but it will be modified. The rebound in the left hand/arm will be (a) performed on only certain "beats" within a given four- or three-beat pattern, and (b) only as high as the initial drop. Hence, after the drop, the left hand/arm will rebound only as high as the original starting position, one or two inches. The drop will be one or two inches, and the rebound will be one or two inches. The beginning location of the left hand/arm will be slightly above the waist and somewhat in line with the left hip.
   c. When performing this exercise, make sure that both hands are relaxed, with palms facing toward the floor. You will note that your hands/fingers will be slightly curved and the fingers slightly spread when they are in a relaxed position.
   d. To start the exercise, begin rebounding with your right hand/arm (mm = 66), and count aloud in groups of four (1, 2, 3, 4, 1, 2, 3, 4, etc.). After a few warm-up patterns, the instructor will have you add the modified left-hand/arm rebound as follows:
      i. The left hand/arm will rebound once only on the first beat of each group of four beats. After four patterns, relax your hands/arms to the side.

ii. After your rest (a couple of seconds), resume your position, begin four beats of rebound with the right hand/arm, and initiate a modified left-hand/arm rebound on the second beat of each group of four beats. After four repetitions, relax, and then resume your conducting position.

iii. Perform four beats with the right hand/arm (remember to keep counting), and with the left, initiate a rebound on the third beat of each pattern. After four repetitions, relax, and resume.

iv. Begin four beats with the right hand/arm, and initiate a left-hand/arm rebound on the fourth beat of each pattern. Complete four repetitions, and then relax.

e. Now, staying with the four-beat pattern:

i. Begin by completing four beats with only the right hand/arm.

ii. Complete the following left-hand/arm modified rebound, remembering to relax after each set of four beat patterns

Beats 1 and 2

Beats 1 and 3

Beats 1 and 4

Beats 2 and 3

Beats 2 and 4

Beats 3 and 4

Beats 1, 2, and 3

Beats 1, 2, and 4

Beats 1, 3, and 4

Beats 2, 3, and 4

f. Now, think and count aloud in groups of three. Using the same procedures as outlined above, complete the following left-hand/arm rebounds:

Beat 1

Beat 2

Beat 3

Beats 1 and 2

Beats 1 and 3

Beats 2 and 3

Assignment

Should you want to further challenge yourself using the parameters provided in this exercise, try switching the roles of the hands/arms.

Observation

As you complete these exercises, are you maintaining and performing appropriate rebound heights for each hand? Are you letting your rebounds fall naturally, or are you inserting a preparation prior to the fall? (No preparation should be initiated prior to the fall.) Do you feel you are developing greater right- and left-hand/arm independence? Notice your directors' and conductors' right- and left-hand/arm independence skills.

PROFESSIONAL KNOWLEDGE: MODELING IN THE MUSIC CLASSROOM

For this component, the focus is to:

- Discuss the different types of modeling within a classroom setting.
- Discuss the teacher as a role model.

The well-known proverb "Imitation is the sincerest form of flattery" refers to paying someone an implied or unspoken compliment. By imitating the actions of others, you show your recognition of specific actions, viewpoints, values, or even simplistic things such as hairstyles or fashion choices. From the moment they are born, babies begin to learn about their environment through observations. This observational learning is sometimes called modeling or indirect learning, as the new behaviors are learned through watching the behaviors and consequences of others.

We are constantly learning from watching others model, and your students will learn by watching you. There are several types of models:

- Visual or physical.
- Positive or negative.
- Student/peer or teacher.
- Verbal or nonverbal.

For this component, we will focus on verbal and nonverbal models. Tait (1992) provides an overview of verbal and nonverbal teaching strategies to use during instruction. Verbal strategies can be divided into three options: professional, experiential, and process. Professional vocabulary originates from the music and can focus on technical, conceptual, or aesthetic aspects. The experiential option focuses on imagery, metaphor, and analogies, whereas process words combine overt and covert behaviors (Tait, 1992, p. 526). Nonverbal communication can also serve multiple functions within the classroom, such as showing emotions, approval or disapproval, values, and attitudes. With a specific focus on the music classroom, Tait divides the most common types of nonverbal modeling into musical, aural, and physical (p. 528). Nonverbal communication can be utilizing one of the three types or in combinations. See figure 6.3 for specific examples of verbal and nonverbal communication.

Type	Term	Example
Verbal	Professional Vocabulary	vibrato, staccato
	Experiential Vocabulary	words used to evoke emotions, colorful words, metaphors
	Process Vocabulary	analyze, imagine, explore, demonstrate
Nonverbal	Music Modeling	demonstration by teacher or peers on an instrument
	Aural Modeling	sing or hum certain segments, speak text in rhythm
	Physical Modeling	use of hand gestures, conducting, etc. to convey meaning

Figure 6.3 Verbal and nonverbal communication in the music classroom.

Eggen and Kauchak (2001) define modeling as "changes in people that result from observing the actions of others" (p. 236). In addition to modeling music behaviors and learning, as a teacher, you will also model your values (e.g., respect, kindness, honesty). Eurich (1995) also reminds readers that one can model respect in the classroom through interactions with adults and students in addition to respecting someone who has the floor when addressing the class (p. 120). Be aware of your ability to be a positive or negative role model. You never know who may choose to imitate you.

Discussion

1. Describe how the process of watching a role model can influence behavior.
2. Describe positive and/or negative role models you have encountered. How are they the same or different?

MODULE 6 REFERENCES

Eggen, P., & Kauchak. D. (2001). *Educational psychology: Classroom connections* (5th ed.). New York, NY: Macmillan.

Eurich, G. (1995). Theory into practice: Modeling respect in the classroom. *Intervention in School and Clinic, 31*(2), 119–121.

Mahmoud, M., & Robinson, P. (2013). Interpreting hand-over-face gestures. http://www.cl.cam.ac.uk/~pr10/publications/acii11f.pdf

Pease, A., & Pease, B. (2006). *The definitive book of body language.* York, NY: Bantam.

Tait, M. J. (1992). Teaching strategies and styles. In R. Colwell (Ed.), *Handbook of research on music teaching and learning* (pp. 697-709). New York, NY: Schirmer.

Visual Scanning—Vocal Exploration—Conducting Crescendos and Diminuendos—Teaching Adolescents

In this module, you will focus on:

- Personal awareness: Visual scanning in a group setting.
- Personal musicianship: Vocal exploration.
- Pre-conducting: Dynamic contrast indications (crescendos and diminuendos).
- Professional knowledge: Teaching adolescents.

PERSONAL AWARENESS: VISUAL SCANNING I

Visual awareness is one of the most important tools educators can use in assessing students' reactions in teaching situations. While there will be additional exercises to help you develop your visual awareness, the following exercises will assist you in group situations.

Classroom Setup

Since this exercise consists of scanning a class, the classroom should be arranged in two or three rows.

Exercises
Exercise 1

This exercise involves scanning from right to left with one row and then left to right on the next row, and so on. Use only the eyes to scan, without moving your head. At this point, you are only scanning the group, not making prolonged eye contact with any one person.

1. Since this first exercise involves scanning using eyes only (movement of the head and body should be restricted), the distance from the group must make this task possible.
2. Stand in front of the class at a distance of about 5 to 10 feet, depending on the class size and the length of the established rows. Each person begins with an elevated posture. Scan the row closest to you, beginning at one end and moving horizontally until you reach the opposite end of the row. Scan the next row in the opposite direction until that row is finished. Continue to scan if additional rows exist. Scan slowly enough that you "notice" each person's eyes. Each person needs to feel "contacted" but not in a prolonged manner.
3. Note that when you scan, you may become aware that your eyes move in "jumps." While it may seem that the visual flow is smooth, it is not, and you may notice one person more than another.
4. Once an individual has completed the exercise, the students can be asked if they felt contacted. If not, have the individual repeat the task.

Exercise 2

This exercise involves scanning using only the head.
1. Standing in front of the group in elevated posture, once again scan the group horizontally. This time, do so by moving only the head and restricting lateral eye movement.
2. Once this is completed by an individual, ask the students if they felt contacted.

Exercise 3

This exercise involves scanning by moving the head and the body.
1. This time, you will scan using both body movement and head movement, while restricting lateral movement of the eyes. You may first want to practice using only body movement (moving or turning your shoulders from left to right or right to left), even though this movement

is usually performed when your neck/head cannot be moved or is uncomfortable to move. Once you feel at ease moving with the body alone, add head movement.

2. Begin by holding your hands up to either side of your face so you can see them within your peripheral vision. Keeping your hands in place, turn toward your right, turning only your shoulders. Continue this process until you have scanned the group.
3. The movement should be a flowing, connective movement, not a disjointed, stop-and-start motion.
4. Assess. Once you are comfortable performing this exercise with your hands up, you can try it without holding hands elevated.

Exercise 4

This scan involves movement of the eyes and the head.

1. Looking at the first row, move your head to the right. Move your eyes to the left until it feels uncomfortable or unnatural, at which point move your head to the left and finish the scan.
2. With your head still facing left, begin scanning the second row. Move your eyes to the right until it feels uncomfortable or unnatural, and then move your head to the right and finish the scan.
3. The movement should be a flowing, connective movement, not a disjointed, stop-and-start motion.
4. Have students evaluate each individual's movements.

Exercise 5

This scan involves using the eyes, the head, and the body and is normally used when working with large groups. Imagine that your rows have been expanded and that you are working with a large group.

1. First, imagine you are continuously scanning with eye movement while assisted with both body and head movement.
2. Now, turn your shoulders to the far left, and begin your scan to the right. At some point, you will want to turn your head. Do this while continuing to scan. Remember, your eyes are also moving within this scan frame. At some point, you will want to engage your body movement as you continue to scan right until you reach the end of your expanded row.

3. Have students evaluate each individual's movements.

If your class is large, you may not be able to complete all exercises with all individuals during one class period. You may choose to have all students complete one exercise before moving to a different lesson segment, or you may wish to have a few students complete all exercises and then repeat this segment in future classes until all students have had practice opportunities.

Assignment

When you are in rehearsal or a classroom, practice these scanning techniques from your seat. When you are among a group of individuals, regardless of the setting, practice initiating your scanning techniques.

Observation

Notice how eye contact and movement differ among your instructors, whether in a classroom, rehearsal, or lecture situation. Teachers want to make eye contact, as it is one of the ways they ascertain whether students comprehend the information they are sending.

PERSONAL MUSICIANSHIP: VOCAL EXPLORATION AND SINGING SENSATIONS

For this component, the focus is to:

- Review breathing that promotes successful singing.
- Discuss using vocal exploration to release tension in the voice.
- Sing a melody with limited pitches (d-r-m-s) in standard notation.
- Perform single-note accompaniments added to a melody using Roman numerals.

Complete four consecutive breath exercises using the balloon analogy and the voiced exhalation process using the consonant *s*, as outlined in the personal musicianship component of module 6. Then perform one additional sequence, and time the length of your exhalation.

Once you can consistently provide breath support to your singing, it is time to focus on producing a relaxed, consistent tone throughout your range. Vocal exploration can serve as a steppingstone to singing without tension. Vocal explorations allow you to discover the "sensation of the singing voice" (Feierabend, 2003), which promotes consistency in vocal production throughout your vocal range.

For the "Ascending Range" exercise, extend your arms in front of you with your hands at waist height. As you slowly raise your hands to slightly above your head, trace the path of this physical upward motion with your voice. Start on any comfortable pitch. As your voice ascends, be sure to maintain a relaxed and light tone throughout. Practice this exercise at different speeds to promote further vocal flexibility.

When singing the melody in figure 7.1, utilizing the sequential steps from previous components, think of performing it with the same relaxed tone used in the vocal exploration activity.

Figure 7.1 "Dinah," traditional notation.

PRE-CONDUCTING: PRECURSOR TO DYNAMIC CONTRAST INDICATIONS

In these exercises, you will use the conducting rebound in the right hand/arm while developing proximity and height movement in the left hand/arm. You will continue to develop independence and the conducting rebound in the right hand/arm. The left-hand/arm movements will serve as a precursor to dynamic contrast indications.

In the following exercises, it is important to monitor carefully each of the movements suggested.

Classroom Setup

All class members can complete either of these exercises simultaneously. Students should stand and allow about one arm's length of space around them. An instructor should initiate each exercise and each step of any given exercise so the class practices as a unit.

Exercises
Exercise 1

1. Establish your conducting posture, and complete the following task:
   a. The left-hand/arm motion described below should be practiced before adding the right-hand/arm rebound. The left hand/arm will begin its motion starting at the right shoulder.
      i. Place your left hand on your right shoulder with the fingertips touching the shoulder joint. The hand/arm will stay at shoulder height throughout this exercise; however, you will move your left hand/arm across and away from your body during the movement as follows:
         The beginning and ending left-hand position will be the right shoulder.
         Move your left hand away from your right shoulder and to your left.
         Halfway through this movement, your left hand will be slightly below and in front of your chin, and your arm will have extended about halfway.
         At the end of the movement, your left hand/arm will be fully extended (as if reaching forward) and will be directly in front of your left shoulder. (Have a very slight bend at the elbow at the completion of your left-hand/arm extension.)

b. The return movement will follow the same path, and your left-hand fingertips will resume their position on the right shoulder joint. Practice this movement several times, using a count of three beats at mm = 69 to attain your position in front of the left shoulder and three beats to return to the right shoulder. The motion should be fluid, graceful, continuous, and smooth.

c. The left-hand movement is also important.

    i. At the beginning of the movement, the palm of the left hand should be facing toward you.

    ii. During the movement to the left, your left hand will begin to turn until your left palm is facing away from you and is in front of your left shoulder.

    iii. The palm should begin to turn toward you on the return movement until it reaches your right shoulder, at which point the palm again faces toward you.

    Practice this movement several times using three beats at mm = 69 to attain your position in front of the left shoulder and three beats to return to the right shoulder. Again, fluid, graceful movement remains the goal, with special attention to the movement and turning of the hand/palm.

d. Once this motion can be completed satisfactorily, add the right-hand rebound, and continue the exercise. Using a tempo of mm = 69, begin to rebound with your right hand/arm. Again, use three beats at mm = 69 to attain your left-hand/arm position in front of the left shoulder and three beats to return to the right shoulder. The left-hand/arm movements should be fluid and graceful and the right-hand/arm rebound appropriately completed. Remember to keep your left-hand/arm movement at shoulder height throughout the exercise.

e. The motion you are completing is a precursor to conducting one measure in 3/4 meter with a crescendo and one measure in 3/4 meter with a diminuendo.

Exercise 2

1. Establish your conducting posture, and complete the following task:

a. The right hand/arm will be performing a conducting rebound, but before initiating the right-hand rebound, the following technique should be practiced with the left hand/arm.

b. Place the left hand/arm slightly above the waist and somewhat in line with the left hip (the beginning conducting position) and with the palm of the left hand facing down/toward the floor. Move the left hand/arm in a circular motion. The left hand/arm will extend forward and up to the height of the left shoulder. Return to the beginning conducting position.

    i. When the left-hand/arm forward motion reaches shoulder height, the returning circular motion will rise slightly at the completion of the circular motion before descending back to the beginning position.

    ii. The resultant arc or circle formed should be completed so it is flowing, graceful, and without pause.

    iii. Practice this movement several times without the right hand, using a count of three beats at mm = 69 to attain your left shoulder position height and three beats to return to the conducting position.

c. The left-hand palm movement is as follows.

    i. The palm of the left hand begins facing the floor but is turned upward upon initiating the movement toward the ceiling.

    ii. Upon completing the forward circular motion, the palm should be turned and face outward, away from the face, until it comes to rest in the conducting position pointing again toward the floor.

    iii. The resultant motion of the palm, hand, and arm should be flowing and without pause.

    iv. Practice this movement several times without the right hand, using a count of three beats at mm = 69 to attain your left shoulder position height and three beats to return to the conducting position.

d. Once the left-palm/hand/arm motion can be successfully completed, add the right-hand rebound motion, using a count of three beats at mm = 69, and then add the left-hand motion. Use three beats to attain your left shoulder position height and three beats to return to the conducting position.

e. When performing this exercise, make sure both hands remain relaxed. You will note that your hands and fingers will be slightly curved and the fingers slightly spread when in a relaxed position.

f. To start the exercise, begin rebounding with your right hand/ arm and count, out loud, in groups of three (1, 2, 3, 1, 2, 3, etc.). After a few warm-up patterns, the instructor will have you add the left-hand/arm movement discussed.

    i. You may want to rest or relax after several measures of this exercise before moving to the next exercise.

    ii. You may also want to have a partner assess your right- and left-hand movements.

g. Once a rest period has been initiated:
   i. Begin with the left hand/arm on the right shoulder, extending for three beats until the left hand/arm is in front of the left shoulder. The palm of the hand gradually turns until it is facing the ceiling.
   ii. Now, instead of returning to the right shoulder, move your hand down into the conducting position. As the hand moves to the conducting position, the palm gradually turns until it is facing the floor.
   iii. You will now be in the conducting position with your left hand/arm. The left hand/arm moves forward and up for three beats, and the palm turns upward.
   iv. Now, instead of returning to the conducting position, move your left hand/arm to the right shoulder with the resultant palm position.
   v. Practice these combinations several times with the right-hand rebound until you feel comfortable.

The idea of these exercises is to prepare you for movements you may encounter in your conducting classes when indicating crescendo and diminuendo or dynamic contrast. Whether these exact motions are used is not of great significance; however, the process of developing the independence needed to perform these and future tasks is important.

Assignment

Try these exercises using four beats to complete the left-hand/arm movements away from the body and four beats back to the body. You can also use different tempi while performing these exercises. Should you want to further challenge yourself and further develop hand/arm independence, try switching the roles of the hands/arms.

Observation

Notice the movements your directors and conductors use when indicating dynamic changes in music.

PROFESSIONAL KNOWLEDGE: TEACHING ADOLESCENTS, "THE UNPREDICTABLES"

For this component, the focus is to:

- Define the term *adolescent*.
- Discuss the physiological, social, and psychological changes during adolescence
- Provide instructional strategies for working with adolescents in the music classroom.

What do you think of when you hear the term *adolescent*? Some refer to adolescents as children in adult bodies, while others think of them as adults in children's bodies. Adolescents are in a transitional stage between childhood and adulthood—a transition that involves physiological, social, and psychological changes. This transitional period typically begins around age 11 and ends during the late teens, although some individuals do not finish the transition until their early 20s.

Just as students enter adolescence, they typically begin middle school. Middle school serves as the bridge between elementary school and high school. A student experiences significant psychological growth during this stage and is in the process of developing his or her identity. This identity is established through real and imagined relationships. "Imagined" refers to how they perceive individuals or the environment. At this stage, students are highly conscious of peer approval, and puberty often becomes a period of self-doubt. While trying to embrace the adult world, adolescents often rebel against many things their parents did or do. Many lifestyle patterns are cemented during this stage.

Adolescents are just beginning to function at the formal operational stage. Formal operational thinking, according to Jean Piaget, includes hypothetical and deductive reasoning skills—the ability to apply logic (see Piaget, 1973). Therefore, students may struggle to make musical connections without teacher guidance. For example, before having students begin new music, an effective teacher will use a specific rhythmic or melodic pattern within the class warm-up and then have students identify those same patterns in a new song. (For more information, see Jean Piaget's theory of cognitive development in the professional knowledge component of module 15.)

How do we embrace these "unpredictables" and create positive learning environments? First, these students need and want adult assistance, even though their overt behaviors may be contradictory. Showing support and interest is crucial. Students often view the value of the subject content in relation to the perceived degree of teacher supportiveness. Music educators—especially those directing ensembles—have opportunities to make connections with their students over multiple semesters and multiple years. This can serve to form loyalties to the ensemble, foster positive self-esteem, and influence future preferences and behaviors.

Second, adolescents want and need to feel productive. They are more successful with hands-on experiences than with lengthy classroom lectures. They are more interested in concrete, immediate goals than in long-term goals. Long-range projects (e.g., composing music, learning concert repertoire, writing reports, etc.) must be segmented. Students need specific strategies and/or templates for personal practice sessions that include specific time frames. For example, requiring students to turn in drafts or segments of compositions (e.g., the main theme, the introduction, the chord progression, etc.) will promote success and lessen anxiety. Rather than having students focus on an entire composition for a playing test, have them focus on a small section of a work. Periodically assessing a student's ability to perform individual scales will be more successful than requiring him or her to perform multiple scales at the end of a term.

Third, adolescents need constant variety within a structured environment. Their reactions change from day to day and sometimes from minute to minute. It is essential to present material in ways that address all the learning modalities—cognitive, affective, and psychomotor. (See module 5 for more information on Bloom's learning domains.) Promoting cooperation, creativity, and critical thinking will assist in keeping them engaged while providing the variety they crave.

Finally, adolescents are observant and vigilant of teachers' actions and conversations. Teachers need to admit when they make a mistake; this sets the stage for students to recognize that mistakes are part of the learning process. Being honest and straightforward works best for providing feedback and praise. Don't sugarcoat your feedback, and remember that blanket responses, such as "great job," "awesome," or "nice work" will not positively affect future performance or serve as a catalyst for change and improvement.

Although adolescents are experiencing many cognitive, physical, and psychological changes, which may result in unpredictable behaviors, they often find music classrooms a safe environment in which to flourish and grow. Music classrooms are highly activity-based and, by the mere nature of the art, address the various learning domains. Maintaining high expectations for behaviors and musicianship—while keeping those expectations reachable, reasonable, and realistic—will promote a positive environment for the music community in your classroom.

Discussion

1. What behavior differences might you notice between music students in middle school and those in high school?
2. What might contribute to those behavior differences?
3. A colleague approaches and shares with you that he or she is struggling to motivate the high school freshman music class. What advice might you provide?

MODULE 7 REFERENCE

Piaget, J. (1973). *Memory and Intelligence.* New York: Basic Books.

SUGGESTED READINGS

Hanna, W. (2007). The new Bloom's taxonomy: Implications for music education. *Arts Education Policy Review, 108*(4), 7–16.
Mooney, C. G. (2000). *Theories of childhood: An introduction to Dewey, Montessori, Erikson, Piaget & Vygotsky.* St. Paul, MN: Redleaf.

Visual Scanning—Vocal Exploration and the Wave—Conducting Cutoff Gestures—Teaching Music in Early Childhood

In this module, you will focus on:

- Personal awareness: Visual scanning in a group setting.
- Personal musicianship: Vocal exploration.
- Pre-conducting: Cutoff gestures.
- Professional knowledge: Teaching music in early childhood.

PERSONAL AWARENESS: VISUAL SCANNING II

In the first set of visual scanning exercises, in module 7, viewing a group of individuals in rows was presented. However, teachers and directors don't scan only by rows but also by groups or sections. For example, a music director may scan a group by instrumentation, while a teacher may scan a class horizontally (by rows), vertically (by columns), or diagonally.

Classroom Setup

These exercises consist of scanning a class vertically, diagonally, and by group or section. For each exercise, a row-and-column arrangement is suggested for implementation purposes. If the class is not large enough to meet the suggested arrangements, individuals should disperse about the room yet maintain an ordered row-and-column setup. Empty chairs or desks can be placed among the rows and columns to represent individuals. As in the earlier visual scanning exercises, you are only scanning individuals, not making prolonged contact with a specific person. The procedure of beginning with eyes alone, then head alone, then head and body, eyes and head, and, finally, eyes, head, and body will again be followed.

Exercises
Exercise 1

For vertical scanning practice, it is best if the class is arranged in three rows of five straight columns. Previously, you scanned by rows (horizontal scanning) beginning from right to left. In vertical scanning, you will view individuals by columns.

1. Begin your scan, for consistency's sake, with the person on the far-right side of the room in the first row, first column. From here, you will scan the first person in the second row, first column, followed by the first person in the third row, first column, and so on.
2. Once a column of individuals has been scanned, proceed to the next column. Begin with the last person in the last row of the second column, scanning vertically to the person in the first row, second column.
3. Move to the next column, and continue until the group has been scanned.
4. Practice this exercise with eyes alone, then head alone, then head and body, then eyes and head, and, finally, with eyes, head, and body.
5. Briefly assess the effectiveness of an individual's eye contact. Ask class members if they felt contacted.

Exercise 2

In diagonal scanning, you will scan using an X pattern. For implementation purposes, it will be assumed that you have three rows and five columns of individuals.

1. Beginning on the far-right side of the group, scan the first person in the first row, first column, followed by the second person in the second row, second column, and, finally, the third person in the third row, third column.

2. Now, scan to your right to the last person in the first row, first column, observing the last person in the second column on your way there. After scanning the last person in the first row, first column, scan to the second person in the second row, second column, and then to the first person in the first row, third column.
3. You will have completed an X scan pattern.
4. Next, scan to the person in the second row, fourth column, and then to the person in the third row, fifth column.
5. Scan now to the person in the first row, fifth column, also observing the person in the second row, fifth column. From here, scan the person in the second row, fourth column, then the person in the third row, third column, and so forth, to complete another X pattern. (See figure 8.1.)

Figure 8.1 Diagonal scanning.

6. Practice this exercise with eyes alone, then head alone, then head and body, then eyes and head, and, finally, with eyes, head, and body.
7. Briefly assess the individual's performance. Did you feel contacted?
8. The idea is to scan in a diagonal sequence, and whatever pattern you choose to use is fine. The pattern described in this exercise is for explanatory purposes and is portrayed in figure 8.1.

Exercise 3

Now you will practice scanning by section or group. For implementation purposes, we will assume that we have four rows of students in four columns. This will form four sections, or four groups, with four people per group. If you would like to separate the sections as shown in figure 8.1 to accustom yourself to this grouping idea, you may do so, but the idea ultimately is to form this type of grouping in your mind, even though a clear separation in a rehearsal or classroom setting does not exist.

1. Begin with the far-right section, and scan the four individuals in that group using horizontal, vertical, or diagonal scanning procedures.
2. Now, move to another section, and scan these four individuals.

3. Continue this process until all individuals in the setting have been scanned.
4. Practice this exercise with eyes alone, then head alone, then head and body, then eyes and head, and, finally, with eyes, head, and body.
5. Assess.

If your class is large, all individuals may not be able to complete all exercises within one class segment. You may choose to have all students complete only one exercise and then move to a different lesson segment, or you may wish to have a few students do all exercises and then repeat this segment in future classes until all students have had a practice opportunity.

Assignment

Practice your scanning techniques when you are in various settings. You should feel that you are capturing more nonverbal information through your scanning techniques.

Observation

Notice how eye contact and movement differ among your instructors, whether in a classroom, rehearsal, or lecture situation. Teachers want to make eye contact, as it is one of the ways they ascertain whether students comprehend the information they are sending.

PERSONAL MUSICIANSHIP: VOCAL EXPLORATION AND THE WAVE

For this component, the focus is to:

- Review the purpose of vocal exploration.
- Sing a melody with limited pitches (d-r-m-s) in standard notation.
- Perform single-note accompaniments added to a melody using Roman numerals.

In the personal musicianship component of module 7, you learned about the importance of producing a relaxed, consistent tone throughout your range. How can vocal exploration activities serve to support this goal? The "Ascending Range exercise in module 7 focused on producing a consistent tone within an ascending pattern.

The following exercise, called "The Wave," focuses on producing a consistent tone while ascending and descending. Extend your right arm across your body at waist height. As you move your hand from left to right, imagine you are riding on a wave. Start on any comfortable pitch. As your arm moves up and down on your wave, follow the same pathway with the voice. Concentrate on maintaining a relaxed, light tone during these ascending and descending vocal explorations. As you complete this exercise several times, remember that a when riding a wave, you ascend at a different rate from when you descend. Be sure to represent this speed fluctuation with your voice, and use plenty of breath support in order to enjoy the long ride.

When singing the melody in figure 8.2—utilizing the sequential steps from previous modules—think of performing the melody with the same relaxed tone used in the vocal exploration activity.

Traditional

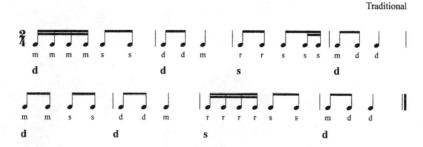

Figure 8.2 "Deedle Deedle Dumpling," stick notation.

PRE-CONDUCTING: CUTOFF GESTURES I

In these exercises, we will use the conducting rebound of the right hand/arm while developing movements in the left hand/arm as preparation for cutoff indications. We will continue to develop independence and enhance conducting rebound in the right hand/arm.

Carefully monitor each of the movements suggested.

Classroom Setup

All class members can complete any of these exercises simultaneously. Students should stand and allow about one arm's length of space around them. An instructor should initiate each exercise and each step of any given exercise so the class practices as a unit.

Exercises
Exercise 1

1. Establish your conducting posture, and complete the following task:
   a. The right hand/arm will perform a conducting rebound, and the left hand/arm will begin its motion starting on the right shoulder. (This pre-conducting cutoff gesture will be used in the pre-conducting exercises in modules 37 and 40 and will be referred to as cutoff gesture A.)
      i. As in the pre-conducting exercise in module 7, place your left hand/arm on your right shoulder, with the tips of the fingers on the shoulder joint. The beginning left-hand/arm position will be the right shoulder. Starting there, move your left hand/arm forward and away from your right shoulder and to your left side. At the beginning of the movement, the palm of the left hand should be facing toward you. Halfway through this movement, your left hand/arm will be slightly below and in front of your chin, and your arm will have extended about halfway. At the end of the movement, your left hand/arm will be directly in front of your shoulder, and your arm will be fully extended but will have a slight bend at the elbow. Once you are at the end of this movement, move your left hand in an upward, clockwise, circular motion.

      At the top of the circular motion, turn the palm of your hand in a downward movement.

      At the end of the circle, close the hand so you are forming a relaxed but closed hand/fist.

The return movement will extend only to approximately the middle of your body (you will not return your left hand/arm to the right shoulder). Your hand will be below (approximately chest height) and in front of your chin.

At the completion of the circular motion, your left hand will be positioned midway between the distance you extended your left hand/arm from your body.

ii. Practice this movement without the right hand (mm = 52).

On the first beat, move the left hand/arm from the right shoulder to the extended left position as described above.

On the second beat, complete the circular motion of the hand, as previously described.

On the third beat, rest, holding the left hand/arm in the relaxed but closed position.

Repeat and practice this movement several times using the tempo mm = 52. Your left-hand/arm motion should be fluid and graceful. Pay special attention to the movement/ turning/closing of the left hand/palm during the exercise.

iii. Once this motion can be completed satisfactorily, add the right-hand rebound, and continue the exercise. Again, using mm = 52 per beat and conceptualizing a three-beats-per-measure grouping: attain your left-hand/arm position in front of the left shoulder, complete the left-hand/palm circular motion and closing of the hand, and rest/hold in the ending position for one beat before repeating the exercise.

b. Begin rebounding with your right hand/arm, and count, out loud, in groups of three (1, 2, 3, 1, 2, 3, etc.). After a couple of warm-up patterns, the instructor will have you add the first left-hand/arm movement discussed.

i. You may want to rest or relax after several measures of this exercise before moving to the next exercise.

ii. You may also want to have a partner assess the right- and left-hand movements.

c. Once the first exercise has been successfully completed, begin the second exercise.

Exercise 2

1. Establish your conducting posture, and complete the task below. (This pre-conducting cutoff gesture will be used in the pre-conducting exercises in modules 38 and 40 and will be referred to as cutoff gesture B.)

a. The right hand/arm will be performing a conducting rebound.
b. The beginning location of the left hand/arm will be slightly above the waist and somewhat in line with your left hip (conducting position). The palm of the left hand should be facing down, toward the floor.

   i. The left hand/arm will move in a circular motion so that the left hand/arm will extend forward and up to left-shoulder height. The return point for this exercise will be midway between the end of your left-hand/arm extension and your body, similar to the return point explained in the first exercise above.

      Starting with your left hand/arm in conducting position, begin your movement with the palm of the left hand facing toward you.

      At the end of the movement, your left hand/arm will be directly in front of your shoulder, and your arm will be fully extended but will have a very slight bend at the elbow. Move your left hand in an upward circular motion.

      At the top of the circular motion, turn the palm of your hand downward. At the end of the circle, close the hand so you are forming a relaxed but closed hand/fist. The return movement will extend to the middle of your body; you will not return your left hand/arm to the conducting position at this point. Your hand will be approximately chest height and below and in front of your chin.

      Upon completion of the circular motion, your left hand will be positioned midway between the distance you extended your left hand/arm and your body. The resultant arc/circle formed should be completed so you can execute with flowing, graceful movements and without pause.

   ii. Practice this movement without the right hand. Once the motion becomes familiar, connect the movement with the metered beat (mm = 52).

c. Begin rebounding with your right hand/arm, and count out loud in groups of three (1, 2, 3, 1, 2, 3, etc.). After a few warm-up patterns, the instructor will have you add the first left-hand/arm movement discussed.

   i. You may want to rest or relax after several measures of this exercise before moving to the next exercise.

   ii. You may also want to have a partner assess the right- and left-hand movements.

d. After successful completion of the second exercise and a brief rest period, perform the next exercise.

Exercise 3

1. Having established your conducting posture and the resultant hand/arm height, complete the following task. (This cutoff gesture will be referred to as cutoff gesture C in the pre-conducting exercises of modules 39 and 40.)

  a. The beginning location of the left hand/arm will be slightly above the waist (conducting position). The palm of the left hand should be facing down, toward the floor. The movement of your left hand/arm will be as follows.

    i. The left hand/arm will move in a horizontal motion at the beginning of the movement and a circular movement at its conclusion.

    ii. The left hand/arm will extend to the side. The return point for this exercise will be approximately midway between the end of your left-hand/arm extension and your body, similar to the return point explained in the previous two exercises.

      Starting with your left hand/arm in conducting position, begin your movement. At the beginning of the movement, the palm of the left hand should be facing toward the floor; however, you should immediately turn it 45 degrees. The hand will now be in a vertical position.

      Move the left hand/arm sideways, in a straight line, until your arm is fully extended, with a slight bend at the elbow.

      Once you finish this movement, move your left hand in an upward circular motion. At the top of the circular motion, turn the palm of your hand in a downward movement. At the end of the circle, close the hand so you are forming a relaxed but closed hand/fist. The return movement will extend only to the middle of your body. You will not return your left hand/arm to the conducting position at this point. Your hand will be at approximately chest height and below and in front of your chin. At the completion of the circular motion, your left hand will be positioned midway between the distances you extended your left hand/arm from your body. The resultant arc or circle formed should be completed so it is flowing, graceful, and without pause.

    iii. Practice this movement, first without the mm = 52 beat, without the right hand. Once the motion becomes familiar, connect the movement with the metered beat as follows:

On the first beat, move the left hand/arm from the conducting position to the horizontally extended position
described above.

On the second beat, complete the circular motion of the
hand, as previously described.

On the third beat, rest, holding the left hand/arm in the
relaxed but closed position.

Repeat and practice this movement several times, using
the tempo mm = 52. Your left-hand/arm motion should
be fluid and graceful. Pay special attention to the move-
ment/turning/closing of the left hand/palm during the
movement.

    iv. Once this motion can be completed satisfactorily, add the
right-hand rebound, and continue the exercise.

  b. Begin rebounding with your right hand/arm, and count, out loud, in
groups of three (1, 2, 3, 1, 2, 3, etc.). After a few warm-up patterns,
the instructor will have you add the first left-hand/arm movement
discussed. You may want to rest or relax after several measures of this
exercise before repeating this or one of the above exercises. You may
also want to have a partner assess the right- and left-hand movements.

Assignment

Try these exercises using four beats to complete the left-hand/arm movements, still using two beats to perform the motion but adding another
beat of rest/hold at the end of the movement. You can also use different
tempi while performing these exercises. Should you want to further challenge yourself using the parameters provided in this exercise, try switching the roles of the hands/arms.

Observation

Notice the movements your directors and conductors use when indicating
cutoffs.

PROFESSIONAL KNOWLEDGE: TEACHING MUSIC IN EARLY CHILDHOOD

For this component, the focus is to:

- Define the term *early childhood.*
- Discuss the nature of effective music environments when working with young children.

Young children do not learn multiple concepts simultaneously but rather in "chunks." Only over time are they able to accommodate more complex thinking. The National Association for the Education of Young Children (NAEYC) has defined early childhood as encompassing birth to age eight. Thanks to psychologists and the continual refinement of learning theories, educators no longer view young children as merely "small adults." Providing music experiences for these youngest musicians requires a different approach. The main difference when working with this age group is to remember to *invite* them to participate in music experiences, rather than *expecting* participation as we do with students in older grades and adults.

A main premise of the NAEYC is to educate teachers, parents, and child-care providers in the importance of developmentally appropriate practice (DAP). At its core, DAP has three main focuses for instruction: age appropriate, individually appropriate, and culturally appropriate (Copple & Bredekamp, 2010). You might be thinking that's what all teaching should have at its core. You are correct. The main consideration when with working with young children is to be aware that their physical, psychological, and social abilities are very different from those of their older counterparts.

Andress (1998), one of the first leading experts in early childhood music, noted the importance of providing young children with music experiences that provide exposure to all the music elements while recognizing they are not ready for mastering advanced terminology. Children use voices, bodies, and everyday items (e.g., toys, spoons, pans) when making music. Through these activities, they learn to identify and manipulate music in learning that eventually leads to identifying and describing the music using traditional terminology and notation. The key to labeling and analyzing—yes, young children can analyze—these experiences is to use terms in their current vocabulary that describe what they are hearing, playing, singing, and so on, rather than using expected terminology. Andress labels this process using "key descriptors" or "general music controls." (See figure 8.3 for a comparison of suggested age-appropriate terminology for the music elements.)

Music Elements	
Traditional Terminology	General Music Controls
Rhythm	short sounds, long sounds, really long, silence
Pitch	high sounds, low sounds, sounds can go up, down, or stay the same
Tempo	fast, slow, getting faster, getting slower
Dynamics	loud, soft, getting louder, getting softer
Form	same, different, almost the same, music "idea"
Timbre	voices can speak, sing, whisper, shout; instruments and animals make different sounds
Style	music you might hear at a parade, music to put baby to sleep
Articulation	smooth, jagged, choppy, separated, jumpy

Figure 8.3 A comparison of traditional terminology and general music controls.

Childhood is not a race. Music development—especially vocal development—for children is a slow process. They need time to hear songs multiple times, and adults need to be willing to sing again and again and again. Children naturally make music; therefore, all their music expressions are to be embraced and encouraged.

Discussion

1. Think about young children you have observed, whether at home or in public spaces (restaurants, parks, etc.), and discuss the differences you noted in how they move in comparison to adults. What about differences in fine motor skills?
2. Go to a public space, and conduct a "child watching" exercise by identifying musical behaviors of young children as they interact with parents and other children.

MODULE 8 REFERENCES

Andress, B. (1998) *Music for young children.* Fort Worth, TX: Harcourt Brace.

Copple, C., & Bredekamp, S. (Eds.). (2010). *Developmentally appropriate practice in early childhood programs serving children from birth through 8* (3rd. ed.). Washington, DC: National Association for the Education of Young Children.

MODULE 9

Connective Eye Contact—Improvisation in Singing—Conducting Cutoff Gestures—Communicating with Students

In this module you will focus on:

- Personal awareness: Visual awareness, eye scanning, and connective eye contact.
- Personal musicianship: Improvisation as a tool for expressive singing.
- Pre-conducting: A continuation of cutoff gestures.
- Professional knowledge: Listening and communicating with students in the classroom.

PERSONAL AWARENESS: VISUAL CONTACT— CONNECTIVE EYE CONTACT

In the visual-scanning exercises in modules 7 and 8, you began to understand how to scan a group. As teachers and directors, we scan individuals in an ensemble or a class and also periodically focus on specific individuals within that group. The eye-contact exercise is similar to that described in the eye-to-eye exercises, only not necessarily maintaining eye contact for as long. This type of eye contact will be called connective eye contact or connective contact.

When you stop scanning and make connective eye contact with an individual for a brief period, it may be to recapture that individual's attention, to address a nonverbal concern that person is sending, or perhaps to assess his or her understanding of a directive or point being made. This serves as another approach you can use to "read" individuals within a group for a number of purposes.

Classroom Setup

This exercise will focus on developing your connective-eye-contact skills with individuals within a group while continuing to expand your eye-scanning skills. Since we will use the techniques presented in modules 7 and 8, the following seating arrangement is suggested: at least three rows of chairs/students with five columns. Again, depending on class size, individuals may need to imagine there are students in the empty chairs.

Exercise

Connective eye contact is established when you stop scanning and look at one individual. When you and that person establish eye contact for at least one second, you have made connective contact. Both you and the individual will be aware that eye contact was made. This awareness can become part of the assessment process.

For this exercise, it is suggested that you use the scanning approaches presented in modules 7 and 8. Now, however, you will want to establish connective contact with individuals in the group. This connection is suggested for every third or fourth person you scan. Thus, using the techniques of horizontal, vertical, diagonal, and/or group or section scanning, you will periodically make connective contact with specific individuals.

For an extension of this exercise, try the scanning and connective-contact procedures using:

- Eyes alone.
- Head alone.
- Head and body.
- Eyes and head.
- Eyes, head, and body.

In combination with:

- Horizontal scanning.
- Vertical scanning.
- Diagonal scanning.
- Group or section scanning.

A brief assessment of each person's performance in these settings is important for individual growth.

If your class is large, you may not be able to complete all exercises with all individuals. You may choose to have all students complete only one exercise before moving to a different lesson, or you may wish to have a few students do all exercises and then repeat this segment in future classes until all students have had participation opportunities.

Assignment

Practice the scanning techniques used in this exercise when you are in small and large groups of people in classrooms, rehearsals, and social gatherings. As you improve your scanning techniques, do you feel you are gathering more information about individuals in each setting than you were previously?

Observation

Notice how eye contact and movement differ among your various instructors, whether in a classroom, rehearsal, or lecture situation. Notice also how many times your teachers and directors make connective eye contact.

PERSONAL MUSICIANSHIP: IMPROVISATION AS A TOOL FOR EXPRESSIVE SINGING

For this component, the focus is to:

- Practice expressive singing using improvisation and poetry.
- Sing a melody with limited pitches (d-r-m-s) in standard notation.
- Perform single-note accompaniments added to a melody using Roman numerals.

In previous personal musicianship components, you performed "Ascending Range" and "The Wave" as tools for promoting relaxed vocal production throughout your range. The following exercise, "Improvising with Poetry," focuses on expressive singing.

Use the traditional nursery rhyme "One Misty Moisty Morning":

One misty moisty morning,
When cloudy was the weather,
I chanced to meet an old man,
Clothed all in leather.
He began to compliment
And I began to grin.
How do you do? How do you do?
How do you do again?

Follow this sequence:

- Read the poem aloud line by line. As a class or in small groups, have each person read one line of the poem. Repeat the poem, as necessary, to allow all to participate.
- Read the poem again, this time focusing on expressivity by incorporating exaggerated vocal inflections.
- Improvise a melody to use with the text. The improvisation can be as simple or complex as you choose. It is sometimes helpful to think of a particular style of music to help spark your creativity. For example, how would you sing this poem if it were performed as part of an opera?

Remember that various poetry styles will prompt different vocal inflections and melodic improvisations. When practicing this exercise individually, experiment with several different poems. Record yourself reading expressively and singing an improvised melody. Analyze your ability to maintain breath support and a relaxed tone.

When singing the melody in figure 9.1—utilizing the sequential steps from previous modules—think of performing the melody with the same expressiveness you used during the poetry activity.

Figure 9.1 "Deedle Deedle Dumpling," standard notation.

PRE-CONDUCTING: CUTOFF GESTURES II

These exercises are an extension of the pre-conducting component in module 8, where you used the conducting rebound in the right hand/arm while developing precursor cutoff indications in the left hand/arm. In the following exercises, carefully monitor each of the suggested movements.

Classroom Setup

All class members can complete either of these exercises simultaneously. Students should stand and allow about one arm's length of space around them. An instructor should initiate each exercise and each step of any given exercise so the class is practicing as a unit.

Exercises
Exercise 1

1. As in the first pre-conducting exercise in module 8, your right hand/arm should be slightly above your waist. Your left hand/arm will begin on the right shoulder. The right hand will be performing a conducting rebound, and the left hand will do the cutoff motion.
2. The left-hand cutoff motion will be completed in two beats. Adding the right hand/arm and using the tempo mm = 52, think in a pattern of three beats per measure/grouping. Complete the left-hand/palm motion beginning on the first beat, with the cutoff completed on beat two, and rest/hold on the remaining third beat. Repeat.
3. Still thinking in groups of three, initiate the left-hand motion on beat two, and complete the cutoff motion on beat three, resting on beat one. Repeat.
4. Perform a cutoff on beat one. Initiate the left-hand motion on beat three, complete the cutoff motion on beat one, and rest on beat two. Repeat.
5. Now, think in groups of four beats per measure. Perform a cutoff on beat two. Initiate the left-hand motion on beat one, and complete the cutoff on beat two, resting on beats three and four Repeat.
6. Still thinking in groups of four, perform a cutoff on beat three, initiate the movement on beat two, complete the cutoff on beat three, and rest on beats four and one. Repeat.
7. Complete a cutoff on beat four by initiating on beat three. Repeat.
8. Compete a cutoff on beat one by initiating on beat four. Repeat.

Exercise 2

Using the procedure outlined above, perform cutoffs on the various beats. Think in both three-beat and four-beat groupings (mm = 52) when performing a cutoff on various beats. For a more detailed description of this exercise, see the pre-conducting exercise in module 8.

The beginning location of the left hand/arm will be slightly above the waist, with the palm facing the floor. Then turn the palm to face you as the arm extends forward and up to shoulder height. At the top of the motion, turn the palm of your hand downward, and complete the cutoff motion while moving to a point approximately at the middle of your body, slightly lower than chest height, and in front of your chin.

Assignment

You can also use different tempi while performing these exercises. Should you want to further challenge yourself using the parameters provided in this exercise, try switching the roles of the hands/arms.

Observation

Notice the movements your directors and conductors use when indicating cutoffs in music.

PROFESSIONAL KNOWLEDGE: LEARNING TO LISTEN

In this component, the focus is to:

- Examine the process involved in listening and communicating with students in the classroom during instruction.

  What I needed as a child in school was a teacher who wanted to hear my voice, my ideas, the words that were always present but never spoken; a teacher who would have given me the support and safety and a space in which to project that voice . . . a teacher who would have valued my voice just because it was mine, not because it provided the right answer. (Jalongo, 2007, p. 1)

Teaching is a reciprocal process between teachers and students; all are learners, and all are teachers. It is one thing to create an environment where students feel comfortable in sharing their responses to questions, thoughts, ideas, and insights. It is quite another environment where the teacher actually listens to student responses and incorporates them within the instruction, whether immediate or delayed. This reciprocal process relies on the teacher's ability to be an effective communicator.

How do you communicate your wants, needs, and emotions to your family? Your friends? Your teachers? The process is different for each setting, but what remains consistent is the desire to share or exchange information and viewpoints and to be understood. "The key to this understanding is listening" (Jalongo, 2007, p. 9). Nelson (2007) asserts that communication serves two purposes: to understand and to build relationships. It's likely that you've experienced a situation where you were talking *to* someone rather than talking *with* someone, and during the exchange you realized the other person wasn't really listening or paying attention.

How do you pay attention? First and foremost, paying attention requires eye contact and purposeful listening. This is easier for some individuals than for others, as it requires a complex chain of events. Your brain has to capture sound while matching it to the movement of the mouth and then match it to your previous knowledge bank to extract the meaning from those sounds. The next step involves listening for vocal inflections that indicate whether the speaker is being earnest, sarcastic, and so on. Listening or paying attention also involves reading the facial expressions, hand gestures, and overall body language of another individual—items you are experiencing within the personal awareness components of this text. Emphasis on eye contact and purposeful listening is merely the first step. What you do with the information received from your students is equally important.

Imagine that you design a stellar music lesson and deliver it with precision and passion. Oh, yes, you are definitely quite proud of yourself. Yet as you begin informal assessments of student comprehension, it becomes painfully clear that they don't understand the concept, either through verbal responses or through performing on an instrument. Now what? Perhaps you've heard teachers say, "We just went over this material. Why weren't you listening?" It is easy to project the blame onto students—and, granted, sometimes they *aren't* listening—but the onus is always on the teacher to deliver material in a manner that makes sense to all learners in the classroom. Listening to students' wrong answers can often provide insight into how to adjust your explanations, definitions, and/or examples to make them more effective. Incorrect responses (wrong answers, performing incorrect rhythms, etc.) result from students' efforts to make connections between their previous knowledge (the known) and new material (the unknown). An effective teacher listens to the vocabulary the students use within their explanations as a guide for presenting the material in alternative ways. It is likely that students have partial comprehension of the material and merely need one or two additional instructional steps to assist their learning. Rather than dismissively saying, "No, that's not right; who else wants to try to answer this question?" take the time to listen to the incorrect responses and use them as steppingstones to form a bridge from the known to the unknown.

How will you react when you observe a student who is upset, frustrated at not understanding the class content, struggling with personal issues, or having experienced a traumatic life event? It is unrealistic to think you'll have all the answers and know all the correct responses—not even veteran teachers can make that claim. "Giving undivided attention or a sympathetic look [can] be just as comforting as my saying the 'right' thing" (Jalongo, 2007, p. 2).

We often hear adults say, "What that child needs is a good talking to." Maybe we should consider rephrasing that to "What that child needs is a good *listening* to."

Discussion

1. Think of instances when you gave correct answers in class and instances when you gave incorrect answers. How did the teacher respond? How did the teacher's responses encourage or discourage you?

2. With a partner or a small group, practice responding to incorrect statements in a way that acknowledges the individual's current knowledge yet provides a steppingstone to new content. Example: "I know a dotted half note is held for three counts, so a dotted quarter note must be held for two counts." The individual knows the note value for the dotted half note, but obviously doesn't understand that the dot's value fluctuates depending on the note it follows.

MODULE 9 REFERENCES

Jalongo, M. R. (2007). *Learning to listen, listening to learn.* Washington, DC: National Association for the Education of Young Children.

Nelson, K. (2007). Young minds in social worlds; Experience, meaning and memory. Cambridge, MA: Harvard University Press.

Visual Awareness and Facial Gestures—Singing Intervals—Conducting the 4/4 Pattern—Goals and Objectives

I n this module, you will focus on:

- Personal awareness: Combining visual awareness with facial gestures.
- Personal musicianship: Maintaining a consistent vocal tone when singing large ascending intervals.
- Pre-conducting: Conducting the 4/4 pattern.
- Professional knowledge: Defining goals and objectives and their purpose in planning classroom instruction.

PERSONAL AWARENESS: COMBINING VISUAL AWARENESS WITH FACIAL GESTURES I

As teachers and directors, we learn to assess individual feedback from a variety of sources, in one-on-one situations and group settings. To develop the skill of "reading" a group, we combine our visual-scanning abilities with expertise at facial interpretation. This is a means of determining whether our message is being received and ascertaining whether students seem focused, understand our message, and so forth.

Classroom Setup

In this exercise, you will observe your classmates and be asked which individuals within the group convey a particular facial expression. The classroom should be arranged in three rows with five columns. If your class contains fewer than 15 individuals, put empty chairs in the rows/columns and randomly fill in the chairs. If you have a larger class, add more rows. To provide no other gestural cues during this exercise, students should sit with their feet flat on the floor shoulders' width apart, with hands crossed or on top of each other and placed on the lap or desktop, and using a relaxed but upright posture (no slumping).

Exercise

1. Have students count off (1, 2, 3, 4, etc.) until each person has an assigned number.
2. For this exercise, the following expressions will be used:
   a. Anger (frowning, squinting, rigid mouth/lips pulled inward, facial muscles generally pulled inward, flared nostrils, etc.).
   b. Confusion/questioning (eyebrows lowered and pulled together but not sloped, one eyebrow may be higher than the other as in a questioning mode, forehead smooth, mouth/lips somewhat relaxed but straight, lips may protrude slightly or be flattened).
   c. Happiness (smiling, wide-open eyes, raised eyebrows, upturned mouth corners, mouth can be slightly open, etc.).
3. To begin the exercise, one individual comes to the front of the class. The instructor selects one of the three expressions (happiness, anger, or confusion/questioning) and three members of the class, by assigned number, to convey that expression. The individual in front of the group should not be informed of either the expression being conveyed or the three individuals conveying the expression.
   a. All individuals begin with a neutral or calm expression.
   b. When the instructor signals, the three individuals selected convey the expression, while all others maintain a neutral/calm pose.
4. The pose is held for a maximum of five seconds. The instructor initiates the count, and the individual in front of the class begins his or her scan of the group.
5. At the end of five seconds, the instructor calls "time," and everyone maintains or returns to a neutral/calm pose.
6. The individual is then asked which three classmates conveyed the expression and what expression was conveyed.

7. This procedure can be repeated for the other two expressions, and then another individual can be selected to come to the front of the class. Once these initial expressions have been performed, the exercise can continue using different expressions. Additional practice can include varying the number of individuals conveying each pose.

Assignment

As you go through your daily activities, make yourself more aware of the facial gestures of others. Notice changes in facial expressions (eyes, forehead, etc.) as activities or conversations change.

Observation

As you observe groups of individuals talking in the hallway, participating in classrooms, listening to directives in ensembles, and so on, notice the expressions on individual faces in the group. What messages are they sending?

PERSONAL MUSICIANSHIP: SINGING
THROUGH LARGE ASCENDING INTERVALS

For this component, the focus is to:

- Practice creating a consistent vocal tone during large ascending intervals.
- Sing a melody with limited pitches (d-r-m-s-l) in stick notation
- Perform single-note accompaniments added to a melody using solfège syllables.

When you are singing, you want to maintain vocal consistency or smoothness, whether in a low register, in a high register, or during passages with large intervalic leaps. To promote a relaxed vocal tone, we will revisit the "Ascending Range" exercise, presented in the personal musicianship component of module 7. Start on the pitch D, and only ascend using a vocal slide (moving through various ascending pitches but not focused on a specific scale) until you reach the pitch A. Repeat the ascending D-to-A pattern several times while focusing on consistent tone production. When confident of your ability to maintain consistency during the vocal slide, perform the interval from D to A without the slide. Alternating between sliding and performing the interval without a slide allows multiple opportunities for you to feel the sensation of smoothness and consistency.

When singing the melody in figure 10.1—utilizing the sequential steps from previous modules—identify the measures that contain a large ascending leap. Concentrate on having your voice flow while maintaining smoothness through the large leap without tension.

Traditional

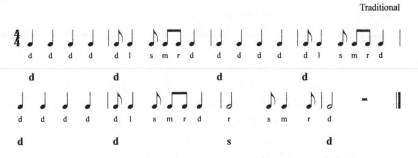

Figure 10.1 "Black Snake," stick notation.

PRE-CONDUCTING: 4/4 CONDUCTING PATTERN

Up to this point, you've kept the right hand/arm in a fixed position. In this exercise, you will begin precursor movements that outline a 4/4 conducting pattern. You will only be using the right hand/arm in this exercise. The left hand/arm will remain in a resting position at the left side of your body.

In the following exercise, carefully monitor the movements suggested.

Classroom Setup

All class members can complete this exercise simultaneously. Students should stand and allow about one arm's length of space around them. An instructor should initiate each exercise and each step of any given exercise so the class practices as a unit.

Exercise

1. Establish your conducting posture, and complete the following task:
   a. As a review, your right-hand/arm rebound has been completed above your waist, on an imaginary plane, in front of or approximately in front of your right thigh. The rebound has been initiated by dropping a relaxed hand in which the fingers were curved and slightly spread/relaxed, with a curved/relaxed palm. The rebound has been initiated with a two- or three-inch drop to your imaginary plane, at which point it has rebounded to a point below your chin/chest.
   b. Continue to begin the rebound in the same position as outlined (above your waist and in front of your right thigh). This position will be referred to as first position.
      i. At a tempo of mm = 72, complete four rebounds in first position, and take note of (1) the relaxed position of your hand and fingers, (2) the position of your right hand in front of your right thigh and above your waist, (3) the drop of two or three inches, (4) your imaginary plane, and (5) your rebound off the plane. Repeat this task until you are completely aware of all these elements. When you have finished, relax and rest.
   c. Move your right hand/arm so it remains above your waist but in front of your left thigh. The hand/fingers will still be relaxed, with a curved palm, and the drop and rebound off your imaginary plane will be the same, except that it is occurring in front of your left thigh. In the 4/4 pre-conducting pattern, this will be referred to as second position.

i. At mm = 72, complete four rebounds in second position, and take note of (1) the relaxed position of your hand and fingers, (2) the position of your right hand in front of your left thigh and above your waist, (3) the drop of two or three inches, (4) your imaginary plane, and (5) your rebound off the plane. Repeat this task until you are completely aware of each element. Once completed, relax and rest.

ii. Now, complete four rebounds in first position and four rebounds in second position, then four rebounds in first position, and so on, without pausing between the two positions. When moving between first and second positions, let the last rebound in first position arc over to second position. (See figure 10.2.) When returning to first position, let the last rebound in second position arc back to first position. (See figure 10.3.)

First Rebound   Last Rebound
in 2nd Position   in 1st Position

Figure 10.2 Rebound from first to second position.

Last Rebound   First Rebound
in 2nd Position   in 1st Position

Figure 10.3 Rebound from second to first position.

d. Next, we will establish third position, which is the right hand/arm being placed to the right of the right hip. Dropping your right hand to your right side and then bringing it straight up will identify this position. Note the distance of the right hand from your right hip.

i. At mm = 72, complete four rebounds in third position, again taking note of your hand/finger position and rebound.

ii. Now, complete four rebounds in second position and four rebounds in third position, without pausing between the two positions, and back again from third to second position. When moving from second to third position, let the last rebound in second position arc to third position, crossing over first position. (See Figure 10.4.)

When moving from third to second position, again let the last rebound arc to the next position. (See figure 10.5.)

2nd Position   1st Position   3rd Position
Last Rebound   First Rebound

Figure 10.4 Rebound from second to third position.

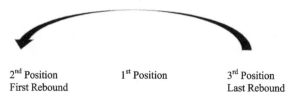

2nd Position   1st Position   3rd Position
First Rebound   Last Rebound

Figure 10.5 Rebound from third to second position

   iii. Once you have successfully accomplished this task, practice moving from first position (four beats), to second position (four beats), to third position (four beats), and then back to first position (four beats), and so on.
  e. Fourth position is halfway between first and third position.
     i. Complete four rebounds in fourth position, and repeat as needed, watching your hand placement, movement, and shape. Now, practice going from fourth to third position and back. (See figure 10.6.)

2nd Position   1st Position   4th Position   3rd Position

Figure 10.6 Rebound from 4th to 3rd and 3rd to 4th Position

    ii. Practice moving from first position (four beats) to second position (four beats) to third position (four beats) to fourth position (four beats) and then back to first position (four beats), and so on. Pay special attention to the distance between your positions and position placement. Make sure first position is in front of your right thigh, second position is in front of your left thigh, and so on.

Assignment

As you begin to feel more at ease with the 4/4 pre-conducting pattern, you can practice this exercise varying the beats in each position (three beats per position, two beats per position, one beat per position). You can also use different tempi while performing these exercises. Should you want to challenge yourself and further develop arm independence, using the parameters provided in this exercise, try switching the roles of the hands/arms.

Observation

Notice the movements your directors and conductors use when conducting the 4/4 pattern.

PROFESSIONAL KNOWLEDGE: GOALS AND OBJECTIVES

For this component, the focus is to:

• Define goals and objectives and their purpose in planning instruction.

Where Am I Headed and How Do I Get There?
Successful teachers spend large amounts of time planning and preparing materials before students enter the classroom. Repertoire choices need to match students' skill levels. Warm-up exercises need to focus on specific topics. You also need to think about the big picture. How will you promote learning for all students? What do you want your students to be able to do at the end of the quarter, the semester, or the year? Remember, even with a full tank of gasoline, you can easily run out of fuel if you don't know your destination and haven't planned accordingly.

Goals and objectives are similar in that they both provide an outline for the expected results of teaching. A goal is a broad or general statement, such as "Through this course, students will develop ways of thinking about music learning and child development that will contribute to career-long growth and success as a music educator." Objectives are specific statements that describe the concept or skill the students should have learned during the lesson. They are intended outcomes that assists students in reaching the broad course goals, such as "Students will be able to define, identify, play, perform, demonstrate, and so on."

An objective—sometimes referred to as a competency—must be able to be assessed by an overt or observable behavior. For example, one cannot assess the following objective: "After reading this component, students will understand the connection between assessment and objectives." As a teacher, you cannot see understanding. Students, however, can demonstrate understanding through observable behaviors: "Students will be able define the terms *assessment* and *objective*." Overt behaviors include terms such as *define, identify, play, perform,* and *demonstrate.*

Objectives can be divided into three categories: cognitive, affective, and behavioral. A cognitive objective is what the students should know. An affective objective identifies what students reflect, think, or care about. A behavioral objective, the most commonly used in lesson planning, is a specific performance skill for students to master. The outcomes of these objectives are the achieved results or behaviors acquired by learners through direct instruction, guided practice, and independent practice. (See figure 10.7.) To simplify the concept of goals and objectives, think of the goal as a semester or year target, while the objectives are the components that can be achieved on a daily basis. The objectives form the foundational building blocks that allow students to gain skill sets for achieving the goal.

Figure 10.7 The relationship between goals and objectives.

Discussion

1. What do you believe are one or two goals that would apply to every music class?
2. In small groups, formulate a goal and a set of objectives for a performing ensemble.
3. Imagine you are teaching an ensemble with students of various grade levels. Your administrator asks how your goals differ for each grade level. How will you respond?

Reading Individuals—Lip Trills in Vocal Warm-Up—Conducting the 3/4 Pattern—Lesson Planning

In this module, you will focus on:

- Personal awareness: Reading individuals within a group.
- Personal musicianship: Using lip trills in the vocal warm-up.
- Pre-conducting: Conducting the 3/4 pattern.
- Professional knowledge: Lesson planning.

PERSONAL AWARENESS: COMBINING VISUAL AWARENESS WITH FACIAL GESTURES II

In the personal awareness component of module 10, you identified particular individuals within a group conveying a particular expression. We will now continue to develop the skill of reading individuals within a group. In this exercise, you will observe your classmates and be asked to identify who communicated an expression and what expression was imparted.

Classroom Setup

The classroom should be arranged in three rows with five columns. If your class contains fewer than 15 individuals, place empty chairs in the rows/columns and randomly fill in the other positions. If you have a larger class, add more rows. Students should sit with their feet flat on the floor, shoulders' width apart, with hands crossed or on top of each other and placed on the lap or desktop, and using a relaxed but upright posture (i.e., no slumping).

Exercise

1. For this exercise, the following expressions will be used (see module 10 to review the elements of each expression):
   a. Anger
   b. Confusion/questioning
   c. Happiness
2. To begin the exercise, one individual comes to the front of the class. In this exercise, three individuals within the group convey all three expressions. The individual in front of the class is *not* informed of the three individuals conveying the expressions during the five-second session.
   a. All individuals begin with a neutral or calm expression.
   b. Three individuals are chosen to convey each of the three expressions. The instructor identifies the individuals and points to one of the three expressions written on a whiteboard, indicating which emotion is to be conveyed by that individual. The individual in front of the group should not be informed of the individuals conveying the expressions.
   c. When the instructor signals, the three individuals selected convey one of the three expressions, as assigned, while all others maintain a neutral/calm pose.
3. The pose should be held for a maximum of five seconds. The instructor initiates the count, and the individual in front of the class begins his or her scan.
4. At the end of five seconds, the instructor calls "time," and everyone maintains or returns to a neutral/calm pose.
5. The individual is then asked which three classmates conveyed an expression and what expression was conveyed.
6. The exercise should be repeated twice. However, in each successive session, one or two additional individuals should be asked to transmit one of the three expressions. Thus, during the second session, four or five individuals will be conveying expressions, and five to seven will be doing so during the third session. This exercise can be performed using a larger number of individuals conveying one of the three expressions if desired.

Assignment

Begin to broaden your awareness of facial expressions. When you are in a group, see how much information you can take in, in the least amount of time, while reading facial expressions.

Observation

As you observe individuals talking in the hallway, participating in classrooms, listening to directives in ensembles, and so on, notice the expressions on their faces. What messages are they sending? Are those messages being received?

PERSONAL MUSICIANSHIP: LIP TRILLS AS A WARM-UP

For this component, the focus is to:

- Discuss and practice lip trills as a tool to relax facial tension.
- Sing a melody with limited pitches (d-r-m-s-l) in standard notation.
- Perform single-note accompaniments added to a melody using Roman numerals.

Lip trills can be a successful way to warm up the voice. These trills also relax facial tension, as it is next to impossible to perform them if your muscles are tense. What is a lip trill? How do you perform it while promoting vocal health? Imagine yourself in a swimming pool, swimming with your head submerged. Now think of the sensation of blowing bubbles underwater. Create that same sensation of blowing lip "bubbles" or lip trills.

The trills should begin after starting your airflow during exhalation, so that the vocal folds are open rather than shut as you start the sound production. Lips, jaw, and throat should all be relaxed. Support the air production by your breath, and do not think of it as being controlled by your lips. Start by producing the bubble sound, and then produce a sound using a single pitch. As you become more successful with creating a relaxed trill, begin to extend the trills through triads and arpeggios.

When singing the melody in see figure 11.1—utilizing the sequential steps from previous modules—concentrate on having your facial muscles remain relaxed throughout.

Figure 11.1 "Black Snake," traditional notation.

PRE-CONDUCTING: 3/4 CONDUCTING PATTERN

In this exercise, you will begin precursor movements that will outline a 3/4 conducting pattern. You will only be using the right hand/arm. The left hand/arm remains in a resting position at the left side of your body. In the following exercise, you should carefully monitor the movements suggested.

Classroom Setup

All members of the class can complete this exercise simultaneously. Students should stand and allow about one arm's length of space around them. An instructor should initiate each exercise and each step of any given exercise so the class practices as a unit.

Exercise

1. The right hand/arm will be performing the task.
   a. At a tempo of mm = 72, complete four rebounds in first position. (First position is the rebound point in front of the right thigh.)
   b. Move your right hand/arm so it remains above your waist but to the right side of your right thigh. This is approximately the same position as the third position in the 4/4 conducting pattern identified in module 10. In the 3/4 pre-conducting pattern, this will be referred to as second position.
      i. At a tempo of mm = 72, complete four rebounds in second position.
      ii. When finished, complete four rebounds in first position, four rebounds in second position, four rebounds back to first position, and four rebounds again in second position. Do not pause between position changes. Once completed, relax and rest. When moving to second position, let the last rebound in first position arc to second position. (See figure 11.2.) When moving back to first position, let the last rebound in second position arc back to first position. (See figure 11.3.)

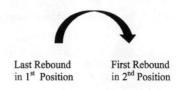

Last Rebound   First Rebound
in 1ˢᵗ Position   in 2ⁿᵈ Position

Figure 11.2 Arc from to second position.

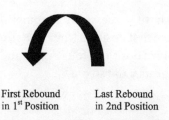

First Rebound   Last Rebound
in 1st Position   in 2nd Position

Figure 11.3 Arc from second to first position.

c. Next, we will establish third position, which is slightly to the left of second position, as shown in figure 11.4.

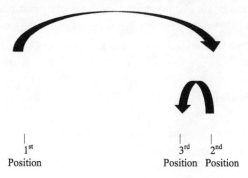

| |
1st
Position

| |
3rd 2nd
Position Position

Figure 11.4 Placement of third position in relation to first and second position.

i. At a tempo of mm = 72, complete four rebounds in third position. Once completed, relax and rest.

ii. Now, complete four rebounds in second position and then four rebounds in third position without pausing between the two positions; return from third to second position. When moving from second to third position, let the last rebound in second position arc to third position. (See figure 11.5.) When moving from third to second position, again let the last rebound arc to the next position. (See figure 11.6.)

1st
Position

3rd   2nd
Position   Position

Figure 11.5 Rebound arc from second to third position.

1st
Position

3rd   2nd
Position   Position

Figure 11.6 Rebound arc from third to second position.

iii. Once you have successfully accomplished this task, practice moving from first position (four beats), to second position (four beats), to third position (four beats), and then back to first position (four beats), and so on.

Assignment

As you begin to feel more at ease with the 3/4 pre-conducting pattern, you can practice this exercise varying the beats in each position (three beats per position, two beats per position, one beat per position). You can also use different tempi while performing these exercises. Should you want to further challenge yourself, try switching the roles of the hands/arms.

Observation

Notice the movements used by your directors and conductors when conducting the 3/4 pattern.

PROFESSIONAL KNOWLEDGE: INTRODUCTION TO LESSON PLANNING

For this component, the focus is to:

- Determine the purpose of lesson plans.
- Understand the importance of balancing student skill levels and teacher expectations.

The Teacher, The Architect. Psychologist Mihaly Csikszentmihalyi (1990) created a flow model that illustrates why the same activity for one individual can be intrinsically rewarding and result in commitment, while another individual may become frustrated and require extrinsic motivators to continue the activity. Flow occurs when the skill level and challenge level are balanced, meaning that as a student's skill level increases, the teacher will increase the challenge level of the content. If a student's skill level is low yet the challenge level of the repertoire is high, he or she may become anxious and frustrated. If the student's skill level is high yet the challenge level of the repertoire is low, he or she may become bored or apathetic.

Teachers have hundreds of lesson-plan formats and rehearsal frame templates from which to choose. Some school administrators may require a specific format, while others allow teachers to choose ones that resonate with their personal teaching style and/or class structure. Because of the great variety of options, we will not present any specific format or template style but rather will focus on constructing lesson sequences that promote musical growth while maintaining that precarious balance between skill level and challenge level.

Your lesson plans serve as a musical road map and include landmarks such as objectives, activities, repertoire, and assessments. After determining the daily objective, you will then select appropriate activities and repertoire that will help students attain the objective. Consider the stress-and-release factor; teachers need to balance segments of concentration (stress) with review, favorite songs, or creative activities that students view as fun (release). Throughout the lesson, there should be assessments—visual, oral/aural, and/or written—that monitor student progress. It is important to remember that the best assessment is embedded within the instruction. Assessments should not get in the way of instruction but rather be integrated within the instruction.

Arnold Palmer is credited with the quote "The road to success is always under construction." Teachers constantly review and rebuild lessons to meet student needs. As the "architect" in your classroom, remember to provide students with lessons that build strong musical foundations, leave room for personal creativity, and balance skill and challenge.

Discussion

1. How will you know if a lesson you designed is too challenging? What behaviors might the students display?
2. How do you feel when you perform repertoire that is not challenging?
3. Some teachers are skillful at creating lessons with various levels of challenge. What are some strategies that you've observed?

MODULE 11 REFERENCE

Csikszentmihalyi, M. (1990). Flow: The psychology of optimal experience. New York: Harper Perennial.

Identifying Facial Gestures—Solfège Syllables—Conducting the 2/4 Pattern—Assessment

In this module, you will focus on:

- Personal awareness: Reading a group while identifying several facial gestures.
- Personal musicianship: Discussing solfège syllables and their relationship to standard notation placement.
- Pre-conducting: Conducting the 2/4 pattern.
- Professional knowledge: Identifying types of assessment.

PERSONAL AWARENESS: COMBINING VISUAL AWARENESS WITH FACIAL GESTURES III

In modules 10 and 11, you were instructed to convey one of three specific expressions. However, in a classroom, you will encounter a variety of expressions at any given time. We will now continue to develop the skill of reading a group as we practice identifying several emotions simultaneously.

In this exercise, you will again observe your classmates and be asked which individuals within the group conveyed particular facial expressions. However, this time, there is a possibility of eight different expressions. You will be asked to identify who communicated an expression and which of the eight expressions was conveyed.

Classroom Setup

The classroom should be arranged in three rows with five columns. If your class contains fewer than fifteen individuals, place empty chairs in the rows/columns and randomly fill in the other positions. If you have a larger class, add more rows. Students should sit with their feet flat on the floor, shoulders' width apart, with hands crossed or on top of each other and placed on the lap or desktop, and using a relaxed but upright posture (no slumping).

Exercise

1. For this exercise, the following eight expressions will be used (see modules 5 and 10 to review the elements of each expression):
   a. Anger
   b. Boredom
   c. Confusion/questioning
   d. Disgust/strong displeasure
   e. Happiness
   f. Relief
   g. Sadness
   h. Surprise
2. To begin the exercise, select an individual to go the front of the class. In this exercise, selected individuals convey one of the eight expressions. The individual in front of the class is *not* informed of the expressions imparted or which individuals are conveying them.
   a. All individuals begin with a neutral/calm expression.
   b. Three individuals are chosen to convey any one of the eight expressions. When the instructor signals, the three individuals selected convey the assigned expression while all others maintain a neutral/calm pose.
3. The pose should be held for a maximum of five seconds. The instructor initiates the count, and the individual in front of the class begins his or her scan.
4. At the end of five seconds, the instructor calls "time," and everyone maintains or returns to a neutral/calm pose.
5. The individual is then asked which of classmates conveyed expressions and to identify the emotion transmitted.
6. This process should be repeated twice, and additional individuals can be asked to transmit one of the eight expressions in successive sessions.

Assignment

Practice reading the facial expressions of individuals in other classes, rehearsals, and settings. The more you practice, the more quickly you become aware of changing expressions.

Observation

As you observe groups of individuals talking in the hallway, participating in classrooms, listening to directives in ensembles, and so on, notice the expressions on individual faces in the group. What messages are they sending? Can you identify those emotions?

PERSONAL MUSICIANSHIP: SOLFÈGE SYLLABLES AND STANDARD NOTATION PLACEMENT

For this component, the focus is to:

- Discuss solfège syllables and their relationship to standard notation placement.
- Sing a melody with limited pitches (s,-t,-d-r-m-s-l) in stick notation.
- Perform single-note accompaniments added to a melody using solfège syllables.

This singing exercise includes the solfège syllable low *ti*, the pitch below *do* (the tonic or tonal center of the melody). Intervalic placement of a solfège syllable can be indicated by using—or not using—a mark following each syllable. The adding of a mark above or below indicates whether it should be sung above or below the tonic. See figure 12.1 for an example of how solfège syllables relate to note placement in standard notation.

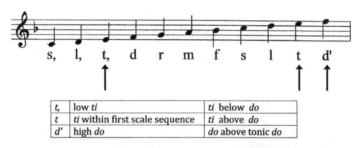

ț	low *ti*	*ti* below *do*	
t	*ti* within first scale sequence	*ti* above *do*	
d′	high *do*	*do* above tonic *do*	

Figure 12.1 Solfège syllable as transferred to standard notation.

Before singing the melody in figure 12.2—utilizing the sequential steps from previous modules—locate the solfège syllables that will be sung below *do*.

Traditional

Figure 12.2 "Paw Paw Patch," stick notation.

PRE-CONDUCTING: 2/4 CONDUCTING PATTERN

In this exercise, you will begin precursor movements that will outline a 2/4 conducting pattern. You will only be using the right hand/arm. The left hand/arm remains in a resting position. In the following exercise, you should carefully monitor your movements.

Classroom Setup

All members of the class can complete this exercise simultaneously. Students should stand and allow about one arm's length of space around them. An instructor should initiate each exercise and each step of any given exercise so the class practices as a unit.

Exercise

This exercise should be practiced at a tempo of mm = 66. Your right hand/ arm rebound begins above your waist, drops to an imaginary plane in front of or approximately in front of your right thigh, and rebounds off the plane.

The rebound in the 2/4 precursor pattern will rebound diagonally, to your right side (with your hand turning slightly to the right), after the initial drop. This will be referred to as first position. (See figure 12.3.)

Initial Drop
and Rebound
in 1st Postion

Figure 12.3 The initial first-position drop and resultant rebound in the 2/4 pattern.

1. Practice a first-position drop and rebound several times. After each drop and rebound, rest, and then begin the drop in the conducting position (drop, rebound, rest, resume).
2. The drop on beat two (second position) of the 2/4 pre-conducting pattern begins at the top of the diagonal rebound. The drop in second position occurs at the same point as the first-position drop. The rebound in second position is vertical. The next first-position drop

occurs at the top of the second-position rebound, and the pattern continues. Note that the rebound after the first-position drop is not as high as the second-position rebound. (See figure 12.4.)

2nd Position Rebound

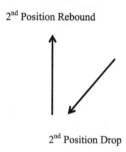

2nd Position Drop

Figure 12.4 The second-position drop and resultant rebound in the 2/4 pattern.

3. Practice a first- and second-position drop and rebound several times. After each drop and rebound, rest, and then begin the drop in the conducting position starting with an initial first-position drop (drop, rebound, rest, resume). After this feels comfortable, continue the pattern without interruption or resting until you have completed several repetitions of the pattern. Note the height of the first-position rebound once the pattern is continued. (See figure 12.5.)

1st Position Drop
and Rebound after
Pattern Continuation

Figure 12.5 First-position drop and resultant rebound in the 2/4 pattern.

Assignment

As you begin to feel more at ease with the 2/4 pre-conducting pattern, you can practice this exercise with varying tempi. Should you want to further challenge yourself, try switching the roles of the hands/arms.

Observation

Notice the movements used by your directors and conductors when conducting the 2/4 pattern. There are various ways to conduct in 2/4, and each conductor has his or her preferred approach. The pattern presented above is a pre-conducting pattern and may or may not be used in a conducting class. The intent of this exercise is simply preparation for future conducting experiences.

PROFESSIONAL KNOWLEDGE: ASSESSMENT

For this component, the focus is to:

• Identify types of assessment.

Assessments are based on the identified goals and objectives for each class. Assessments provide teachers with information regarding whether the students have actually acquired the desired skill or outcome. Assessments can only be created after the identification of specific objectives. An objective states what the students will be able to identify, play, perform, demonstrate, and so on. If you don't know what you want them to do, then you don't know what to assess.

You learned in module 9 that objectives designate the desired outcome or skill a student should be able to demonstrate after direct instruction, guided practice, and independent practice. Assessments are used to determine if the learners have attained the skills (behavioral objectives), attitudes (affective objectives), and knowledge (cognitive objectives) outlined in the objective.

Assessments are the tools used to evaluate student learning and/or mastery. Just as there are different types of objectives, there are different types of assessments. Assessments can be formal or informal. Assessments that result in numerical or quantifiable data (e.g., percentiles) are termed formal. A standardized test or a test used to compare individuals within the same class, school district, state, and so on, is a formal assessment. Informal assessments include items such as checklists, rubrics, group projects, presentations, and demonstrations. Informal assessments are generally used to inform the teacher of future instructional needs, are nonstandardized, and are not used to compare one student with another.

Assessments are also categorized by the terms *diagnostic, formative,* and *summative.* In the music classroom, an audition would be a diagnostic assessment. The audition helps you determine an individual's current skill level and also identifies instructional needs. When reading about the differences in formative and summative assessments, the following example from educational researcher Robert Stake is often used to provide a simplistic clarification: "When the cook tastes the soup, that's formative. When the guests taste the soup, that's summative" (Scriven, 1991, p. 169). Formative assessments monitor student learning and provide feedback during the lesson or rehearsal. It in-*forms* the teacher about which skills still need further focus and is the foundation for *form*-ing future lessons.

Summative assessments provide students with feedback on whether they achieved the objectives. Typically conducted at the end of a project, unit, or semester, this provides a *sum*-mary for the student and the teacher. Playing tests, written tests, and letter grades assigned to students at the end of the semester are summative assessments.

You were reminded that objectives must be created before assessments. Equally important is to remember that the assessment tool used must meet the purpose of the assessment and be connected to objectives. For example, if your goal was to evaluate a student's ability to compose a song using the 12-bar blues chord progression, the assessment should focus on the compositional techniques used to create the song but not to evaluate a student's ability to "perform" the composition. Performing a song is a separate skill from composing a song.

The sequence in figure 12.6 will help you organize and memorize the assessment terms discussed in this module.

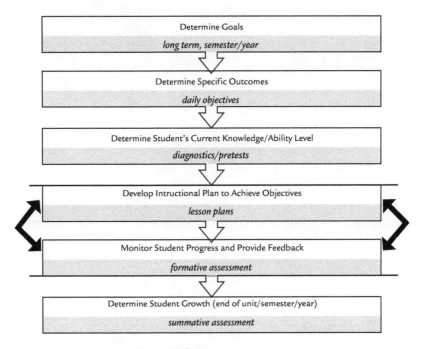

Figure 12.6 Assessment sequence.

Discussion

1. What is assessment? Why is it needed?
2. What are the types of assessment?
3. Make a list of the various types of assessments you've experienced within your various music classes.
4. With a partner or a small group, compare your responses and then determine whether they were informal or formal assessements. Then categorize them by diagnostic, formative, and/or summative.

MODULE 12 REFERENCE

Scriven, M. (1991). Evaluation thesaurus (4th ed.). Newbury Park, CA: Sage.

Emotions—Resonance through Humming—Preparatory Gestures in 4/4—Motivation

In this module, you will focus on:

- Personal awareness: Identifying individual emotions in a classroom setting.
- Personal musicianship: Discovering resonance through humming.
- Pre-conducting: Conducting a preparatory gesture on the downbeat in 4/4 meter.
- Professional knowledge: Motivation.

PERSONAL AWARENESS: COMBINING VISUAL AWARENESS WITH FACIAL GESTURES IV

In module 12, you were instructed to convey one of eight expressions, or if you were in front of the class, you were asked to identify the three people who displayed one of three expressions. In a classroom, everyone conveys some type of expression.

In this exercise, you will again observe your classmates but will now be asked to identify the particular facial expression each member conveyed. Since all members of the class will be participating in conveying an expression, the number of different expressions will be limited to two. The instructor will select two from the eight different possibilities. When you are in front of the class, you will be asked which of two expressions individuals in the class conveyed.

Classroom Setup

The classroom should be arranged in three rows with five columns. If your class contains fewer than 15 individuals, place empty chairs in the rows/ columns. If you have a larger class, add more rows. Students should sit with their feet flat on the floor, shoulders' width apart, with hands crossed or on top of each other and placed on the lap or desktop, and using a relaxed but upright posture (no slumping).

Exercise

1. For this exercise, the following eight expressions will be used (see modules 5 and 10 to review the elements of each expression):
   a. Anger
   b. Boredom
   c. Confusion/questioning
   d. Disgust/strong displeasure
   e. Happiness
   f. Relief
   g. Sadness
   h. Surprise
2. To begin the exercise, one individual comes to the front of the class. The instructor chooses two expressions from the eight listed above for class members to transmit. The individual in front of the class *is* informed of the two expressions selected.
   a. All individuals begin with a neutral/calm expression.
   b. The instructor informs all class members which two expressions to convey. Each class member, other than the individual in front of the class, decides which of the two expressions he or she wishes to communicate.
   c. When the instructor signals, the expressions are conveyed by each class member.
3. The pose should be held for a maximum of five seconds. The instructor initiates the count, and the individual in front of the class begins his or her scan.
4. At the end of five seconds, the instructor calls "time," and everyone returns to a neutral/calm pose.
5. The individual is then asked which of his or her classmates conveyed which of the two expressions.
6. This exercise should be repeated with two different expressions.

7. All members of the class should have the opportunity to stand in front of the group and identify the number of individuals conveying the two expressions.

Assignment

Additional expressions, other than the eight suggested, can be used. It should be noted that an 80 percent to 100 percent identification rate is rare, given the time frame, but the idea of these exercises is to heighten individual awareness of classroom dynamics.

Observation

As you observe groups of individuals talking in the hallway, participating in classrooms, listening to directives in ensembles, and so on, notice the expressions on individuals' faces. Can you identify those emotions?

PERSONAL MUSICIANSHIP: DISCOVERING RESONANCE THROUGH HUMMING

For this component, the focus is to:

- Discuss the importance of resonance.
- Sing a melody with limited pitches (s,-t,-d-r-m-s-l) in standard notation.
- Perform single-note accompaniments added to a melody using Roman numerals.

Vocal resonance occurs when sound waves are amplified in the hollow spaces of your body. These spaces—or cavities—are referred to as resonators and include head, nasal passages, mouth, throat, and chest. It is important to remember that vocal projection results from resonance and not from forcing or pushing yourself to sing more loudly. Building resonance develops a full sound free of tension.

Humming, when performed correctly, can be a successful strategy for assisting you in discovering your resonance space. It is important that you hum with relaxed lips and an open throat. (See figure 13.1 for a basic physical outline of the larynx.) Tight lips cause facial tension and may reduce the connection between breath and resonance, so be sure to keep your lips relaxed.

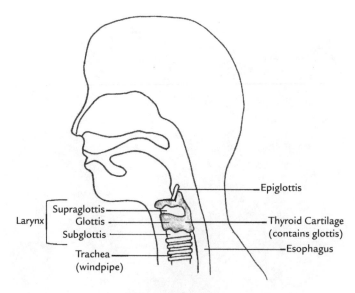

Figure 13.1 The larynx.

Before singing the melody in figure 13.2—with solfège and a chordal accompaniment—hum the melody, and focus on creating vocal resonance by lifting the soft palate, keeping the larynx low, and using breath support.

Figure 13.2 "Paw Paw Patch," standard notation.

PRE-CONDUCTING: PREPARATORY GESTURE FOR THE DOWNBEAT IN 4/4 METER

In this exercise, we will introduce the pre-conducting preparatory gesture, which is the precursor to downbeat, pickup, and so on. The preparatory gesture indicates tempo, style, and other elements. You will focus on the preparatory gesture only as an indicator of tempo in this exercise. As in the pre-conducting exercises in modules 10, 11, and 12, you will be using only the right hand/arm. The left hand/arm remains in a resting position.

Carefully monitor your movements, and have other members of your group provide feedback concerning the appropriateness of your upbeat gesture.

Classroom Setup

All members of the class can complete this exercise simultaneously. Students should stand and allow about an arm's length of space around them. An instructor should initiate each activity and each step of any given task so the class is practicing as a unit. However, as individuals become more proficient in completing the elements, it is suggested that they form small groups of three or four individuals and conduct preparatory gestures for others. This will be discussed later.

Exercise

1. Establish your conducting posture, use a tempo of mm = 69, review the 4/4 conducting pattern, and complete the following.
   a. The preparatory gesture will begin one beat prior to the downbeat. Since the downbeat in a 4/4 conducting pattern occurs on beat one (referred to as first position in the 4/4 pre-conducting pattern), the preparatory beat begins on beat four (fourth position) of the pattern.
      i. In this preparatory gesture for the downbeat, the rebound will be diagonal, to your left side, to first position. The hand will rebound to the top of the first-position pattern. (See figure 13.3.) Once the rebound height is attained, the right hand is dropped without pause and in the same tempo and continuous motion as was initiated at the beginning of the fourth-position drop. (See figure 13.4.)

Rebound after the Initial
4th-Position Drop

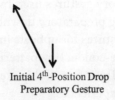

Initial 4th-Position Drop
Preparatory Gesture

Figure 13.3 The fourth-position preparatory gesture for a downbeat in 4/4: initial drop and rebound.

Rebound and Downbeat Drop

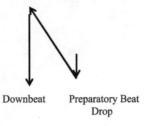

Downbeat   Preparatory Beat
Drop

Figure 13.4 Preparatory gesture for a downbeat in 4/4: initial drop, rebound, and downbeat

    ii. Practice the preparatory gesture and downbeat several times. After each preparatory gesture and downbeat, rest, and then repeat the gesture. Check your fourth-position preparatory position, drop, and rebound.

    iii. To aid in your performance of the preparatory gesture, breathe in tempo (mm = 69) while completing the drop/rebound and downbeat motion. Inhale at the beginning of the initial drop/rebound, and exhale during the downbeat drop.

    iv. Keep your movements continuous (no pauses) and in the same tempo throughout the preparatory gesture and downbeat.

2. Once you have successfully completed this task, form groups of three or four individuals. With one person serving as the conductor, conduct the preparatory gesture. Have the group breathe with you and sing "ahhh" on a mutually agreed-upon pitch at the downbeat. Repeat this process several times for each conductor, and then have another conductor perform the task. Provide feedback/evaluation information after each preparatory gesture.

Assignment

As you begin to feel more at ease with the preparatory gesture for a downbeat in 4/4 meter, you can practice this exercise with varying tempi.

Observation

Notice the preparatory gestures used by your directors and conductors. We will be exploring preparatory downbeat gestures in 3/4 and 2/4 and then preparatory gestures for upbeats in later exercises. The pattern presented above is a pre-conducting pattern and may or may not be used in a conducting class. The intent of this exercise is simply to prepare you for future conducting experiences.

PROFESSIONAL KNOWLEDGE: MOTIVATION

For this component, the focus is to:

• Define motivation.
• Discuss various strategies for motivating students.

Dwight Eisenhower said, "Leadership is the art of getting someone else to do something you want done because he wants to do it."

What motivated you to participate in music? What motivated you to enroll in college? What motivated you to come to class today? Not all students begin music study because *they* are motivated to learn, but rather some start because their parents wanted them to participate. Whether or not it was your choice to begin studying music, somewhere during your journey, you maintained or generated the desire and the interest to continue.

Through instruction, a music teacher conveys the specific kinesthetics of making music, which results in students being able to relate the abstract and artistic ideas of music through performance. Learning is a complicated process, which can be interesting, challenging, and sometimes frustrating. Even during the occasions when your music study ended up being more difficult than enjoyable, you continued to play. What became your motivation?

There are two types of motivation: external and internal. External motivation results when goals originate from an external source rather than yourself. Perhaps when you were young, your parents connected your allowance with practicing your instrument; that would be external motivation. Your practice was tied to parental influence and/or mandates. Internal motivation is the key to success, as one has to have the personal desire to continue learning. Klickstein (2009, p. 105) cites the great tenor Placido Domingo as saying, "My strength is my enthusiasm." Klickstein believes that "internal motivation opens the creative spigot" and suggests five strategies that can fuel internal motivation: "clarify goals, kindle devotion, inspire yourself, master basic skills, and be productive."

Think of motivation as at three-part equation: subject or task interest + desire = motivation. Your interest and your desire are equal partners. As teachers, we have to provide students with learning experiences that promote internal interest and personal desire. It is intrinsic motivation or the personal desire factor that serves as a crucial component of goal setting. If you don't want to do something—whether learning an instrument, memorizing song lyrics, or something else—then it is likely you will exert little effort and not attain that goal. The effectiveness of learning experiences can also depend on the ways in which we interact with students. The more you can connect with your students and support their learning, the more confident they will become with the task. Confidence serves to increase engagement and motivation, which result in "more successful learners" (Dombro, Jablon, & Stetson, 2011, p. 8).

It is likely that during your lifetime, many people will ask you how you became motivated to start in music. Maybe a more insightful question would be what motivates you to continue playing music.

Discussion

1. Think of instances in your music training where an adult—either a parent or a teacher—used external motivation to get you to complete a task.
2. What is problematic about only relying on extrinsic motivation?
3. With a partner or a small group, discuss ways to promote internal motivation.

MODULE 13 REFERENCES

Dombro, A. L., Jablon, J., & Stetson, C. (2011). *Powerful interactions: How to connect with children to extend their learning.* Washington, DC: National Association for the Education of Young Children.

Klickstein, G. (2009). *The musician's way: A guide to practice, performance, and wellness.* New York, NY: Oxford University Press.

Identifying Expressions—Building Triads—Preparatory Gestures in 3/4—Learning Theories

In this module, you will focus on:

- Personal awareness: Identifying expressions within a class.
- Personal musicianship: Building triads with solfège.
- Pre-conducting: Conducting the preparatory gesture on the downbeat in 3/4 meter.
- Professional knowledge: Learning theories.

PERSONAL AWARENESS: COMBINING VISUAL AWARENESS WITH FACIAL GESTURES V

In module 13, you were instructed to convey one of eight particular expressions, or if you were in front of the class, you were asked to identify the people who conveyed an expression. We will continue to develop the skill of reading a group as we practice identifying more than two emotions at a time.

In this exercise, you will again observe your classmates. Since all class members will be conveying an expression, the number of different expressions will be limited. The instructor will select from the eight different possibilities.

Classroom Setup

The classroom should be arranged in three rows with five columns. If your class contains fewer than 15 individuals, place chairs in the rows/columns and randomly fill in the other positions. If you have a larger class, add more rows. Students should sit with their feet flat on the floor, shoulders' width apart, with hands crossed or on top of each other and placed on the lap or desktop, and using a relaxed but upright posture (no slumping).

Exercises
Exercise 1

1. For this exercise the following eight expressions will be used (see modules 5 and 10 to review the elements of each expression):
   a. Anger
   b. Boredom
   c. Confusion/questioning
   d. Disgust/strong displeasure
   e. Happiness
   f. Relief
   g. Sadness
   h. Surprise
2. To begin the exercise, one individual comes to the front of the class. The instructor chooses three expressions from which members of the class can elect one. The individual in front of the class *is* informed of the three expressions being conveyed.
   a. All individuals begin with a neutral/calm expression.
   b. The instructor informs all class members which three expressions are to be used. Each class member, other than the individual in front of the class, decides which of the three expressions he or she wishes to communicate.
   c. When the instructor signals, the expressions are conveyed by each class member.
3. The pose should be held for a maximum of five seconds. The instructor initiates the count, and the individual in front of the class begins his or her scan.
4. At the end of five seconds, the instructor calls "time," and everyone returns to a neutral/calm pose.
5. The individual is then asked which of his or her classmates conveyed which of the three expressions.
6. This exercise should be repeated with three different expressions.

7. All members of the class should have the opportunity to stand in front of the group and identify the number of individuals conveying the three expressions.

Exercise 2

1. Again, eight expressions are possible, but now each individual conveys one of four facial gestures selected by the instructor.
2. One individual comes to the front of the class and is informed of the four expressions to be conveyed. The conveyance time frame will be five seconds. The procedure outlined above should be used.

Assignment

Different facial expressions can be added to the exercise, and the number of expressions presented at one time can also be increased. It should be noted that an 80 percent to 100 percent identification rate is rare, given the time frame, but the idea of these exercises is to heighten individual awareness of classroom dynamics.

Observation

As you observe groups of individuals talking in the hallway, participating in classrooms, listening to directives in ensembles, and so on, notice the expressions on individual faces in the group. What messages are they sending? Can you identify those emotions?

PERSONAL MUSICIANSHIP: BUILDING TRIADS WITH SOLFÈGE

For this component, the focus is to:

- Discuss building triads with solfège syllables.
- Practice singing and outlining various triads using solfège.
- Sing a melody with limited pitches (s,-d-r-m-f-s) in stick notation.
- Perform one-note accompaniments to a melody using solfège syllables.

All previous modules have used one-note accompaniments to promote independent part singing. Before applying accompaniments using chords, what follows is a brief exercise to increase familiarity with building triads using solfège syllables. A triad is a chord made up of three notes with the distance of a third separating them. The root *tri* means "three," while the root *ad* means "relationship"; therefore, when they are "stacked up," the notes are separated by the relationship of a third. For example, the relationship of *do* to *mi* is an interval of a major third, while the relationship of *mi* to *so* is an interval of a minor third.

Figure 14.1 outlines triads used when singing a *do*-centered melody in a major key. Select a pitch for *do* (e.g., B♭ below middle C), and practice singing each column of triads with solfège and hand signs. You might be more successful singing all the triads that create major triads (e.g., triads built on *do, fa,* and *so*) before moving to the minor triads. Eventually, you should be able to sequence through these triads with ease; therefore, repeated practice is recommended.

I	ii	iii	IV	V	vi	vii
so	la	ti	do	re	mi	fa
mi	fa	so	la	ti	do	re
do	re	mi	fa	so	la	ti

Figure 14.1 Solfège and chords for *do* center (major).

Sing the melody in figure 14.2,—utilizing the sequential steps from previous modules.

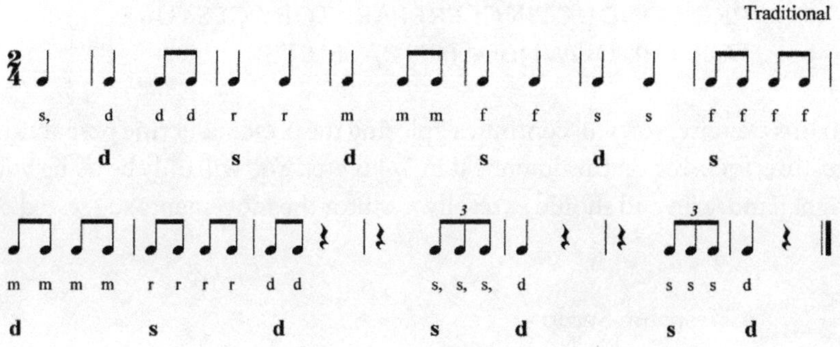

Figure 14.2 "Frog in a Bog," stick notation.

PRE-CONDUCTING: PREPARATORY GESTURE FOR THE DOWNBEAT IN 3/4 METER

In this exercise, you will continue exploring the pre-conducting preparatory gesture, focusing on the downbeat in 3/4 meter. You will only be using your right hand/arm and should carefully monitor the movements suggested.

Classroom Setup

All class members can complete this exercise simultaneously. Students should stand and allow about one arm's length of space around them. An instructor should initiate each activity and each step of any given task so the class practices as a unit. However, as individuals become more proficient in completing the elements in this activity, it is suggested that they form small groups of three or four individuals and conduct preparatory gestures for others.

Exercise

1. Establish your conducting posture and a tempo of mm = 69.
   a. The first gesture begins one beat prior to the downbeat. Since the downbeat in a 3/4 conducting pattern occurs on beat one or first position, the preparatory beat begins on beat three or the third position in the pattern.
      i. In this preparatory gesture for the downbeat, the rebound will be diagonal, to your left side. The hand will rebound to the top of the first-position pattern. (See figure 14.3.) Once the rebound height is attained, the right hand is immediately dropped in the same tempo and continuous motion as it was initiated. (See figure 14.4.)

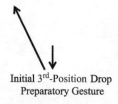

Rebound after the Initial
3rd-Position Drop

Initial 3rd-Position Drop
Preparatory Gesture

Figure 14.3 The third-position preparatory gesture for a downbeat in 3/4: initial drop and rebound.

Rebound and Downbeat Drop

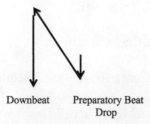

Downbeat   Preparatory Beat
Drop

Figure 14.4 Preparatory gesture for a downbeat in 3/4: initial drop, rebound, and downbeat.

ii. Practice the preparatory gesture and downbeat several times. After each preparatory gesture and downbeat, rest before repeating the gesture. Check your third-position preparatory position, drop, and rebound.

iii. Using your breath can help your performance of the preparatory gesture. In tempo (mm = 69), inhale at the beginning of the initial drop/rebound, and exhale during the downbeat drop.

iv. Keep your movements continuous (no pauses) and in the same tempo throughout the preparatory gesture and downbeat.

v. Once you have successfully completed this task, form groups of three or four individuals. With one person serving as the conductor, perform the preparatory gesture. Have the group breathe with you and sing "ahhh" on a mutually agreed-upon pitch at the downbeat. Repeat this process several times for each conductor, and then have another conductor perform the task. Provide feedback/evaluation information after each preparatory gesture.

Assignment

As you begin to feel more at ease with the preparatory gesture for a downbeat in 3/4 meter, you can practice this exercise varying the tempi.

Observation

Notice the preparatory gestures used by your directors and conductors. We will be exploring preparatory downbeat gestures in 2/4 meter and preparatory gestures for upbeats in later exercises. The pattern presented above is a pre-conducting pattern and may or may not be used in a conducting class. The intent of this exercise is in preparation for future conducting experiences.

PROFESSIONAL KNOWLEDGE: LEARNING THEORIES

For this component, the focus is to:

- Explore the difference between stage theories and phase theories.

"Theory links the teacher to the child learner, as it relates teaching events to learning processes and demonstrated learning outcomes" (Campbell & Scott-Kassner, 2006, p. 17). The world of psychology is a long, winding path full of modalities, instruction theories, phase and stage theories, reinforcement strategies, and so much more. In this module you will explore two learning theories and their application to music education.

Throughout your education, you will study many different learning theories. Some multilevel theories, from developmental psychology, are stage-dependent, meaning that children pass through stages of intellectual growth as they mature. Individuals' development—both psychological and physical—throughout their lives form the parameters of their ability to process information. Think of a small infant; obviously, he or she cannot learn to play a drum if he or she can't physically hold a mallet or maintain the attention span required to learn to repeat rhythmic patterns.

Some stages are based on phases of learning, with "scaffolding" used as a tool to support the learning of new concepts. In scaffolding, a teacher uses earlier stages of learning to provide the foundation for more complex learning. Think of how builders and painters use scaffolds in order to reach beyond what they couldn't reach without assistance. In music, think of how one needs to understand the concept of a steady beat before having the cognitive ability to subdivide the beat and determine the duration of different notes (quarter note, eighth notes, sixteenth notes, etc.). Children—and many adults—do not learn multiple concepts at one time but rather learn in "chunks," with the chunks serving as the foundation for more complex learning.

Phase and stage theories have several things in common:

- They involve how individuals manage new information (intellectual stimuli).
- Processing new information—in our case, music content—serves the dual purpose of assisting in mastering the current level of thinking while simultaneously preparing the learner for the next, more advanced, level of cognitive processing.

- Learning develops in a successive order but not always with discrete delineations from each step to the next, whether from one "stage" to the next or one "phase" to the next.
- When an individual experiences new information, the brain categorizes or compares the new material with known information based on common attributes. In other words, both stage theory and phase theory use the known as steppingstones stones to making sense of the unknown.

Discussion

1. Make a list of psychologists you have studied or have heard referred to in classes.
2. Explain to a partner or a small group the rationale for learning about psychology and psychologists in a music education class.
3. Think of a specific music skill (e.g., playing the clarinet), and make a list of the foundational knowledge needed to perform a solo.

MODULE 14 REFERENCE

Campbell, P. S., & Scott-Kassner, C. (2006). *Music in childhood: From preschool through the elementary grades* (3rd ed.). Belmont, CA: Thomson.

Identifying Expressions—Triads Using Inversions—Preparatory Gestures in 2/4—Jean Piaget

I n this module you will focus on:

- Personal awareness: Identifying expressions within a class setting.
- Personal musicianship: Building triads using inversions.
- Pre-conducting: Conducting the preparatory gesture on the downbeat in 2/4 meter.
- Professional knowledge: Jean Piaget's cognitive stage theory and its applications to music learning.

PERSONAL AWARENESS: COMBINING VISUAL AWARENESS WITH FACIAL GESTURES VI

In module 14, you were asked to identify the people who conveyed one of three or more expressions. You were informed of the expressions being transmitted. In this exercise, you will not be informed of the expressions selected.

All class members will be conveying an expression. The number of different expressions transmitted will be limited, but the instructor can select from the eight different possibilities. When you are in front of the class, you will be asked which expressions were being transmitted and which individuals expressed those emotions.

Classroom Setup

The classroom should be arranged in three rows with five columns. If your class contains fewer than 15 individuals, place chairs in the rows/columns and randomly fill in the other positions. If you have a larger class, add more rows. Students should sit with their feet flat on the floor, shoulders' width apart, with hands crossed or on top of each other and placed on the lap or desktop, and using a relaxed but upright posture (no slumping).

Exercises
Exercise 1

1. For this exercise, the following eight expressions will be used (see modules 5 and 10 to review the elements of each expression):
   a. Anger
   b. Boredom
   c. Confusion/questioning
   d. Disgust/strong displeasure
   e. Happiness
   f. Relief
   g. Sadness
   h. Surprise
2. To begin the exercise, one individual comes to the front of the class. Each individual conveys the expressions. The individual in front of the class is *not* informed of the two expressions being conveyed.
   a. All individuals begin with a neutral/calm expression.
   b. The instructor selects two expressions and informs class members which two expressions are to be used. Each class member, other than the individual in front of the class, decides which of the two expressions he or she wishes to communicate.
   c. When the instructor signals, the expressions are conveyed by each class member.
3. The pose should be held for a maximum of five seconds. The instructor initiates the count, and the individual in front of the class begins his or her scan.
4. At the end of five seconds, the instructor calls "time," and everyone returns to a neutral/calm pose.
5. The individual is then asked what two expressions were being transmitted and which of his or her classmates conveyed which of the two expressions.
6. This exercise should be repeated with two different expressions.

7. All members of the class should have the opportunity to stand in front of the group and identify the number of individuals conveying each of the two expressions.

Exercise 2

1. Again, eight expressions are possible, and each individual will convey one of three facial gestures selected by the instructor.
2. One individual comes to the front of the class and is *not* informed of the three expressions being conveyed. The procedure outlined above should be used.

Assignment

Different facial expressions can be added to the exercise, and the number of expressions presented at one time can also be increased. It should be noted that an 80 percent to 100 percent identification rate is rare, given the time frame, but the idea of these exercises is to heighten individual awareness of classroom dynamics.

Observation

As you observe groups of individuals talking in the hallway, participating in classrooms, listening to directives in ensembles, and so on, notice the expressions on individual faces in the group. What messages are they sending?

PERSONAL MUSICIANSHIP: BUILDING TRIADS USING INVERSIONS

For this component, the focus is to:

- Review the definition of a triad.
- Sing a melody with limited pitches (d-r-m-f-s) in stick notation.
- Create triads and perform them as accompaniments to a melody using solfège syllables.

With a partner, define *triad*, including the definition of the roots *tri* and *ad*

Our singing exercises, up to this point, have been associated with two-chord accompaniments (*do* and *so*; I and V). Using the two syllables *do* and *so* to build triads will result in the following triads: *do, mi, so* and *so, ti, re*. (See figure 15.1 for the staff notation representations.) The problem with root-position chords is the difficulty of promoting smooth voice leading. By inverting the triads, keeping the same basic entities but stacking in a different order, the outcome provides smooth voice leading and avoidance of awkward leaps. Refer again to figure 15.1, and notice how the second example makes part singing much more accessible.

Figure 15.1 Two-chord accompaniments in root and inverted positions.

Sing the melody in figure 15.2, and add chordal accompaniment that includes appropriate voice leading. (This will require at least four people to perform all parts, with three singing triads and one singing the melody.)

Traditional

Figure 15.2 "Oats and Beans," stick notation.

PRE-CONDUCTING: PREPARATORY GESTURE
FOR THE DOWNBEAT IN 2/4 METER

In this exercise, you will explore the preparatory gesture for the downbeat in 2/4 time. You will be using only the right hand/arm. The left hand/arm remain in a resting position. You should carefully monitor the movements suggested.

Classroom Setup

All class members can complete this exercise simultaneously. Students should stand and allow about one arm's length of space around them. An instructor should initiate each activity and each step of any given task so the class practices as a unit. As individuals become more proficient in completing the elements in this activity, it is suggested that they form small groups of three or four individuals and conduct preparatory gestures for others.

Exercise

1. Establish your conducting posture and a tempo of mm = 69.
   a. In this preparatory gesture for the downbeat in 2/4 meter, the rebound will be vertical. The hand will rebound to the top of the first-position pattern and then be dropped from that height. (See figure 15.3.) Once the rebound height is attained, the right hand is dropped without pause and in the same tempo and continuous motion as it was initiated at the beginning of the second-position drop. (See figure 15.4.)

2ⁿᵈ-Position **Drop**

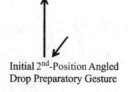

Initial 2ⁿᵈ-Position Angled
Drop Preparatory Gesture

Figure 15.3 The second-position preparatory gesture for a downbeat in 2/4: initial drop and rebound.

Rebound and Downbeat Drop

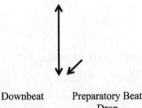

Downbeat   Preparatory Beat
                          Drop

Figure 15.4 Preparatory gesture for a downbeat in 2/4: initial drop, rebound and downbeat drop, downbeat.

b. Practice the preparatory gesture and downbeat several times. After each preparatory gesture and downbeat, rest before repeating the gesture. Check your second-position preparatory position, drop, and rebound.

c. Breathe in tempo (mm = 69) while completing the drop/rebound and downbeat motion. Inhale at the beginning of the initial drop/rebound, and exhale during the downbeat drop.

d. Keep your movements continuous (no pauses) and in the same tempo throughout the preparatory gesture and downbeat.

e. Once you have successfully completed this task, form groups of three or four individuals. With one person serving as the conductor, perform the preparatory gesture. Have the group breathe with you and sing "ahhh," or some other vowel/syllable, on a mutually agreed-upon pitch at the downbeat. Repeat this process several times for each conductor, and then have another conductor perform the task. Provide feedback/evaluation information after each preparatory gesture.

Assignment

As you begin to feel more at ease with the preparatory gesture for a downbeat in 2/4 meter, you can practice this exercise varying the tempi.

Observation

Notice the preparatory gestures used by your directors and conductors. The pattern presented above is a pre-conducting pattern and may or may not be used in a conducting class.

PROFESSIONAL KNOWLEDGE: JEAN PIAGET

For this component, the focus is to:

- Understand Jean Piaget's cognitive stage theory and its applications to music learning.

Swiss biologist Jean Piaget wrote, "The principal goal of education in the schools should be creating men and women who are capable of doing new things, not simply repeating what other generations have done." Theories of development provide teachers with information regarding learning, learning development, and how individual learning needs change throughout the maturation process. In module 14, you explored the differences between stage and phase learning theories. We will now examine the stage theory outlined by Piaget.

Piaget's work provides educators with a framework for understanding two main concepts: (1) why children interact differently with objects at various ages and (2) why children respond and construct personal meaning differently from adults. Piaget viewed children as "little philosophers" or "little scientists," creating and building their own theories of knowledge. Through analysis of what children were *unable* to do, Piaget used this negative information as a tool for understanding how to teach children during each stage progression. Piaget made the following basic assumptions about children:

- They do not think like adults.
- They learn by becoming involved with concrete objects.
- They learn intrinsically (from within), not extrinsically (from without).
- They evolve intellectually through the generative nature of prior experience and the quality of current experience.
- They learn through the adaptation of new schemas (formation of concepts; categorizing perceived data) (as summarized in Andress, 1998, p. 3).

Piaget designated four stages of intellectual development: sensorimotor, preoperational, concrete operational, and formal operational (see figure 15.5). The stages are loosely connected with age levels, but it is important to realize that all individuals progress at different paces.

As children progress through these stages, they adapt and modify the varying levels to best understand their environment. Each stage is a necessary step toward the next stage of learning. The knowledge obtained from each stage may be altered or discarded during the progression.

Stage	Age	Description	Music
Sensorimotor	0–2	Child learns from random behavior, repetition, association, trial and error	Able to recognize mothers voice; respond to repetitive motions (rocking/bouncing); stimulation of senses through sound and movement
Preoperational	2–7	Development of motor and language skills; cannot distinguish between possibility and necessity; creative thinking predominates	Focus on motor skill development – keeping steady beat, playing rhythms, moving to music, often uses musical instruments in nontraditional ways
Concrete Operational	7–11	Logical thinkers	Symbols (notation) related to music can be taught and understood; Students can recognize and comprehend changes in music; can anticipate what will happen next in the music
Formal Operational	11+	Abstract reasoning is being developed	Students able to "think beyond the page." Able to improvise, compose, make personal choices regarding expression and dynamics

Figure 15.5 Piaget's stages and connections to Music.

Although Piaget found these four stages and age correlations to be approximate (individual age, stage growth, and overlap of stages depend on the individual child), music educators benefit greatly in knowing approximate ages for best introducing musical concepts and elements to students and what to expect at the different grade levels.

During all stages, children need to make sense of their environment. *Assimilation* is defined as taking in stimuli (information, ideas, or culture) and understanding fully. An example would be that when babies learn that the grab-and-thrust pattern allows them to pick up a toy, they then use the same pattern to pick up other objects. The new information fits into their database of knowledge. But what happens when they encounter something they cannot assimilate? A child sees an animal with four legs, and the parent explains, "That is a dog." The child sees another animal with four legs and promptly points and says, "Dog." The parent responds, "No, that is a cat, not a dog." In this case, the child could not assimilate or incorporate previous data but rather needed to incorporate the process of accommodation.

Accommodation requires one to modify his or her thinking to incorporate new information, new perceptual data. In the example, new information has revealed that animals with four legs can be dogs or cats. *Equilibrium* occurs when accommodation and assimilation are balanced (see figure 15.6).

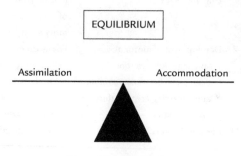

Figure 15.6 Equilibrium.

Now let's use an example of assimilation, accommodation, and equilibrium from the music classroom.

- Assimilation: A student learns the fingering for G on a recorder. The student tries that same fingering on flute, which results in the same pitch.
- Accommodation: The student tries the same fingering on a clarinet, which results in a different pitch. The same fingering may result in a different note or sound.
- Equilibrium: The student realizes that fingerings transfer to some instruments but not to all.

Piaget believed that education should teach students how to accumulate useful knowledge, how to learn, and how to be innovative. They should learn to check, verify, and repeat the process. This perspective allows for student discovery through engagement—through doing or "musicking." In music education, these two components are essential for understanding and experiencing music. In relating music education to the cognitive processes of the developing child, Piaget's stages are relevant and useful.

Discussion

Working with a partner or a small group, do the following:
1. Review the four stages outlined by Piaget.

2. Review the terms *assimilation, accommodation,* and *equilibrium.*
3. Provide a musical example of assimilation, accommodation, and equilibrium.

MODULE 15 REFERENCE

Andress, B. (1998). *Music for young children.* New York, NY: Harcourt Brace.

Facial and Body Gesture Awareness—Chord Building—Preparatory Gestures in 4/4—Jerome Bruner

In this module, you will focus on:

- Personal awareness: Facial and body gesture awareness.
- Personal musicianship: Chord building with Roman numerals.
- Pre-conducting: Conducting the preparatory gesture for the anacrusis in 4/4 meter.
- Professional knowledge: Jerome Bruner's cognitive development theory and its applications to music learning.

PERSONAL AWARENESS: FACIAL AND BODY GESTURE AWARENESS I

According to Widrich (2013), your body expresses emotion better than your face. Based on four separate studies completed in Princeton, it was found that individuals more accurately identified an emotion based on body language alone, or in combination with facial expressions, more often than with facial expression alone. So while facial expressions are extremely valuable in judging people's emotions, the addition of body language adds an important dimension to this process.

We will now explore this combination of facial and body gestures. As an instructor, you will need to be aware of facial expressions and body expressions such as crossed hands, arms, and legs. In this exercise, you will again observe your classmates conveying one of two facial expressions in addition to one of two body gestures. The facial expression will be happiness or disgust/strong displeasure, and the body gesture used will be crossed/not crossed arms.

According to Allan and Barbara Pease (2004), when someone crosses his or her arms on the chest, it has a universally negative connotation. Such a gesture is seen as an attempt to put a barrier between the person and someone or something the person does not like. It carries a defensive or negative meaning almost universally and is usually interpreted as not receptive, disagreeable, or ill at ease. In contrast, not crossing one's arms or hands in any manner is generally interpreted as being receptive, at ease, and open.

All class members will be participating in this exercise. The number of different expressions transmitted will be limited to disgust/strong displeasure or happiness. A description of both expressions is provided. In addition, two body gestures will be given: arms crossed over the chest or arms not crossed.

Classroom Setup

The classroom should be arranged in three rows with five columns. If your class contains fewer than 15 individuals, place chairs in the rows/columns and randomly fill in the other positions. If you have a larger class, add more rows. Students should be seated in a relaxed but upright posture (no slumping), with their feet flat on the floor, shoulders' width apart.

Exercise

1. For this exercise, the following two facial expressions will be used:
   a. Disgust/strong displeasure (eyes are squinted slightly, eyebrows are flat and may be pulled inward slightly, forehead is flat, mouth is closed with corners upturned, lips are moderately tense).
   b. Happiness (smiling, wide-open eyes, raised eyebrows, upturned mouth corners, mouth can be slightly open, etc.).

2. The following two body gestures will be used:
   a. Arms crossed over the chest.
   b. Arms not crossed (the palm of each hand is placed either on the desktop or on the legs, right hand on right thigh and left hand on left thigh).
3. To begin the exercise, one individual comes to the front of the class. In this exercise, each individual conveys one of the two facial expressions and one of the two body expressions.
   a. All individuals begin with a neutral/calm facial expression and in a neutral body position (arms and hands uncrossed).
   b. Each member of the class decides which facial expression and which body gesture he or she wishes to communicate.
   c. When the instructor signals, the expressions are conveyed.
4. The facial and body pose should be held for a maximum of five seconds. The instructor initiates the count, and the individual in front of the class begins his or her scan.
5. At the end of five seconds, the instructor calls "time," and everyone returns to a neutral/calm pose.
6. The individual in front of the class is then asked to identify those individuals transmitting either the disgust/strong displeasure facial expression or the happiness facial expression and then to identify those individuals with arms crossed or arms not crossed. There is a possibility of four combinations:
   a. Happiness with arms not crossed.
   b. Happiness with arms crossed.
   c. Disgust/strong displeasure with arms not crossed.
   d. Disgust/strong displeasure with arms crossed.
7. This exercise should be repeated.
8. All class members should have the opportunity to stand in front of the group and complete the exercise.

Assignment

Different facial expressions, other than those suggested, can be added to the exercise. Your success rate of identification is not important, but your heightened awareness of classroom dynamics is significant.

Observation

As you observe groups of individuals talking in the hallway, participating in classrooms, listening to directives in ensembles, and so on, notice the expressions on individual faces and the bodily gestures being conveyed with the arms. What messages are they sending?

PERSONAL MUSICIANSHIP: CHORD BUILDING WITH ROMAN NUMERALS

For this component, the focus is to:

- Review the purpose of chord inversions.
- Sing a melody with limited pitches (s,- d-r-m-f-s) in standard notation and with Roman numerals.
- Perform chordal accompaniments to a melody using Roman numerals and inversions.

This component focuses on building triads from Roman numerals. The solfège syllables and inversions outlined in module 15 remain the same; therefore, your ears will not hear any difference, even though your eyes are viewing Roman numerals. Refer to figure 16.1, and explain to a neighbor why the V chord is written as an inversion. Also identify the inversion.

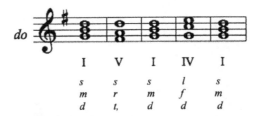

Figure 16.1 Chord-building Examples, *do*-center or major.

Sing the melody in figure 16.2, and add chordal accompaniment as indicated by the Roman numerals. Be sure to include appropriate voice leading. (This will require at least four people to perform all parts, with three singing triads and one singing the melody.)

Traditional

Figure 16.2 "Oats and Beans," standard notation.

PRE-CONDUCTING: PREPARATORY GESTURE
FOR THE ANACRUSIS IN 4/4 METER

Often, a preparatory gesture needs to be provided for a beat other than the downbeat. For example, a preparatory gesture is required for an upbeat, also labeled an anacrusis or a pickup. In this exercise, we will introduce the pre-conducting preparatory gesture for an upbeat/anacrusis/pickup in 4/4 meter. This preparatory gesture can indicate tempo along with style, and so on, but in this exercise, we will focus on the preparatory gesture only as an indicator of tempo. You will only be using the right hand/arm in this exercise. You should carefully monitor your movements as suggested.

Classroom Setup

All class members can complete this exercise simultaneously. Students should stand and allow about one arm's length of space around them. An instructor should initiate each activity and each step of any given task so the class practices as a unit. However, as individuals become more proficient in completing the elements in this activity, it is suggested that they form small groups of three or four individuals and conduct preparatory gestures for others.

Exercise

1. Establish your conducting posture and a tempo of mm = 69.
   a. The preparatory gesture for an anacrusis begins one beat prior to the anacrusis. Since the anacrusis in a 4/4 conducting pattern occurs on beat four or fourth position, the preparatory beat begins on beat three
      i. For this preparatory gesture, the initial drop begins in third position, with the rebound going to your left side, to fourth position. The hand will rebound to the top of the fourth-position pattern. (See figure 16.3.) Once the rebound height is attained, the right hand is dropped without pause, in the same tempo, to complete the upbeat/anacrusis/pickup movement. (See figure 16.4.)

Rebound after the Initial
3rd-Position Drop

Initial 3rd-Position Drop
Preparatory Gesture

Figure 16.3 The third-position preparatory gesture for an upbeat/anacrusis/pickup in 4/4: initial drop and rebound.

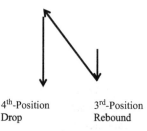

4th-Position   3rd-Position
Drop   Rebound

Figure 16.4 Third-position rebound and fourth-position drop.

ii. Practice the preparatory gesture and upbeat/anacrusis/pickup several times. After each preparatory gesture and upbeat/anacrusis/pickup, rest before repeating the gesture. Check your preparatory position, drop, and rebound.

iii. Inhale at the beginning of the initial drop/rebound, and exhale during the upbeat/anacrusis/pickup drop. Keep your movements continuous (no pauses) and in the same tempo throughout the preparatory gesture and anacrusis.

iv. Once you have successfully completed this task, form groups of three or four individuals. With one person serving as the conductor, conduct the preparatory gesture. Have the group breathe with you and sing a neutral syllable on a mutually agreed-upon pitch at the upbeat/anacrusis/pickup. Repeat this process several times for each conductor, and then have another conductor perform the task. Provide feedback/evaluation information after each preparatory gesture.

Assignment

As you begin to feel more at ease with the preparatory gesture for the anacrusis in 4/4 time, you can practice this exercise at varying tempi.

Observation

Notice the preparatory gestures used by your directors and conductors. The pattern presented above is a pre-conducting pattern and may or may not be used in a conducting class.

PROFESSIONAL KNOWLEDGE: JEROME BRUNER

For this component, the focus is to:

- Understand Jerome Bruner's cognitive development theory and its applications to music learning.

"Teachers who think about what they do, and are informed by theory, are deeply committed to leading children to their maximal musical development" (Campbell & Scott-Kassner, 2013, p. 18). In module 15, the emphasis was on Piaget's stages of learning. We will now examine the cognitive development theory defined by psychologist Jerome Bruner. He outlined how learners can demonstrate understanding or meaning as they move through the stages, and although this is *related* to maturation, it is not *dependent* on maturation. Bruner believes that learners of all ages can learn new material by processing it through three representation modes: enactive, iconic, and symbolic.

Bruner's theory is considered a constructivist view of learning, as the learners are active in the process. Bruner's framework is often called a "spiral curriculum" or "discovery learning," with learners applying their current knowledge base to make sense of new ideas and concepts, using the known to make sense of the unknown as they construct their learning. "Students learn through exploration and problem solving; subject matter can be taught to children through age-appropriate experiences and can be embellished through repeated exposure" (Campbell & Scott-Kassner, 2013, p. 20). Each set of instructions in the "spiral" is intended to strengthen the foundation for further learning or to provide the "scaffolding" necessary to move to the next step.

Now let's explore what is meant by enactive, iconic, and symbolic, by using a music-listening example that includes alternating meters of two and three. *Enactive* is "the act of doing," and in this case, it could be moving your body to the music to show whether you recognize the meter as two (marching) or three (swaying). *Iconic* means using "pictorial representations" to show your understanding. Think of having a sheet of paper with rectangles, and the students place either two dots or three dots on each rectangle to show their understanding of the meter. The dots represent the beats, and the rectangles represent individual measures. *Symbolic*, the final stage of the process, includes standard notation and writing the meter changes on the music, adding bar lines where appropriate. (See figure 16.5 for a comparison of the three representation modes.)

Enactive: Body movements that represent meter in 2 or meter in 3

Iconic: Pictures that represent measures with 2 beats versus measures with 3 beats

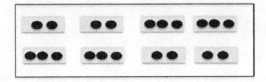

Symbolic: Students write in the appropriate bar lines and time signatures

Figure 16.5 Modes of representation, example.

In summary, Bruner follows three basic principles in regard to instructional practice:

1. Student readiness should match the experiences and content prepared by the teacher.
2. Instruction should be organized in a manner that builds on foundational learning before attempting more complex content—learning follows a "spiral."
3. Instruction should facilitate the ability of the learners to generalize and draw conclusions. Current instruction serves as a scaffold to future learning.

Discussion

1. With a partner or a small group, review the following terms:
   a. Modes of representation
   b. Constructivist learning
   c. Spiral curriculum
   d. Scaffolding
2. With a partner or a small group, provide another musical example using the three modes of representation. (e.g., rhythms, pitches, dynamics, texture)

MODULE 16 REFERENCES

Campbell, P. S., & Scott-Kassner, C. (2013). *Music in childhood: From preschool through the elementary grades.* Boston, MA: Schirmer.

Pease, A., & Pease, B. (2004). *The definitive book of body language.* London: Orion House.

Widrich, L. (2013). The secrets of body language: Why you should never cross your arms again. http://blog.bufferapp.com/improve-my-body-language-secrets

Identifying Facial and Body Expressions—Singing Ascending Leaps—Preparatory Gestures in 3/4—Asking Good Questions

I n this module, you will focus on:

- Personal awareness: Identifying facial and body expressions.
- Personal musicianship: Practicing small ascending leaps.
- Pre-conducting: Conducting the preparatory gesture for the anacrusis in 3/4 meter.
- Professional knowledge: Asking good questions.

PERSONAL AWARENESS: FACIAL AND BODY GESTURE AWARENESS II

In this component, we will continue to develop awareness of both facial and body expressions. In module 16, you were asked to identify individuals who had one of two facial expressions and one of two body gestures. In this exercise, you will again observe one of two body gestures, but one more facial gesture will be added. The body gesture will be hands folded or not folded, and the facial expressions will be confusion/questioning, disgust/strong displeasure, or happiness.

When someone folds his or her hands, the connotation is similar to that of folding one's arms, putting a barrier between the person and someone or something else (Pease & Pease, 2004). Folding one's hands is a defensive gesture and is often used when an individual feels threatened or ill at ease. A classic example of defensive hand crossing is when someone is standing and crosses or folds his or her hands in front of himself or herself. In contrast, not folding one's hands, in any manner, is generally interpreted as being receptive, at ease, and open (Pease & Pease, 2004).

Classroom Setup

The classroom should be arranged in three rows with five columns. If your class contains fewer than 15 individuals, place empty chairs in the rows/columns and randomly fill in the other positions. If you have a larger class, add more rows. Students should be seated in a relaxed but upright posture (no slumping), with their feet flat on the floor, shoulders' width apart.

Exercise

All class members will be participating in this exercise. The number of different expressions transmitted will be limited to confusion/questioning, disgust/strong displeasure, or happiness. A description of these expressions is provided. In addition, two body gestures will be given: hands folded or not folded. If you are in sitting in a chair with an attached desk or at a table, the suggested folded-hands position is to place one hand over the other, palms down, in the middle of the desktop or table. If you are in a chair without an attached desk or table, the hands should be folded on your lap. For unfolded hands, place the hands, palms down, apart from each other on the flat surface. If you are in a chair without a desk, place hands, palms down, on your thighs, right hand on the right thigh and left hand on the left thigh.

1. For this exercise the following three facial expressions will be used:
   a. Confusion/questioning (eyebrows lowered and pulled together but not sloped, one eyebrow may be higher than the other as in a questioning mode, smooth forehead, mouth/lips somewhat relaxed but straight, lips may protrude slightly or be flattened, etc.).
   b. Disgust/strong displeasure (eyes are squinted slightly, eyebrows are flat and may be pulled inward slightly, forehead is flat, upturned lips in which the corners of the mouth are turned up and the mouth is closed, lips are moderately tense).
   c. Happiness (smiling, wide-open eyes, raised eyebrows, upturned mouth corners, mouth can be slightly open, etc.).

2. The following two body gestures will be used:
   a. Hands folded.
   b. Hands not folded.
3. To begin the exercise, one individual comes to the front of the class. In this exercise, each individual conveys one of the three facial expressions and one of the two body expressions.
   a. All individuals begin with a neutral/calm facial expression and in a neutral body position.
   b. Each member of the class decides which facial expression, chosen from the three above, and which hand position he or she wishes to communicate.
   c. When the instructor signals, the expressions are conveyed.
4. The facial and body pose should be held for a maximum of five seconds. The instructor initiates the count, and the individual in front of the class begins his or her scan.
5. At the end of five seconds, the instructor calls "time," and everyone returns to a neutral/calm pose.
6. The individual in front of the class is then asked to identify those individuals transmitting either the confusion/questioning, the disgust/strong displeasure, or the happiness facial expression and identify those individuals with hands folded or not folded. There is a possibility of six combinations:
   a. Confusion/questioning with hands folded.
   b. Confusion/questioning with hands not folded.
   c. Disgust/strong displeasure with hands folded.
   d. Disgust/strong displeasure with hands not folded.
   e. Happiness with hands folded.
   f. Happiness with hands not folded.
7. This exercise should be repeated.
8. All class members should have the opportunity to stand in front of the group and complete the exercise.

Assignment

Different facial expressions, other than those suggested, can be added to the exercise. Remember, the accuracy of gesture identification is not as important as the act of becoming aware of the gestures conveyed in a classroom. As teachers and conductors, you want to be aware of nonverbal feedback, and the idea of these exercises is to heighten individual awareness of those responses.

Observation

As you observe groups of individuals talking in the hallway, participating in classrooms, listening to directives in ensembles, and so on, notice the expressions on individual faces and the body gestures being conveyed with their hands. What messages are they sending?

PERSONAL MUSICIANSHIP: PRACTICING SMALL ASCENDING LEAPS

For this component, the focus is to:

- Perform a warm-up designed to practice small ascending leaps.
- Sing a melody with limited pitches (d-r-m-s-l) in stick notation.
- Perform chordal accompaniments to a melody using solfège syllables.

Singers can typically maintain vocal consistency during stepwise melodic passages with more accuracy than during melodic passages with small and large leaps. For the purpose of this text, a small leap refers to intervals of a perfect fifth or less. The warm-up exercise in figure 17.1 includes an ascending small leap followed by a descending stepwise motion. Notice the use of the vowel switch to "oo" on the fermata. This vowel switch encourages the soft palate to lift and helps you feel the resonance shift. Be sure to continue your breath support during the stepwise descent while keeping your soft palate raised. Try bending your knees slightly during the leap; this will also help you remain relaxed rather than forcing your voice through the leap. For each repetition of the warm-up, begin the pattern one half step higher.

SiNG,   "ah" _____

Sequence through all vowels to practice maintaining
a relaxed and open tone

NG-ah; NG-ee; NG-I; NG-oh; NG-oo

Figure 17.1 Warm-up for practicing small ascending leaps.

Sing the melody in figure 17.2, and add chordal accompaniment as indicated by the solfège syllables. Be sure to include appropriate voice leading. (This will require at least four people to perform all parts, three singing triads and one singing the melody.) Focus on creating vocal consistency between the two notes that form the ascending leap in measure 5.

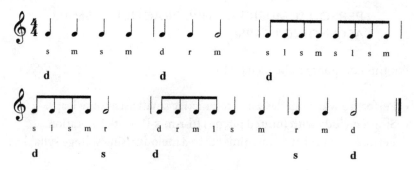

Figure 17.2 "Firefly," stick notation.

PRE-CONDUCTING: PREPARATORY GESTURE FOR THE ANACRUSIS IN 3/4 METER

In this exercise, you will continue working with the pre-conducting preparatory gesture for an upbeat/anacrusis/pickup. You will work with the preparatory gesture for an upbeat/anacrusis/pickup in 3/4 meter and will focus on the preparatory gesture only as an indicator of tempo. You will only be using the right hand/arm in this exercise. You should carefully monitor the movements suggested.

Classroom Setup

All class members can complete this exercise simultaneously. Students should stand and allow about one arm's length of space around them. An instructor should initiate each activity and each step of any given task so the class practices as a unit. As individuals become more proficient at completing the elements in this activity, they should form small groups of three or four individuals and conduct preparatory gestures for others.

Exercise

1. Establish your conducting posture and a tempo of mm = 69. The right hand/arm will be performing the task.
   a. The preparatory gesture for the anacrusis in 3/4 begins on beat two or second position.
      i. In this preparatory gesture for the upbeat/anacrusis/pickup, the initial drop begins in second position, with the rebound going to your left side. (See figure 17.3.) Once the rebound height is attained, the right hand is dropped without pause, in the same tempo, to complete the upbeat/anacrusis/pickup movement. (See figure 17.4.)

Rebound after the Initial

2nd-Position Drop

Initial 2nd-Position Drop
Preparatory Gesture

Figure 17.3 The second-position preparatory gesture for an anacrusis in ¾: initial drop and rebound.

2nd-Position

Rebound

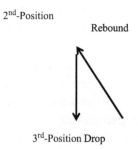

3rd-Position Drop

Figure 17.4 Second-position rebound and third-position drop.

ii. Practice the preparatory gesture and upbeat/anacrusis/pickup several times. After each preparatory gesture and upbeat/anacrusis/pickup, rest before repeating the gesture. Check your -position preparatory position, drop, and rebound.

iii. Inhale at the beginning of the initial drop/rebound, and exhale during the upbeat/anacrusis/pickup drop. Keep your movements continuous (no pauses) and in the same tempo throughout the preparatory gesture and anacrusis.

iv. Once you have successfully completed this task, form groups of three or four individuals. With one person serving as the conductor, conduct the preparatory gesture. Have the group breathe with you during the preparatory gesture and sing a vowel on a mutually agreed-upon pitch at the upbeat/anacrusis/pickup. Repeat this process several times for each conductor, and then have another conductor perform the task. Provide feedback/evaluation information after each preparatory gesture.

Assignment

As you begin to feel more at ease with the preparatory gesture for an upbeat/anacrusis/pickup in 3/4 meter, you can practice this exercise with varying tempi.

Observation

Notice the preparatory gestures used by your directors and conductors. The pattern presented above is a pre-conducting pattern and may or may not be used in a conducting class.

PROFESSIONAL KNOWLEDGE: ASKING GOOD QUESTIONS

For this component, the focus is to:

- Refine your ability to ask good questions in the classroom setting.

"Understanding questioning strategies and practicing with a peer can improve teachers' questioning skills" (Vogler, 2008). Your ability to be effective in the classroom can be enhanced by thinking about the types of questions to ask your students.

Here are three problematic questions:

- Does everyone understand?
- Do you want to play the Sousa march?
- Do you want to volunteer to come up to the board?

Let's look at the first one. The teacher has guided students through a lesson with new content and then asks, "Does everyone understand?" You might be asking yourself why this is problematic. Teachers overuse that question and often do not receive true feedback from the students regarding their comprehension of the new material. After a teacher poses that question, the common response is a bunch of heads bobbing up and down in a yes motion. What about the student who doesn't understand? If a student thinks most classmates understand the new concept, he or she may be reluctant to admit confusion. In the body awareness components of this book, you are practicing being more perceptive about facial expressions. Although the students are saying yes and/or performing a yes gesture, do their facial expressions portray understanding, or do you see confusion or frustration?

The second and third questions above are problematic in a different manner. When a teacher asks questions such as these, he or she does not expect the response from students to be a no. Rather, the teacher is expecting the students to say yes, as the intent was merely to inform the students about which music selection they would be playing next or which student should come to the board and write an answer. The problem with asking a question rather than giving a directive is that you offer students the opportunity to say no. Chances are, even if they respond negatively, you will still move forward to play the piece you intended or have the specified student come to the board. With these types of "questions of futility," you open yourself up to power struggles with students. If you give them the option to make a decision (yes or no) but do not acknowledge their responses, the students soon recognize that (1) you really don't want their opinions, and (2) they don't truly have a voice in the classroom. Once you begin to examine the nuances of asking questions in the classroom, you will realize that there are few instances that require asking a yes/no question, as those types of questions do not require students to reflect, analyze, or compare.

Teachers constantly ask students questions to assess comprehension and to monitor and adjust their pacing and content delivery. This has been a common practice for centuries. The only other instructional strategy that teachers use more than questions is lecturing (Black, 2001). "Teachers ask about 300–400 questions per day and as many as 120 question per hour" (Vogler, 2008). Rather than use questions as merely organizational tools—what selection to play next or what student to come to the board—think of them as a way to motivate your students and encourage exploration.

In addition to routine or procedural questions, there are four other basic types of questioning strategies: cognitive memory, convergent thinking, divergent thinking, and evaluative thinking (Hunt, Wiseman, & Touzel, 2009, p. 127). Cognitive memory questions are based on rote memory (e.g., "Name a composition written by Beethoven"). This is based on selective recall. Convergent thinking requires students to recall, process, and analyze data to form an answer. It is still a simplistic questioning strategy, in that typically there is one correct response to the question. The answer depends on the use of deduction rather than creativity. Divergent thinking allows for more than one answer to a question. Teachers may ask students to brainstorm ideas for creating various accompaniments to melodies (e.g., instrumentation, chords, ostinato, etc.). This process involves creative thinking on the part of students rather than mere recall. Evaluative thinking is what we should strive for in the classroom, as it is based on judgments, values, and choices.

You can develop your ability to ask effective questions through awareness, knowledge, and practice. "Once honed, verbal questioning becomes an efficient formative assessment tool, helps students make connections to prior knowledge, and stimulates cognitive growth" (Vogler, 2008).

Discussion

1. With a partner or a small group, brainstorm two or three questions that focus on music content for each of the following questioning strategies: cognitive memory, convergent thinking, divergent thinking, and evaluative thinking.

2. Select one class this week to track the number of times a teacher or director asks questions of the class.
3. Select a different class to track the number of times a teacher or director asks a "question of futility."

MODULE 17 REFERENCES

Black, S. (2001). Ask me a question: How teachers use inquiry in the classroom. *American School Board Journal, 188*(5), 43–45.

Hunt, G., Wiseman, D., & Touzel, T. (2009). *Effective teaching: Preparation and implementation.* Springfield, IL: Charles C. Thomas.

Pease, A., & Pease, B. (2004). *The definitive book of body language.* London: Orion House.

Vogler, K. E. (2008). Asking good questions. *Educational Leadership, 65*(9).

Body Expression Awareness—Singing Large Ascending Leaps—Preparatory Gestures in 2/4—Teaching Flexibility

I n this module, you will focus on:

- Personal awareness: Facial and lower-body expression awareness.
- Personal musicianship: Practicing large ascending leaps.
- Pre-conducting: Conducting the preparatory gesture for an anacrusis in 2/4 meter.
- Professional knowledge: Flexibility in teaching.

PERSONAL AWARENESS: FACIAL AND BODY GESTURE AWARENESS III

In our personal awareness exercises so far, the primary focus has been on the upper half of the body (face, arms, hands). However, as music instructors, we know the importance of proper body posture, and this includes the legs and feet. Not crossing one's legs and having one's feet flat on the floor form a desired playing or singing position. In this component, we will develop awareness of both facial and lower-body postures.

Pease and Pease (2004) state that the legs, ankles, and feet offer information about someone's attitude. If people cross their legs, they are indicating that they are not comfortable with the situation, are closing themselves off, are being defensive or submissive, or fear that some sort of attack is imminent. If people want to leave a situation their dominant foot points in the direction they want to go. The tapping of a foot, a restless leg, or swaying from side to side can indicate a person's intention to leave the room or 'get away.' (Pease & Pease, 2004). Uncrossed legs mean basically the opposite: openness, comfort, or dominance. Individuals who cross or lock their ankles are mentally biting their lips and are most likely holding back a negative emotion or expressing uncertainty or fear (Pease & Pease, 2004).

In these exercises, you will focus on gestures of the legs (crossed and uncrossed), ankles (crossed and uncrossed), and feet (tapping and not tapping) but not simultaneously. You will also use three facial expressions: confusion/questioning, disgust/strong displeasure, and happiness. When you are in front of the group, you will be asked to identify individuals' facial and body gestures. All class members will be participating in these exercises. The number of different expressions transmitted will be limited to confusion/questioning, disgust/strong displeasure, or happiness.

In exercise 1, the directive to cross or not cross the legs will be given. The suggested legs-crossed position is to place either the right or left leg over the knee of the other leg. (There is also a legs-crossed position, the "figure-our" position, in which the ankle of one leg contacts the upper portion of the knee of the other leg. That position is not recommended for this exercise.)

For exercise 2, the suggested crossed-ankle position is to place either the right or left ankle over the other ankle.

In exercise 3, foot tapping replaces the leg or ankle crossing: with legs and feet shoulders' width apart and one foot flat on the floor, tap the other foot.

Depending on the size of the class, completion of the exercises in this component may require more than one class session.

Classroom Setup

The classroom should be arranged in three rows with five columns. If your class contains fewer than 15 individuals, place empty chairs in the rows/columns and randomly fill in the other positions. If you have a larger class, add more rows. Students should be seated in a relaxed but upright posture (no slumping), with their feet flat on the floor, shoulders' width apart.

Exercises
Exercise 1

1. For this exercise, the following three facial expressions will be used:
   a. Confusion/questioning.
   b. Disgust/strong displeasure.
   c. Happiness.
2. The following two body gestures will be used:
   a. Legs crossed.
   b. Legs not crossed.
3. To begin the exercise, one individual comes to the front of the class. All other classmates convey one of the three facial expressions and one of the two leg positions.
   a. All individuals begin with a neutral/calm facial expression and in a neutral body position (feet flat on the floor and legs not crossed).
   b. Each member of the class decides which facial expression, chosen from the three above, and which leg position he or she wishes to communicate.
   c. When the instructor signals, the expressions are conveyed.
4. The facial and body pose should be held for a maximum of five seconds. The instructor initiates the count, and the individual in front of the class begins his or her scan.
5. At the end of five seconds, the instructor calls "time" and everyone returns to a neutral/calm pose.
6. The individual in front of the class is then asked to identify those individuals transmitting the confusion/questioning, the disgust/strong displeasure, or the happiness facial expression and identify those individuals with legs crossed or not crossed. There is a possibility of six combinations:
   a. Confusion/questioning with legs crossed.
   b. Confusion/questioning with legs not crossed.
   c. Disgust/strong displeasure with legs crossed.
   d. Disgust/strong displeasure with legs not crossed.
   e. Happiness with legs crossed.
   f. Happiness with legs not crossed
7. This exercise should be repeated.
8. All class members should have the opportunity to stand in front of the group and complete the exercise.

Exercise 2

1. To begin the exercise, one individual comes to the front of the class. In this exercise, each individual conveys one of the three facial expressions and

one of the two ankle positions. The procedure outlined above should be followed for this exercise, except that ankle crossing replaces leg crossing.

Exercise 3

1. To begin the exercise, one individual comes to the front of the class. In this exercise, each individual conveys one of the three facial expressions and one of the two foot-tapping positions. The procedure outlined above should be followed for this exercise, except that foot tapping replaces leg or ankle crossing.

Assignment

Different facial expressions, other than those suggested, can be added to the exercises. Remember, the accuracy of gesture identification is not as important as the act of becoming aware of the gestures being conveyed in a classroom. As teachers and conductors, you want to be aware of individuals' nonverbal feedback, and the idea of these exercises is to heighten individual awareness of those responses.

Observation

As you observe groups of individuals talking in the hallway, participating in classrooms, listening to directives in ensembles, and so on, notice the expressions on individual faces and the body gestures being conveyed with their legs, ankles, and feet. What messages are they sending?

PERSONAL MUSICIANSHIP: PRACTICING LARGE ASCENDING LEAPS

For this component, the focus is to:

- Perform a warm-up designed to practice large ascending leaps.
- Sing a melody with limited pitches (d-r-m-s-l) in standard notation.
- Perform chordal accompaniments to a melody using Roman numerals and solfège syllables.

In module 17, you practiced a warm-up designed to maintain vocal consistency during a melodic passage with small ascending leaps. A large leap is any interval that exceeds a perfect fifth. The warm-up exercise in figure 18.1 includes an ascending large leap followed by a descending arpeggiated pattern. Notice the use of the vowel switch to "hoy" on the fermata. This helps prevent over-adduction of the vocal folds with the octave leap and can help connect the breath from the low abdominal muscles instead of constricting the throat with a glottal stop. This vowel switch encourages the soft palate to lift and helps you feel the resonance shift. Be sure to continue your breath support during the descent while focusing on keeping your soft palate raised.

> Imagine you are serving a volleyball. On the first note, "ah," pantomime tossing the ball up with one hand. As you switch the vowel to "hoy" swing your other hand around as if "hitting" the ball. Then have your arm follow through and move downward to mirror the descending arpeggiated pattern in the warm-up. This will help you to remain relaxed rather than "forcing your voice" through the octave leap. (Nokes, 2014)

For each repetition of the warm-up, begin the pattern one half step higher.

ah   hoy _____

Figure 18.1 Warm-up for practicing large ascending leaps.

Sing the melody in figure 18.2, and add chordal accompaniment as indicated by the Roman numerals. Be sure to include appropriate voice leading. (This will require at least four people to perform all parts, three singing triads and one singing the melody.) Focus on creating vocal consistency between the two notes that form an ascending leap followed by a descending pattern in measure 5.

Figure 18.2 "Firefly," stick notation.

PRE-CONDUCTING: PREPARATORY GESTURE FOR THE ANACRUSIS IN 2/4 METER

In this exercise, you will continue working with the pre-conducting preparatory gesture for an upbeat/anacrusis/pickup in 2/4 meter. You will only be using the right hand/arm in this exercise. You should carefully monitor the movements suggested.

Classroom Setup

All class members can complete this exercise simultaneously. Students should stand and allow about one arm's length of space around them. An instructor should initiate each activity and each step of any given task so the class practices as a unit. As individuals become more proficient in completing the elements in this activity, they should form small groups of three or four individuals and conduct preparatory gestures for others.

Exercise

1. Establish your conducting posture and a tempo of mm = 69.
   a. Since the anacrusis in a 2/4 conducting pattern occurs on beat two or second position, the preparatory gesture begins on beat one, first position, or the downbeat.
      i. In this preparatory gesture for the anacrusis, the initial drop begins in first position. (See figure 18.3.) Once the rebound height is attained, the right hand is dropped without pause, in the same tempo, to complete the upbeat/anacrusis/pickup movement. (See figure 18.4.)

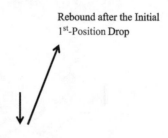

Rebound after the Initial
1st-Position Drop

Initial 1st-Position Drop
Preparatory Gesture

Figure 18.3 The first-position preparatory gesture for an anacrusis in 2/4: initial drop and rebound.

2nd-Position
Rebound

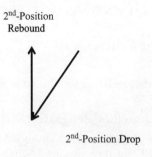

2nd-Position
Rebound

2nd-Position **Drop**

Figure 18.4 Second-position drop and rebound.

ii. Practice the preparatory gesture and upbeat/anacrusis/pickup several times. After each preparatory gesture and upbeat/anacrusis/pickup, rest before repeating the gesture.

iii. Inhale at the beginning of the initial drop/rebound, and exhale during the upbeat drop. Keep your movements continuous (no pauses) and in the same tempo throughout the preparatory gesture and anacrusis.

iv. Once you have successfully completed this task, form groups of three or four individuals. With one person serving as the conductor, conduct the preparatory gesture. Have the group breathe with you during the preparatory gesture and sing a vowel on a mutually agreed-upon pitch at the upbeat/anacrusis/pickup. Repeat this process several times for each conductor, and then have another conductor perform the task. Provide feedback/ evaluation information after each preparatory gesture.

Assignment

As you begin to feel more at ease with the preparatory gesture for an upbeat/anacrusis/pickup in 2/4 meter, you can practice this exercise with varying tempi.

Observation

Notice the preparatory gestures used by your directors and conductors. The pattern presented above is a pre-conducting pattern and may or may not be used in a conducting class.

PROFESSIONAL KNOWLEDGE: FLEXIBILITY

For this component, the focus is to:

• Discuss the importance of being flexible in teaching.

The expression "as the crow flies" designates the shortest distance between two points on a map (see figure 18.5). Although it serves as a general guide, this designation is not helpful to someone who is driving a car and constrained to existing roadways. As teachers, we know that students need to move from point A to point B, but that distance is sometimes lengthened depending on each student's current knowledge base, learning style, personality, and other factors. It is important to remember that although goals and objectives in the music classroom may appear straightforward ("as the crow flies"), the pathway for each student will be slightly altered, with learners and teachers encountering detours and even some mountains to climb along the way. The ability to be flexible—defined as being "ready and able to change so as to adapt to different circumstances" (*New Oxford American Dictionary*)—enables you to accept, and even sometimes embrace, the alternative routes.

Figure 18.5 Distance between A and B.

When you are teaching, you will have few "typical" days. The reality is that most days, you will have interruptions, disruptions, and malfunctioning technical equipment and musical instruments. Learning to be flexible can have many benefits. First and foremost, it likely will reduce your stress level. Another benefit, maybe not as obvious, is that you model for your students the ability to adapt and make alternative decisions.

> Effective teaching is variable. Effective teachers use a variety of strategies and a range of methods, and they change and refine these over time. They do not teach the same way and use the same instructional repertoire year after year. (Christenbury, 2010–2011)

There is no clear, definitive, linear path from point A to B in education or in teaching—not in learner outcomes, communication between teachers and students, or progressing from a college student to a professional teacher (see figure 18.6). The ability to be flexible and to embrace the detours you encounter will help as you continue on your journey to becoming a professional teacher.

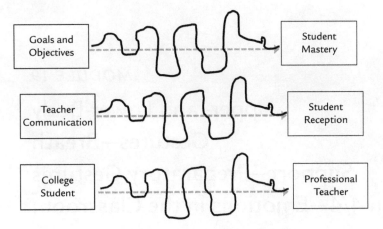

Figure 18.6 No linear paths in education.

Discussion

1. With a partner or a small group, discuss events this week that have required you to be flexible.
2. Take time to reflect on your ability to encounter change and to adapt. Are you comfortable with change, or does it make you nervous or anxious?
3. During classes this week, watch your teachers and note times when they are flexible or inflexible. How do they react? How do their facial expressions change? (For example, maybe one teacher's lectures required technology, but the equipment wasn't working, and the teacher reacted to that situation.)

MODULE 18 REFERENCES

Christenbury, L. (2010–2011). The flexible teacher. *Educational Leadership, 68*(4), 46–50.
Nokes, C. D. (2014). Unpublished vocal warmup. Used with permission.
Pease, A., & Pease, B. (2004). *The definitive book of body language.* London: Orion House.

Upper- and Lower-Body Gestures—Breath Support—Preparatory Gestures in 4/4—Emotions in the Classroom

In this module, you will focus on:

- Personal awareness: Upper- and lower-body gestures.
- Personal musicianship: Increasing breath support.
- Pre-conducting: Conducting a preparatory gesture to begin on beat two in 4/4 meter.
- Professional knowledge: The effect of emotions in the classroom.

PERSONAL AWARENESS: FACIAL AND BODY GESTURE AWARENESS IV

The emphasis of these exercises will be on gestures from the upper half of the body (arms, hands) and the lower half of the body (legs, ankles, and feet). Facial expressions will not be included. As music teachers and directors, you will need to be constantly aware of embouchures and other facial areas and also of hand and arm positions and sitting postures.

In these exercises, we will focus on upper-body gestures (arms crossed and uncrossed, hands crossed and uncrossed) and lower-body gestures (legs crossed and uncrossed, ankles crossed and uncrossed, feet tapping and not tapping). When you are in front of the group, you will be asked to identify individuals' body gestures. All class members will be participating in these exercises.

In exercise 1, the hand, arm, leg, and ankle (crossed or not crossed) and the feet (one foot tapping or no feet tapping) will be used. To review the suggested positions for each of these body gestures, see module 18.

For exercise 2, we will combine or use the two upper- and the three lower-body positions simultaneously.

Depending on the size of the class, completion of the exercises in this component may require more than one class session.

Classroom Setup

The classroom should be arranged in three rows with five columns. If your class contains fewer than 15 individuals, place chairs in the rows/columns and randomly fill in the other positions. If you have a larger class, add more rows. Students should be seated in a relaxed but upright posture (no slumping), with their feet flat on the floor, shoulders' width apart.

Exercises
Exercise 1

1. This exercise will use the following upper- and lower-body gestures:
   a. Arms crossed.
   b. Arms not crossed.
   c. Legs crossed.
   d. Legs not crossed.
2. To begin the exercise, one individual comes to the front of the class. All other classmates will convey one of the two arm gestures and one of the two leg gestures.
   a. All individuals begin with a neutral body position (feet flat on the floor and legs not crossed).
   b. Each member of the class decides which upper- and lower-body positions, chosen from the list above, he or she wishes to convey.
   c. When the instructor signals, the gestures are conveyed.
3. The body gestures should be held for a maximum of five seconds. The instructor initiates the count, and the individual in front of the class begins his or her scan.
4. At the end of five seconds, the instructor calls "time," and everyone returns to a neutral/calm pose.

5. The individual in front of the class is then asked to identify those individuals' body gestures. There is a possibility of four combinations:
   a. Arms and legs crossed.
   b. Arms not crossed, legs not crossed.
   c. Arms not crossed, legs crossed.
   d. Arms crossed, legs not crossed.
6. All class members should have the opportunity to stand in front of the group and complete the exercise.
7. This exercise should be repeated using arms (crossed or not crossed) and ankles (crossed or not crossed).
8. After the exercise is repeated using arms and ankles, it should be repeated one more time using arms (crossed or not crossed) and feet (one foot tapping or no feet tapping).
9. After the exercise using arms (crossed or not crossed) and feet (one foot tapping or no feet tapping), complete the exercise using hands (crossed and uncrossed) with legs (crossed and uncrossed), followed by hands (crossed and uncrossed) with ankles (crossed and uncrossed), followed by hands (crossed and uncrossed) with feet (tapping and not tapping).

Exercise 2

1. To begin the exercise, one individual comes to the front of the class. In this exercise, each individual conveys one of the two upper-body gestures or one of the three lower-body gestures. The procedure outlined above should be followed.
2. There is a possibility of 24 combinations:
   a. Hands crossed, legs crossed.
   b. Hands crossed, legs not crossed.
   c. Hands crossed, ankles crossed.
   d. Hands crossed, ankles not crossed.
   e. Hands crossed, one foot tapping.
   f. Hands crossed, feet idle.
   g. Hands not crossed, legs crossed.
   h. Hands not crossed, legs not crossed.
   i. Hands not crossed, ankles crossed.
   j. Hands not crossed, ankles not crossed.
   k. Hands not crossed, one foot tapping.
   l. Hands not crossed, feet idle.
   m. Arms crossed, legs crossed.
   n. Arms crossed, legs not crossed.

o. Arms crossed, ankles crossed.
p. Arms crossed, ankles not crossed.
q. Arms crossed, one foot tapping.
r. Arms crossed, feet idle.
s. Arms not crossed, legs crossed.
t. Arms not crossed, legs not crossed.
u. Arms not crossed, ankles crossed.
v. Arms not crossed, ankles not crossed.
w. Arms not crossed, one foot tapping.
x. Arms not crossed, feet idle.

3. All class members should have the opportunity to stand in front of the group and complete the exercise.

Assignment

In exercise 2, there are numerous combination possibilities, and the complexity of keeping track of them becomes increasingly challenging. However, your focus should be both on awareness and on developing your own system for tracking the various gestures in a classroom setting. Again, the accuracy of gesture identification is not as important as becoming aware of the gestures conveyed in a classroom and developing a system whereby you can best track those gestures.

Observation

As you complete these exercises, you should become increasingly aware of your colleagues' nonverbal gestures and messages. Are verbal and nonverbal messages always in agreement, or are mixed messages being sent? We will continue to explore such possibilities in later exercises.

PERSONAL MUSICIANSHIP: SPRINKLER HOSE WARM-UP

For this component, the focus is to:

- Perform a warm-up designed to increase breath support.
- Sing a melody with limited pitches (s,-l,-d-r-m) in stick notation.
- Perform chordal accompaniments to a melody using solfège syllables.

The focus in this component now returns to breath support. Begin by inhaling for four counts and then exhaling for four counts. After repeating the inhalation and exhalation exercise, increase the number by two with each consecutive repetition (inhale for six, exhale for six; inhale for eight, exhale for eight). Now that you are consciously thinking about your breathing, you will practice an exercise that promotes awareness of how long you can sustain the exhalation. This awareness will improve your ability to sustain longer passages of music.

Think of a sprinkler that uses a rotary-gear head, which allows users to program the rotation distance of the arc. As the sprinkler reaches the final distance in the rotation, it returns quickly to the original position to begin watering the area again. To perform the "Sprinkler Hose" warm-up, always use a silent inhalation breath, and imagine you are filling a balloon within your body. During exhalation, voice the sound "ch" using a steady beat while bringing one arm across your body. When you feel yourself running out of air, increase the tempo of your "ch" sounds while having your arm change directions and return across your body to its original position.

Sing the melody in figure 19.1, and add chordal accompaniment as indicated by the solfège syllables. Be sure to include appropriate voice leading. (This will require at least four people to perform all parts, three singing triads and one singing the melody.)

North Carolina Folk Song

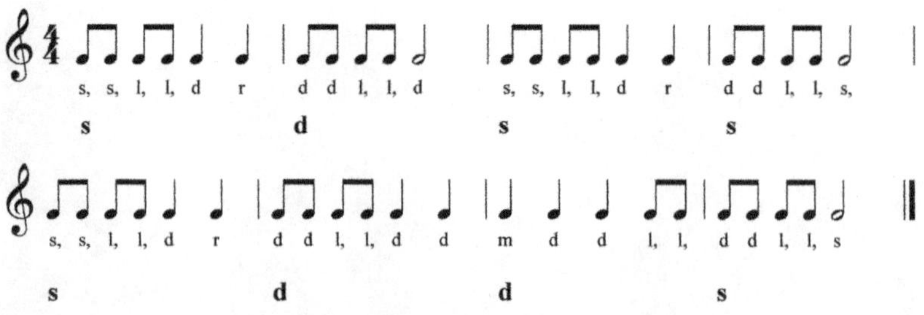

Figure 19.1 "Ridin' of a Goat," stick notation.

PRE-CONDUCTING: PREPARATORY GESTURE
TO BEGIN ON BEAT TWO IN 4/4 METER

To this point, you've explored pre-conducting preparatory gestures for the downbeat and the upbeat/anacrusis/pickup. At times, you will need to have your ensembles begin on a beat other than an upbeat or downbeat, such as after a fermata. In this exercise, we introduce the pre-conducting preparatory gesture for such beats that occur in 4/4 meter. You will only use the right hand/arm in this exercise. You should carefully monitor the movements suggested.

Classroom Setup

All class members can complete this exercise simultaneously. Students should stand and allow about one arm's length of space around them. An instructor should initiate each activity and each step of any given task so the class is practicing as a unit. As individuals become more proficient in completing the elements in this activity, they should form small groups of three or four individuals and conduct preparatory gestures for others.

Exercise

1. Establish your conducting posture and a tempo of mm = 69.
   a. This is a pre-conducting precursor exercise to the preparation gesture to begin on beat two in a 4/4 meter. The preparatory gesture begins one beat prior to beat two or second position, hence the preparatory gesture will begin on beat one or first position.
      i. The preparatory drop begins in first position, with the rebound going to your left side, to second position. As in prior exercises, the preparatory drop begins one or two inches above your imaginary rebound plane. The preparatory drop and subsequent rebound will prepare you to begin on beat two or second position. (See figure 19.2.) Once the rebound height is attained, the right hand is dropped without pause, in the same tempo, to complete the movement (starting your ensemble on the second beat, second position, in a 4/4 measure). (See figure 19.3.)

Rebound after the Initial
1st-Position Drop

Initial 1st-Position Drop
Preparatory Gesture

Figure 19.2 The first-position preparatory gesture beginning on the second beat in 4/4.

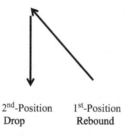

2nd-Position   1st-Position
Drop   Rebound

Figure 19.3 First-position rebound and second-position drop.

ii. Practice the preparatory gesture several times. After each preparatory gesture, rest before repeating the gesture.
iii. Inhale at the beginning of the initial drop/rebound, and exhale
during the drop. Keep your movements continuous (no pauses)
and in the same tempo throughout the preparatory gesture.
iv. Once you have successfully completed this task, form groups
of three or four individuals. With one person serving as the
conductor, conduct the preparatory gesture. Have the group
breathe with you and sing a vowel on a mutually agreed-upon
pitch on the second beat. Repeat this process several times for
each conductor, and then have another conductor perform the
task. Provide feedback/evaluation information after each preparatory gesture.

Assignment

As you begin to feel more at ease with the preparatory gesture, you can
practice this exercise with varying tempi.

Observation

Notice the preparatory gestures used by your directors and conductors. We will continue exploring preparatory gestures in later exercises. The pattern presented above is a pre-conducting pattern and may or may not be used in a conducting class.

PROFESSIONAL KNOWLEDGE: EMOTIONS IN THE CLASSROOM

For this component, the focus is to:

- Examine the effects of emotions on classroom climate.

Many teachers identify classroom management as their top priority. Before we examine classroom management in later modules, it is important to first consider emotion, defined as "a natural instinctive state of mind deriving from one's circumstances, mood, or relationship with others" (*New Oxford American Dictionary*). Ginott (1975) asserted that emotions are considered part of our genetic heritage. "*Fish swim, birds fly, and people feel*" (Ginott, 1975, p. 1; italics in original).

The brain's limbic system—located at the base of the brain—controls or processes our emotions. Emotional processing occurs before information moves into the frontal lobe of the cerebrum, the section of the brain that controls cognitive processing. "If information processing is short-circuited to the emotional center before the thinking center, long-term memory and deep learning is significantly impaired" (Hardiman, online). Think of a time when you crammed for an exam. You learned the material while being stressed, and though you passed the exam when you took it, a few weeks later you couldn't recall the information well enough to pass the exam again. Your long-term recall was affected by your negative emotional state. Teachers who incorporate teaching strategies for promoting positive emotional states can enhance long-term memory and cognitive processing.

Emotions are usually categorized as negative or positive. Positive emotions include enjoyment, excitement, and confidence, while negative emotions include frustration, stress, anxiety, and fear. Teachers need to understand that if a student is experiencing a negative emotion, it will affect his or her performance. "Only when children *feel right can they think clearly, and act right*—in this case concentrate, pay attention, and be able to listen" (Ginott, Ginott, & Goddard, 2003, p. 17; italics in original). Teachers need to make a conscious effort not to overlook or underestimate the power of students' feelings, which "must be taken seriously, even though the situation itself is not very serious" (Ginott, Ginott, & Goddard, 2003, p. 7). A teacher may not be as worried about a student's "bad-hair day," ripped pants from playing on the playground, or the often-heard "She doesn't like me," but these are *real* emotions to the student and need to be recognized.

It is essential for teachers to create an environment that promotes learning while assisting students in managing and directing their own learning. This sounds great, but it is not easy to accomplish. Teachers are busy with course content, assessments, managing large groups of students, and more, which makes creating a positive atmosphere or environment seem like another added chore. Yet research shows a correlation between a "warm" classroom climate and students' learning and social behaviors (Elias & Arnold, 2006). Therefore, it is important to make the effort to listen to students' feelings and validate them by acknowledging them as real. It doesn't require you to endorse or promote those types of emotions but rather to accept that until a student's negative emotions become more positive, learning and social behaviors may be problematic.

How can we provide a positive and warm classroom climate that promotes positive emotions? Maximize any opportunity that promotes positive communication and sense of community in the classroom. Nurture all learners, and provide an atmosphere where they feel secure, without fear of ridicule or personal safety.

> I have come to the frightening conclusion that I am the decisive element. It is my personal approach that creates the climate. It is my daily mood that makes the weather. I possess tremendous power to make life miserable or joyous. I can be a tool of torture or an instrument of inspiration. I can humiliate or humor, hurt or heal. In all situations, it is my response that decides whether a crisis is escalated or de-escalated, and a person is humanized or de-humanized. If we treat people as they are, we make them worse. If we treat people as they ought to be, we help them become what they are capable of becoming. (Ginott, 1975, p. 15)

Discussion

1. Think of a time when you experienced a warm or positive classroom environment. How would you describe it to a classmate? Can you pinpoint what made it warm?
2. With a partner or a small group, create a scenario in which a student is upset or displaying a negative emotion. Then formulate an appropriate teacher response, one that acknowledges the student's emotion but could diffuse it.

MODULE 19 REFERENCES

Coalition for Psychology in Schools and Education. (2006). *Report on the Teacher Needs Survey.* Washington, DC: American Psychological Association.

Elias, M. J., & Arnold, H. A. (Eds.). 2006. *The educator's guide to emotional intelligence and academic achievement: Social-emotional learning in the classroom.* Thousand Oaks, CA: Corwin.

Ginott, H. G. (1975). *Teacher and child: A book for parents and teachers.* New York, NY: Macmillan.

Ginott, H. G., Ginott, A., & Goddard, W. (2003). *Between parent and child.* New York, NY: Three Rivers.

Hardiman, M. M. (2012). Brain-targeted teaching. http://www.braintargetedteaching.org

Mixed or Congruent Messages—Articulators in Vocal Production—Preparatory Gestures in 4/4—Teacher Emotions

In this module, you will focus on:

- Personal awareness: Identifying mixed or congruent messages as transmitted through facial and body gestures.
- Personal musicianship: Articulators in vocal production.
- Pre-conducting: Conducting the preparatory gesture to begin on beat three in 4/4 meter.
- Professional knowledge: Examining the effects of emotions with an emphasis on teacher emotions.

PERSONAL AWARENESS: FACIAL AND BODY GESTURE AWARENESS V

As we develop our abilities to read body language, we must remember not to interpret a solitary gesture in isolation from other gestures or circumstances. For example, on a cold day, you might cross your arms and legs and put your chin down; you aren't necessarily indicating defensiveness but simply trying to stay warm (Pease & Pease, 2004). We must consider the setting in addition to all gestures transmitted. People often send mixed messages (Melcrum.com, 2013). Verbal messages aren't always in agreement with body language. When asked to complete a task by a superior, you may reply,

"OK, I'd be happy to do that," when in reality you wouldn't be happy to perform the task. Yet did your body language say you didn't want to do it? Allan and Barbara Pease note that based on research studies, nonverbal signals carry about five times more impact than verbal messages and that when the two are not in agreement, most people rely on the nonverbal and disregard the verbal information. Talk-show host Phil McGraw (Dr. Phil) extolled the importance of nonverbal communication when he said that 7 percent of communication is verbal, while 93 percent is nonverbal (McGraw, 2013). The importance of body language can't be ignored.

In order to assist you in developing a more complete approach to assessing body language, you will be asked in the following exercise to determine whether an individual's facial and body gestures convey a mixed or congruent message.

We will focus on facial expressions, upper-body gestures (arms crossed and uncrossed, hands with palms up or palms down), and lower-body gestures (legs crossed and uncrossed, ankles crossed and uncrossed, feet tapping and not tapping). When you are in front of the group, you will be asked whether an individual sent a mixed or a congruent message.

In this exercise, two facial expressions will be used: happy/satisfied and unhappy/discontented. The upper-body gestures of hands and arms (crossed or not crossed) and the lower-body gestures of legs and ankles (crossed or not crossed) and feet (one foot tapping or no feet tapping) will also be used. The suggested positions for these body gestures were detailed in earlier modules.

Classroom Setup

The classroom should be arranged in three rows with five columns. If your class contains fewer than 15 individuals, place empty chairs in the rows/columns and randomly fill in the other positions. If you have a larger class, add more rows. Students should be seated in a relaxed but upright posture (no slumping), with their feet flat on the floor, shoulders' width apart.

Exercise

1. Congruent messages are indicated when both the facial expression and the upper- and lower-body gestures are communicating the same emotion, as follows:
   a. A happy/satisfied facial expression with arms/hands not crossed (upper-body gestures), legs/ankles not crossed, and no foot tapping (lower-body gestures).

b. An unhappy/discontented facial expression with arms/hands crossed (upper-body gestures), legs/ankles crossed, or one foot tapping (lower-body gestures).

2. Mixed messages, for purposes of this exercise, are sent when either facial expressions or upper- or lower-body gestures do not communicate the same emotion, as follows:

   a. A happy/satisfied facial expression with arms/hands crossed (upper-body gestures), legs/ankles crossed, or either foot tapping (lower-body gestures).

   b. An unhappy/discontented facial expression with arms/hands not crossed (upper-body gestures), legs/ankles not crossed, and no foot tapping (lower-body gestures).

3. When the instructor signals, one individual comes to the front of the class, and each class member determines whether he or she wants to transmit a congruent or a mixed message as defined above.

4. The gestures should be held for a maximum of five seconds. The instructor initiates the count, and the individual in front of the class begins his or her scan.

5. At the end of five seconds, the instructor calls "time," and everyone returns to a neutral/calm pose.

6. The individual in front of the class is then asked to identify those individuals who transmitted a congruent or a mixed message.

7. All class members should have the opportunity to stand in front of the group and complete the exercise.

8. This exercise can be repeated as time permits.

Assignment

Becoming aware of and being able to read body language helps provide a clearer picture of an individual's intentions. Practice your awareness skills by muting the volume on your television and seeing how accurately you can predict the emotions conveyed through body language alone. You can then check your accuracy by turning the volume up.

Observation

As you complete these exercises, you should become increasingly aware of your colleagues' nonverbal gestures and messages. Are their messages congruent or mixed?

PERSONAL MUSICIANSHIP: GETTING TO KNOW YOUR ARTICULATORS

For this component, the focus is to:

- Discuss articulators in vocal production.
- Sing a melody with limited pitches (s,-l,-d-r-m) in standard notation.
- Perform chordal accompaniments to a melody using Roman numerals and solfège syllables.

Articulators allow you to shape your mouth to form various sounds that when combined in patterns create words within a language. Your articulators include your lips, teeth, tongue, and palate. When speaking and/or singing, you should not feel your consonants voiced within your neck, as that will not produce a full sound and will eventually cause vocal fatigue and discomfort. Tongue-twisters are useful for promoting articulation flexibility. Keep in mind that the goal is to perform the text with precision yet free of tension.

Perform the tongue-twister "Peter Piper" at different speeds. This exercise focuses on performing the consonant "p" with precision:

> Peter Piper picked a peck of pickled peppers.
> A peck of pickled peppers Peter Piper picked.
> If Peter Piper picked a peck of pickled peppers,
> Where's the peck of pickled peppers Peter Piper picked?

Start a collection of tongue-twisters to use in your future classroom. Be sure to include a variety of consonants.

Sing the melody in figure 20.1, and add chordal accompaniment as indicated by the Roman numerals. Be sure to include appropriate voice leading. (This will require at least four people to perform all parts, three singing triads and one singing the melody.)

North Carolina Folk Song

Figure 20.1 "Ridin' of a Goat," standard notation.

PRE-CONDUCTING: PREPARATORY GESTURE TO BEGIN ON BEAT THREE IN 4/4 METER

In this exercise, we introduce the pre-conducting preparatory gesture to begin on beat three (third position) in 4/4 meter. You will only be using the right hand/arm in this exercise. You should carefully monitor the movements suggested.

Classroom Setup

All class members can complete this exercise simultaneously. Students should stand and allow about one arm's length of space around them. An instructor should initiate each activity and each step of any given task so the class is practicing as a unit. As individuals become more proficient, they should form small groups of three or four individuals and conduct preparatory gestures for others.

Exercise

1. Establish your conducting posture and a tempo of mm = 69 .
   a. This is a pre-conducting precursor exercise to the preparation gesture to begin on beat three in a 4/4 meter. The preparatory gesture begins on beat two or second position.
      i. The initial preparatory drop begins in second position, with the rebound going to your right side, to third position. The initial preparatory drop and subsequent rebound will prepare you to begin on beat three or third position. (See figure 20.2.) Once the rebound height is attained, the right hand is dropped without pause, in the same tempo, to complete the movement (starting your ensemble on the third beat, third position, in a 4/4 measure). (See figure 20.3.)

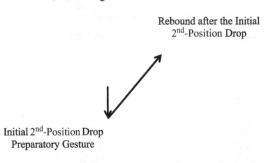

Rebound after the Initial
2nd-Position Drop

Initial 2nd-Position Drop
Preparatory Gesture

Figure 20.2 The second-position preparatory gesture to begin on the third beat in 4/4 meter.

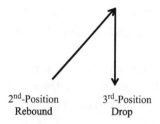

2nd-Position   3rd-Position
Rebound   Drop

Figure 20.3 Second-position rebound and third-position drop.

ii. Practice the preparatory gesture several times. After each practice, rest before repeating the gesture. Check your second-position preparatory position, drop, and rebound and subsequent third-position drop.

iii. Inhale at the beginning of the initial drop/rebound, and exhale during the drop. Keep your movements continuous (no pauses) and in the same tempo throughout the preparatory gesture.

iv. Once you have successfully completed this task, form groups of three or four individuals. With one person serving as the conductor, conduct the preparatory gesture. Have the group breathe with you and sing a vowel on a mutually agreed-upon pitch on the third beat. Repeat this process several times for each conductor, and then have another conductor perform the task. Provide feedback/evaluation information for each performer.

Assignment

As you begin to feel at ease with the preparatory gesture, you can practice this exercise varying the tempi.

Observation

Notice the preparatory gestures used by your directors and conductors. We will continue exploring preparatory gestures in 3/4 meter in a later exercise.

PROFESSIONAL KNOWLEDGE: TEACHERS HAVE EMOTIONS

For this component, the focus is to:

- Continue examining the effects of emotions in the classroom with an emphasis on teacher emotions.

"Emotion is a subjective feeling state, which can influence perception, thinking, and behaviour; usually accompanied by facial and bodily expressions; often has arousing and motivational properties" (Ekman, 1992). In module 19, the discussion focused on the impact of student emotions in the classroom and how they affect learning and social behaviors. This component will focus on teacher emotions. Neville (2013) recognized the need to acknowledge the role played by emotions in the classroom:

> Theories of teaching and learning used to ignore the role of emotions in the class-room, assuming that they were a sort of waste product that got in the way of the brain's more important functions like cognition, memory, decision-making and planning. It is no longer possible to make this assumption [because] in normal human function-ing cognition and emotion are fully integrated. (pp. 21–22)

Our temperaments and past experiences account for how we react or show emotions. Family, environmental, and cultural factors influence an individual's perceptions of how to—or how *not* to—display emotion within specific situations.

Teaching can be a rewarding profession, but you will encounter days when you may be discouraged or frustrated. No individual—whether a teacher or another specialist—can be happy, satisfied, and enthused about their profession 100 percent of the time. Your coping mechanisms and your ability to manage stress will be major factors in your sustainability as a teacher. "Individuals who are strongly committed to teaching but lack the necessary coping and emotional self-regulation skills to manage stress are candidates for exhaustion and burnout" (Hoy, 2013, p. 265).

Self-regulation is a necessity in the education field. The Collaborative for Academic, Social and Emotional Learning (CASEL) outlines five interrelated social and emotional skills needed for social and emotional learning:

- *Self-awareness*: the ability to accurately recognize one's emotions and thoughts and their influence on behavior. This includes accurately assessing one's strengths and limitations and possessing a well-grounded sense of confidence and optimism.

- *Self-management*: the ability to regulate one's emotions, thoughts, and behaviors effectively in different situations. This includes managing stress, controlling impulses, motivating oneself, and setting and working toward achieving personal and academic goals.
- *Social awareness*: the ability to take the perspective of and empathize with others from diverse backgrounds and cultures, to understand social and ethical norms for behavior, and to recognize family, school, and community resources and supports.
- *Relationship skills*: the ability to establish and maintain healthy and rewarding relationships with diverse individuals and groups. This includes communicating clearly, listening actively, cooperating, resisting inappropriate social pressure, negotiating conflict constructively, and seeking and offering help when needed.
- *Responsible decision making*: the ability to make constructive and respectful choices about personal behavior and social interactions based on consideration of ethical standards, safety concerns, social norms, the realistic evaluation of consequences of various actions, and the well-being of self and others. (CASEL, 2013, p. 9)

Awareness of the importance of emotions in the classroom and your self-regulatory skills will be beneficial as you enter the profession.

Discussion

1. Think of a time when you witnessed a teacher express a negative emotion in the classroom. How did that make you feel as a student learner?
2. Reflect on situations and or experiences when you felt yourself becoming stressed or frustrated. How were these occasions similar or different?
3. With a partner or a small group, create a list of strategies for managing stress, frustration, and/or anger in the classroom.

MODULE 20 REFERENCES

CASEL. (2013). *CASEL guide: Effective social and emotional learning programs.* http://www.casel.org/preschool-and-elementary-edition-casel-guide

Ekman P. (1992). An argument for basic emotions. *Cognition and Emotion, 6*(3–4), 169–200.

Hoy, A. W. (2013). A reflection on the place of emotion in teaching and teacher education. In M. Newberry, A Gallant, & P. Riley (Eds.), *Emotion and school: Understanding how the hidden curriculum influences relationships, leadership, teaching and learning* (pp. 255–270). Bingley, UK: Emerald.

McGraw, P. (2013). Mixed signals. http://www.drphil.com/articles/article/318

Melcrum.com. (2013). Avoiding mixed messages: Understand the impact of body language. https://www.melcrum.com/research/strengthen-leader-communication/avoiding-mixed-messages-understand-impact-body-language

Neville, B. (2013). The enchanted loom. In M. Newberry, A. Gallant. & P. Riley (Eds.), *Emotion and school: Understanding how the hidden curriculum influences relationships, leadership, teaching and learning* (pp. 3–23). Bingley, UK: Emerald.

Pease, A., & Pease, B. (2004). *The definitive book of body language.* London: Orion House.

Wind Instrument Body Gestures—Raising the Soft Palate—Conducting Preparatory Gestures—Learning Communities

I n this module, you will focus on:

- Personal awareness: Awareness of body gestures when playing wind instruments of the band.
- Personal musicianship: Raising the soft palate.
- Pre-conducting: Conducting the preparatory gesture to begin on beat two in 3/4 meter.
- Professional knowledge: Creating learning communities within your classrooms.

PERSONAL AWARENESS: FACIAL AND BODY GESTURE AWARENESS VI

Whether we are vocal or instrumental instructors, we will, as music directors, be working with instrumentalists. As instrumental directors, we check embouchures (facial awareness), instrument holds (upper- and lower-body awareness), bow holds (upper-body awareness), hand/finger placements (upper-body awareness), and postures (upper- and lower-body awareness). One of our greatest assessment tools is the ability to quickly evaluate an instrumentalist's external facial and body language. As you have discovered, correcting physical issues, assessed through facial and body positioning awareness, can solve many playing problems.

In this exercise, you will be an instrumental instructor, and the class will be your group. Your students will not use instruments but will mimic playing and holding instruments. We will focus on wind instruments in this module. The emphasis will be on identifying improper embouchures, instrument holds, hand/finger placements, and postures.

Classroom Setup

All class members will be participating in this exercise. The classroom arrangement and criteria for assessment will be discussed in the exercise. Because of the amount of time it takes to complete and adequately assess each "director," it is suggested that at least two sessions be allotted for all individuals to complete this exercise.

Exercise

In this exercise, it will be assumed that half of the class is playing woodwind instruments (limited here to clarinet and flute) and the other half is playing brass instruments (limited here to trumpet and horn). Assignment of students to instruments should be divided equally, one-fourth for each designated instrument. Seating should be in two semicircle rows, with the woodwinds in front of the brass. The suggested seating order for the first semicircle is clarinets to the left of the director and flutes to the right of the director. The suggested seating order for the second semicircle is trumpets to the left of the director and horns to the right of the director. In a 16-member group with a director, the setup would be as presented in figure 21.1.

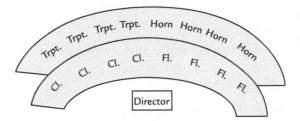

Figure 21.1 Suggested seating arrangement for trumpet, horn, clarinet, and flute.

Assessment criteria are as follows:

Embouchure
   All instruments
     Positive:
- Cheeks not puffed out
     Negative:
- Cheeks puffed out

Instrument hold and hand/finger placement

   Trumpet
     Positive:
- Imaginary instrument held in left hand
- Right-hand index, middle, and ring fingers placed over imaginary valves
- Fingers curved over valves
     Negative:
- Reversed hands, imaginary instrument held in right hand
- Left-hand index, middle, and ring fingers placed over imaginary valves
- Fingers not curved over valves

   Horn
     Positive:
- Imaginary instrument held with right hand in bell
- Left-hand index, middle, and ring fingers over imaginary valves
- Fingers slightly curved over valves
     Negative:
- Reversed hands, imaginary instrument held with left hand in bell
- Right-hand index, middle, and ring fingers placed over imaginary valves
- Fingers not curved over valves

   Clarinet
     Positive:
- Imaginary instrument placed between legs
- Left hand placed above right hand
- Fingers curved over imaginary keys
     Negative:
- Imaginary instrument clearly not placed between legs (off to right or left side)

- Right hand placed above left hand
- Fingers not curved over keys

Flute

   Positive:

- Imaginary instrument held to right side of body
- Instrument parallel to floor (for purposes of this exercise)
- Left hand placed closest to face or to the left of right hand
- Fingers slightly curved over imaginary keys

   Negative:

- Imaginary instrument is held to left side of body
- Instrument not parallel to floor, held very high or very low (for purposes of this exercise)
- Right hand placed closest to face/to the left of left hand
- Fingers straight and not slightly curved over imaginary keys

Posture

   All instruments

   Positive:

- Students seated using relaxed but upright posture (no slumping or arching back uncharacteristically)
- Feet flat on floor
- Feet shoulders' width apart

   Negative:

- Students slumping or back uncharacteristically arched forward
- Feet not flat on floor, pulled back or tucked under the chair, or one or both legs extended, causing a foot or both feet not to be flat on floor
- Feet not shoulders' width apart (for purposes of this exercise), ankles crossed

1. To begin the exercise, the class should be arranged and students assigned to the various instruments as suggested above. One class member serves as the director of the group. When the instructor signals, each class member determines whether he or she wants to transmit a positive or negative embouchure, a positive or negative instrument hold, a positive or negative hand/finger placement, and/or a positive or negative posture.
2. There are three trials/assessment periods for each director. For the first trial, it is suggested that only instrument hold and hand/finger placement be assessed; however, the instrument class should display all portions of the instrument hold and hand/finger placement, embouchure, and posture

during each trial. On the second trial, embouchure should be added, and on the third trial, posture should be added in order to assess all elements.

3. The instrument poses should be held for a maximum of 10 seconds. The instructor initiates the count, and the individual in front of the class begins his or her scan.

4. At the end of 10 seconds, the instructor calls "time," and everyone returns to a neutral/calm pose.

5. The director is then asked to assess the various factors being considered, positive or negative. Feedback should also be provided for the director. Because of the amount of time it takes to complete and adequately assess each director, it is suggested that at least two sessions be allotted for all individuals to complete this exercise.

6. All class members should have the opportunity to stand in front of the group and complete the exercise.

7. This exercise can be repeated as time permits.

Assignment

The ability to quickly assess embouchures, instrument holds, hand/finger placements, and postures is a fundamental skill for instrumental music teaching. Being able to diagnose criteria in a short period of time is essential. Obviously, many instruments and issues with instrumental performance were not addressed in this exercise, such as tonguing, breathing, and so forth. As you improve your diagnostic assessment skills, think of other criteria you may want to add to your evaluation rubric. You should include other woodwind and brass instruments to your observation experience and develop criteria for assessment of those instruments.

Observation

As you complete observations in various environments—whether in elementary, middle, or high school or in community or university settings—see how accurately you can assess the factors considered in this exercise. As you study various groups, think about the types of things you might address as a director.

PERSONAL MUSICIANSHIP: SMELL THE FLOWERS

For this component, the focus is to:

• Discuss inhalation for raising the soft palate.
• Perform an exercise for raising the soft palate.
• Sing a melody with limited pitches (s,-l,-d-r-m-s-l) in stick notation.
• Perform chordal accompaniments to a melody using solfège syllables.

Think about how you take a breath before and during singing. What do you notice? How does it feel? Do you make any sound? Voice teachers and choral directors constantly remind singers to raise their soft palates. What is the soft palate? One purpose of the soft palate is to close off your nasal passages during sneezing and swallowing. The scientific name for the soft palate is *velum*, which in Latin means "veil." Hence the mantra of voice teachers to "lift/raise your soft palate."

In the next few modules, you will practice several strategies for lifting the soft palate. The first is "Smell the Flowers." Begin by closing your mouth, and then inhale deeply through your nose as if you are smelling fragrant flowers. Repeat the inhalation process, concentrating on feeling the air go down your throat. The soft palate rises to allow the air to move through your throat.

Sing the melody in figure 21.2, and add chordal accompaniment as indicated by the solfège syllables. Be sure to include appropriate voice leading. (This will require at least four people to perform all parts, three singing triads and one singing the melody.) As you inhale to sing, remember to raise the soft palate.

Traditional

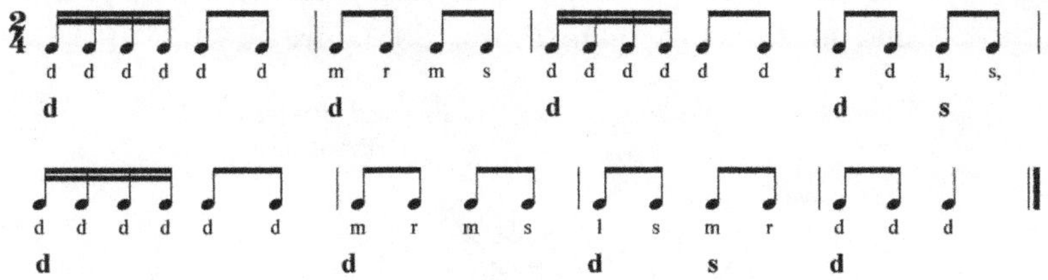

Figure 21.2 "Chicken on a Fence Post," stick notation.

PRE-CONDUCTING: PREPARATORY GESTURE
TO BEGIN ON BEAT TWO IN 3/4 METER

In this exercise, we introduce the pre-conducting preparatory gesture to begin on beat two (second position) in 3/4 meter. You will only be using the right hand/arm in this exercise. You should carefully monitor the movements suggested.

Classroom Setup

All class members can complete this exercise simultaneously. Students should stand and allow about one arm's length of space around them. An instructor should initiate each activity and each step of any given task so the class is practicing as a unit. As individuals become more proficient at completing the elements in this activity, they should form small groups of three or four individuals and conduct preparatory gestures for others.

Exercise

1. Establish your conducting posture and a tempo of mm = 69.
   a. This is a pre-conducting precursor exercise to the preparation gesture to begin on beat two in a 3/4 meter. The preparatory gesture begins on beat one or first position.
      i. The initial preparatory gesture drop begins in first position, with the rebound going to your right side, to second position. (See figure 21.3.) Once the rebound height is attained, the right hand is dropped without pause, in the same tempo, to complete the movement (starting your ensemble on the second beat, second position, in a 3/4 measure. (See figure 21.4.)

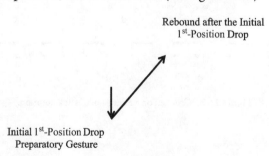

Rebound after the Initial
1st-Position Drop

Initial 1st-Position Drop
Preparatory Gesture

Figure 21.3 The first-position preparatory gesture to begin on the second beat in 3/4 meter.

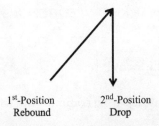

1st-Position   2nd-Position
Rebound   Drop

Figure 21.4 First-position rebound and second-position drop.

ii. Practice this preparatory gesture several times. After each preparatory gesture, rest, then repeat.

iii. Inhale at the beginning of the initial drop/rebound, and exhale during the second-beat drop. Keep your movements continuous (no pauses) and in the same tempo throughout the preparatory gesture.

iv. Once you have successfully completed this task, form groups of three or four individuals. With one person serving as the conductor, conduct the preparatory gesture. Have the group breathe with you and sing a vowel on a mutually agreed-upon pitch on the second beat. Repeat this process several times for each conductor, and then have another conductor perform the task. Provide feedback/evaluation information for each conductor.

Assignment

As you begin to feel at ease with the preparatory gesture, you can practice this exercise at varying tempi.

Observation

Notice the preparatory gestures used by your directors and conductors.

PROFESSIONAL KNOWLEDGE: CREATING COMMUNITY

For this component, the focus is to:

- Explore ways to create learning communities within your classrooms.

Psychologists have explored how individuals learn individually and within group settings. These groups are sometimes called learning communities or communities of practice. *Community* is defined as "a feeling of fellowship with others, as a result of sharing common attitudes, interests, and goals" (*New Oxford American Dictionary*). Woolfolk (2004) describes a community of practice as a "social situation or context in which ideas are judged useful or true" and individuals become connected by their common endeavors (p. 600). The strength of learning communities is dependent on a teacher's ability to encourage all to participate and to ensure that all voices in the room are heard. This is no small feat and requires great sensitivity on the part of the teacher.

A sensitive teacher listens. A sensitive teacher encourages. A sensitive teacher is empathetic. A sensitive teacher is a successful communicator. Teachers must have passion for their subject and for their students. By being sensitive to student needs and viewing them as unique and valued individuals, teachers have the power to make learning enjoyable and rewarding.

Classrooms are filled with diverse learners. This requires teachers to search constantly for activities, content-delivery strategies, and repertoire to engage all learners. We often want to dive into the deep end of the pool and focus on class content and music repertoire. Before addressing class content, though, one must first wade into the shallow end and build a caring classroom community. Students must feel that they belong and are valued. How do we do that?

- Take the time to build strong teacher-student relationships; get to know them. What are their likes and dislikes? Greet them as they enter the classroom. Comment on a new haircut, new shoes, and so on.
- Promote team effort, and provide opportunities for group work and collaboration. Think of posters that advertise the importance of teamwork, such as "T-E-A-M: Together Everyone Achieves More."
- Value the contributions of class members, and encourage all students to participate by capitalizing on their strengths and interests.

- Model respect at all times. It is important for teachers to be respectful to all members of the learning community—students, teachers, administrators, and parents.
- Reflect on the visual appeal of your classroom.

Building community does not occur only at the beginning of the year or the semester, but it is created by constant attention and commitment. Every day you enter a classroom, *you* have the power to strengthen the learning community.

Discussion

1. How do you perceive your ideal school community? Your ideal classroom community?
2. Music classrooms involve group music-making opportunities, but how do we ensure that all voices are heard in our learning communities?
3. Throughout your classes this week, observe your teachers, and watch for times when they are successful in encouraging class members to participate. Compile a list of the strategies.

MODULE 21 REFERENCE

Woolfolk, A. (2004). *Educational psychology* (9th ed.). Boston: Pearson Education.

Body Gestures— Soft Palate—Independence while Conducting—Advocacy Statements

In this module, you will focus on:

- Personal awareness: Continued awareness of body gestures when playing wind instruments of the band.
- Personal musicianship: Additional exercises to raise the soft palate.
- Pre-conducting: Developing independence while conducting a 4/4 pattern.
- Professional knowledge: Formulating advocacy statements.

PERSONAL AWARENESS: FACIAL AND BODY GESTURE AWARENESS VII

This is a continuation of the personal awareness component in module 21, where you became an instrumental instructor and the class was your group. Because of the number of elements in that component, it was suggested that it be continued to allow ample time for all class members to complete the exercise. This component is a repeat of the component in module 21. As before, the emphasis is on identifying improper embouchures, instrument holds, hand/finger placements, and postures.

Classroom Setup

As in module 21, the seating should be in two semicircle rows with the woodwinds in front of the brass. The suggested order for the first semicircle (woodwinds) is clarinets to the left of the director and flutes to the right. The suggested order for the second semicircle is trumpets to the left of the director and horns to the right. In a 16-member group with a director, the setup would be as presented in figure 22.1.

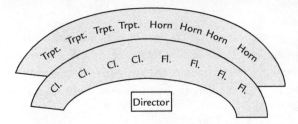

Figure 22.1 Suggested seating arrangement for trumpet, horn, clarinet, and flute.

Exercise

The same procedure and assessment criteria detailed in module 21 should be used here.

Assignment

The ability to quickly assess embouchures, instrument holds, hand/finger placements, and postures is a fundamental skill for instrumental music teaching. In addition to the woodwind and brass instruments used in this exercise, you should also explore assessment criteria for other woodwind and brass instruments and percussion.

Observation

As you study various groups of instruments, think about the types of things you might address as a director.

PERSONAL MUSICIANSHIP: BE SURPRISED

For this component, the focus is to:

- Review raising the soft palate.
- Perform an exercise for raising the soft palate.
- Sing a melody with limited pitches (s,-l,-d-r-m-s-l) in standard notation.
- Perform chordal accompaniments to a melody using Roman numerals and solfège syllables.

The soft palate consists of several muscles. In addition to being vital during swallowing and sneezing, the lifting of the soft palate during singing has many benefits. If you have heard someone referring to a singer's voice as sounding nasal, it is likely that he or she was not singing with a raised soft palate.

There exist as many explanations and imagery suggestions for how to raise the soft palate as there are teachers. The important thing is to find one that works for you. In module 21, you practiced raising your soft palate with the "Smell the Flowers" exercise. This exercise is "Be Surprised." Begin with your mouth closed. Imagine you've just heard a loud, unexpected sound right behind you. The sound surprised you and caused you to open your mouth and inhale quickly. Practice being surprised several more times, and concentrate on the sensation of a raised palate.

Sing the melody in figure 22.2, and add chordal accompaniment as indicated by the Roman numerals. Be sure to include appropriate voice leading. (This will require at least four people to perform all parts, three singing triads and one singing the melody.) Concentrate on singing with a raised soft palate.

Traditional

Figure 22.2 "Chicken on a Fence Post," standard notation.

PRE-CONDUCTING: DEVELOPING
INDEPENDENCE WHILE CONDUCTING
THE 4/4 PATTERN

The craft of conducting involves planning, analyzing, rehearsing, providing feedback, and a host of other skills. The pre-conducting skills you are developing through these exercises focus on one conducting element: developing coordination and independence of basic arm, hand, body, and head movements.

In this exercise, you will begin to develop independence while conducting a 4/4 pattern. Focus on having the 4/4 conducting pattern become automatic, in the sense that you will be able to conduct the pattern while doing other actions. Eventually, you will be asked to combine right- and left-hand motions, which will require conducting independence. We will only be using the right hand/arm in this exercise. You should carefully monitor the movements suggested.

Classroom Setup

All class members can complete this exercise simultaneously. Students should stand and allow about one arm's length of space around them. An instructor should initiate each activity and each step of any given task so the class is practicing as a unit. As individuals become more proficient in completing the elements in this activity, they should form small groups of three or four individuals and conduct preparatory gestures for others.

Exercise

1. Establish your conducting posture and a tempo of mm = 69–72.
   a. Your rebound can now be lowered, not as high as previously performed, but you should still maintain the sensation of dropping to an imaginary plane and rebounding off that plane. Try rebounding about three or four inches after every beat drop. Practice your 4/4 pattern independently, and proceed to the next step once you are comfortable with the pattern.
   b. As a group, begin conducting the 4/4 pattern at the suggested tempo. The instructor should ask one of the following questions, to which you should give a response as you continue conducting. Keep a steady beat. Maintain the flow, consistency, and smoothness of the rebound throughout the exercise. The group should simultaneously respond to each question. Once a question is asked and a response given, another question should be asked and another response given, and so on.

    i. What is your name? (Say it, and then spell it.)
   ii. What are your address and telephone/cell number?
  iii. What is one of your favorite things to do?
  iv. What are two of your favorite movies?
   v. Different questions can be created in place of the above questions and/or additional questions asked. The questions should be simplistic, as the intent is to multitask but not to recall complex content knowledge.
  vi. Stop and rest once this part of the exercise is completed.
c. Form groups of two to four people. An instructor has all individuals begin conducting the 4/4 pattern and tells you when to begin.
   i. Each individual, in turn, asks a question of another individual in each group, while conducting the 4/4 pattern.
  ii. After a few rounds of questions have been asked, stop and rest. Each individual should, in turn, introduce himself or herself while conducting. For example:

> "Hello, I'm _____. I'm a _____ major with additional interests in _____. My principal performing instrument is _____. I want to become a (teacher/performer/conductor, etc.) because _____. I became interested in music when/because _____. Some of my favorite composers are _____."

The script does not need to be identical to the one above, but the introduction should contain elements of teaching, musical interests, and so on.
  iii. After each round, remember to assess and/or receive feedback on your performance.

Assignment

Continue to practice the 4/4 conducting pattern until it becomes so natural that you do not have to give it your full attention and it becomes automatic. You can practice this exercise with varying tempi. Should you want to further challenge yourself, try reading while conducting. This can be done in groups or individually.

Observation

Notice how various conductors have developed their ability to conduct the 4/4 pattern while performing a multitude of other tasks.

PROFESSIONAL KNOWLEDGE: ADVOCACY PRACTICE

For this component, the focus is to:

- Practice formulating advocacy statements.

Advocacy is defined as "public support for or recommendation of a particular cause or policy" (*New Oxford American Dictionary*). There will be times during your career when you will need to advocate for music education. You might be thinking, "I just want to teach music. I don't want to be a salesperson." Advocating for music education can occur in formal situations, such as with an administrator or a school board member. It can also occur in informal situations, such as at a dinner party or at a community park.

Music education plays a crucial role in the education of children. One has to be able to speak knowledgeably and passionately about music education in order to create a community of supporters for music programs and to ensure that music remains within the core curriculum.

A partner/small-group activity will provide an opportunity for you to practice your advocacy skills.

Partner/Small-Group Activity

For this activity, divide the class into six groups. For smaller classes, you can complete the activity with partners. Each small group or set of partners will do the following:

1. Formulate a response to the questions and/or scenario assigned to the group (see list below).
2. Determine the target audience (parent, administrator, coworker, etc.).
3. Present responses to the class.

Questions/scenarios

- You teach at a middle school where students have to choose between participating in chorus, orchestra, or band, as the classes all meet at the same time of day. What is your recommendation about the schedule conflicts?

- There is no string program in your school district. You are asked, "Why do you want to initiate one?" What is your response?
- The marching band is fully funded. You want to start a concert band. What would be your rationale?
- Prepare a justification for the existence of general music/nonperformance classes as a part of a balanced secondary-school (grades 7–12) program.
- Your school has a "no religious music" policy. How will you approach changing the policy to ensure that students experience a balanced choral program?
- Your principal does not understand why you have sectional rehearsals as a part of your schedule. What is your rationale?
- The school board intends to eliminate music for kindergarteners as taught by the music specialist. What is your response and course of action?

Body Gestures Playing Bowed String Instruments—Relaxed Vocal Tone—Independence in Conducting 3/4—Applying Knowledge in the Classroom

I n this module, you will focus on:

- Personal awareness: Continued awareness of body gestures when playing bowed string instruments of the orchestra.
- Personal musicianship: Creating an open, relaxed vocal tone.
- Pre-conducting: Developing independence while conducting the 3/4 pattern.
- Professional knowledge: Applying knowledge, attitudes, and skills from other learning situations to the music education classroom.

PERSONAL AWARENESS: FACIAL AND BODY GESTURE AWARENESS VIII

Acting as instrumental woodwind and brass directors in modules 21 and 22, you heightened your awareness of criteria established for embouchures, instrument and hand/finger placements, and postures. In this exercise, you will heightened your awareness of bowed string instruments. Specifically, you will be assessing the following:

- Instrument hold, which for the violin and viola involves jaw/facial and upper-body awareness and for the cello and double bass involves upper- and lower-body awareness.
- Bow holds (upper-body awareness).
- Arm/hand/finger placement (upper-body awareness).
- Posture (upper- and lower-body awareness).

As you discovered in previous exercises, many physical issues can be assessed through facial and body positioning awareness. With bowed string instruments, many people believe that even more issues can be assessed to assist performance practice.

In this exercise, you will once again become an instrumental instructor, and the class will be your group. Your class will not use instruments but will again mimic playing and holding instruments. The emphasis in these exercises will be on identifying improper instrument holds, bow holds, hand/finger placements, and postures.

Classroom Setup

All class members will be participating in this exercise. The classroom arrangement will be discussed at the beginning of the exercise. Because of the amount of time it takes to complete and adequately assess each "director," it is suggested that at least two sessions be allotted for all individuals to complete this exercise.

Exercise

In this exercise, the focus will be on bowed string instruments. It will be assumed that two-thirds of the class will be playing an upper-string instrument (violin or viola) and one-third will be playing a lower-string instrument (cello or double bass). The instrumentation assignment in a class of 10 individuals would be one director, three violins, three violas, two cellos, and one double bass. In a class of 19, the instrumentation assignment would be doubled except for the director. Seating should be in a semicircle with homogeneous groupings. In a 16-member group with a director, the setup would be as presented in figure 23.1.

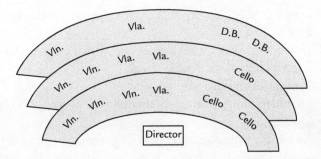

Figure 23.1 Suggested seating arrangement for bowed string instruments, 15 players and director.

Assessment criteria are as follows:

Instrument hold and posture
Upper strings

Positive:
- Elevated sitting posture evident (no slumping or arching back uncharacteristically)
- Instrument on left side of body
- Instrument parallel to floor
- Instrument over collarbone and left shoulder (see arm/hand/ finger placement; position of arm/hand should be to side of body)
- Eyes looking down imaginary fingerboard
- Shoulder and head relaxed, shoulder or head not raised, head not bent/lowered

Negative:
- Elevated sitting posture not evident (back uncharacteristically arched, slumping, feet not flat on floor)
- Instrument held on right side of body
- Instrument not parallel to floor (too high/extreme elevation or too low/drooping so elbow rests on ribs)
- Instrument in front of body rather than collarbone and left shoulder (also see arm/hand/finger placement)
- Eyes not looking down imaginary fingerboard/angle
- Shoulder and head not relaxed, shoulders raised or head bent/ lowered

Lower strings

Positive:
- Elevated sitting (cello) or standing (double bass) posture evident (back not uncharacteristically arched, not slumped, feet flat on floor at shoulders' width, and additionally for double

bass, feet at 10 o'clock and 2 o'clock position, with left foot more forward than right)
- Instrument neck on left side of body (imaginary neck of instrument on left side of person's neck)
- Eyes/head forward
- Shoulders and head relaxed, shoulders not raised, head not bent/lowered
- Imaginary cello contacts knees (legs should be shoulders' width apart), double bass contacts inside of left leg and hip area (double bass stance should be at 10 o'clock and 2 o'clock position)

   Negative:
- Elevated sitting (cello) or standing (double bass) posture not evident (back uncharacteristically arched, slumping, feet not flat on floor at shoulders' width, and, additionally for double bass, feet not at a 10 o'clock and 2 o'clock position, and/or left foot not slightly forward of right)
- Instrument on right side of body (imaginary neck of instrument on right side of person's neck)
- Eyes/head looking at or pointed toward imaginary fingerboard
- Shoulders raised and/or head bent/lowered
- Legs not shoulders' width apart to hold cello, double bass stance not appropriate to hold instrument (see also posture)

Bow hold
   All strings
      Positive:
- Imaginary bow held in right hand
- Bow-hand fingers curved
- Bow-hand thumb curved and across from second finger
      Negative:
- Imaginary bow held in left hand
- Bow-hand fingers not curved/straight
- Bow-hand thumb not curved and/or not across from second finger

Arm/hand/finger placement
   Upper strings
      Positive:
- Left arm relaxed with elbow lower than wrist. elbow not touching/resting on individual's body
- Left wrist straight
- Left elbow positioned directly under imaginary instrument
- Fingers curved over imaginary string on fingerboard

- Left thumb straight, not curved, thumb points up to ceiling and forms a V shape with other fingers

  Negative:
- Arm/hand/fingers reversed, using right arm/hand/fingers
- Left arm not relaxed, elbow touching/resting on individual's body/ribs
- Left elbow not positioned directly under imaginary instrument
- Left wrist not straight, bent inward or outward
- Fingers straight, pointing up. not over imaginary string on fingerboard
- Left thumb curved, thumb not pointing to ceiling and/or not forming a V shape

  Lower strings

  Positive:
- Left arm relaxed with elbow slightly lower than wrist but not touching body of person or instrument
- Left wrist straight
- Fingers arched/curved over imaginary string on fingerboard
- Left thumb straight and across from middle finger of left hand

  Negative:
- Arm/hand/fingers reversed, using right arm/hand/fingers
- Left arm not relaxed, elbow not lower than wrist and/or touching/resting on body/ribs of person or instrument
- Left wrist not straight, bent inward or outward
- Fingers not arched/curved, straight, and/or not over imaginary string on fingerboard
- Left thumb not straight but curved and/or not across from middle finger of left hand

1. To begin the exercise, the class should be arranged and students assigned to the various instruments as suggested above. One class member serves as the director of the group. When the instructor signals, each class member determines whether he or she wants to transmit a positive or negative bow hold, a positive or negative instrument hold, a positive or negative hand/finger placement, and/or a positive or negative posture.
2. There are three trials/assessment periods for each director. For the first trial, it is suggested that only instrument hold and posture be assessed; however, the string class should display all portions of the instrument hold, posture, bow hold, and left arm/hand/finger placement during each trial. On the second trial, the bow hold should be added; and on

the third trial, arm/hand/finger placement should be added in order to assess all elements.

3. The instrument poses should be held for a maximum of 10 seconds. The instructor initiates the count, and the individual in front of the class begins his or her scan.

4. At the end of 10 seconds, the instructor calls "time," and everyone returns to a neutral/calm pose.

5. The director is then asked to assess the various factors being considered, positive or negative. Feedback should also be provided for the director. Because of the amount of time it takes to complete and adequately assess each director, it is suggested that at least two sessions be allotted for all individuals to complete this exercise.

6. All class members should have the opportunity to stand in front of the group and complete the exercise.

7. This exercise can be repeated as time permits.

Assignment

The ability to quickly assess instrument and bow holds, arm/hand/finger placements, and postures is a fundamental skill for instrumental music teaching. Being able to diagnose criteria in a short period of time is essential. You will note, however, that identifying all possible problems in a short time is impossible. The goal of this exercise is to increase your awareness of the many things you should assess on a constant basis.

Observation

As you complete observations in various environments—whether in elementary, middle, or high school or in community or university settings—see how accurately you can assess the factors considered in this exercise. As you improve your observation skills, add various components of string performance practice to your skill set and develop assessment criteria. As you observe various groups, think about the types of things you might address as a director.

PERSONAL MUSICIANSHIP: SING AH

For this component, the focus is to:

- Review raising the soft palate.
- Perform an exercise for raising the soft palate.
- Sing a melody with limited pitches in stick notation.
- Perform chordal accompaniments to a melody using solfège syllables.

The tongue and the soft palate are used when forming the sound "ng" (as in "sing"). Sing the word "sing" on a comfortable pitch, and sustain the "ng" for several seconds. As you sustain the sound, listen to the quality of your voice. Follow the word "sing" with "ah" (as in "ah, this is so interesting learning about my soft palate"). Notice how the voice quality changes when forming the "ah." It is likely you heard a more open and resonant sound, all thanks to raising your soft palate. Singing the melody in figure 23.2 will help you concentrate on creating an open, relaxed tone.

Figure 23.2 SiNG AH.

Select a melody from a previous module, and add chordal accompaniment as indicated by the solfège syllables. Be sure to include appropriate voice leading. (This will require at least four people to perform all parts, three singing triads and one singing the melody.) Focus on singing with an open, relaxed tone.

PRE-CONDUCTING: DEVELOPING INDEPENDENCE WHILE CONDUCTING THE 3/4 PATTERN

In module 22, you began to develop right-hand/arm independence while conducting the 4/4 pattern. You may have discovered that this task improved with repetition. Continue to conduct the 4/4 pattern while performing other tasks to improve independence.

In this exercise, you will begin to develop independence of motion using a 3/4 pattern. Focus on having the 3/4 conducting pattern become automatic, in the sense that you will be able to conduct the pattern while doing other actions. You should carefully monitor the movements suggested.

Classroom Setup

All class members can complete this exercise simultaneously. Students should stand and allow about one arm's length of space around them. An instructor should initiate each activity and each step of any given task so the class is practicing as a unit. As individuals become more proficient in completing the elements in this activity, they should form small groups of three or four individuals and conduct preparatory gestures for others.

Exercise

1. Establish your conducting posture and a tempo of mm = 69–72.
   a. Your rebound should now emulate the motion described in module 22. Practice your 3/4 pattern independently or as a group, and when comfortable, proceed to the next step.
   b. As a group, begin conducting the 3/4 pattern at the suggested tempo. The instructor asks one of the following questions, to which you should give a response as you continue conducting. Keep a steady beat. Maintain the flow, consistency, and smoothness of the rebound throughout the exercise. The group should simultaneously respond to each question. Once a question is asked and a response given, another question should be asked and another response given, and so on.
      i. What is your name? (Say it, and then spell it.)
      ii. What are your address and telephone/cell number?
      iii. What is one of your favorite things to do?
      iv. What are two of your favorite movies?

Different questions can be created in place of the above questions and/or additional questions asked. The questions should be simplistic, as the intent is to multitask but not to recall complex content knowledge. Stop and rest once this part of the exercise is completed.

c. Form groups of two to four people. An instructor has all individuals begin conducting the 3/4 pattern and tells you when to begin.

i. Each individual, in turn, asks a question of another individual in each group, while conducting the 3/4 pattern.

ii. After a few rounds of questions have been asked, stop and rest. Each individual should, in turn, introduce himself or herself while conducting. For example:

"Hello, I'm _____. I'm a _____ major with additional interests in _____. My principal performing medium is _____. I want to become a (teacher/performer/conductor, etc.) because _____. I became interested in music when/because _____. Some of my favorite composers are _____."

The script does not need to be identical to the one above, but the introduction should contain elements of teaching, musical interests, and so on.

iii. After each round, remember to assess and/or receive feedback on your performance.

Assignment

Continue to practice the 3/4 conducting pattern until it is so natural that you do not have to give it your full attention and it becomes automatic. You can practice this exercise with varying tempi. Should you want to further challenge yourself, try reading while conducting. This can be done in groups or individually.

Observation

Notice how various conductors have developed their ability to conduct the 3/4 pattern while performing a multitude of other tasks.

PROFESSIONAL KNOWLEDGE: TRANSFER OF LEARNING

For this component, the focus is to:

- Begin applying knowledge, attitudes, and skills from other learning situations to the music education classroom.

"Transfer is the application of knowledge learned in one setting or for one purpose to another setting and/or purpose" (Gagne, Yekovich, & Yekovich, 1993, p. 235). Transfer of learning occurs when an individual's prior knowledge and skills affect the processing of new knowledge and skills. Every time you learn something new, it forms a building block for future learning. Transferring information from one context to another involves creative thinking. How can you use what you already know and apply it to this situation? "Transfer of learning is essentially the crux of all learning" (Leberman, Mcdonald, & Doyle, 2006, p. ix).

Partner/Small-Group Activity

For this activity, divide the class into small groups. For smaller classes, you can complete the activity with partners. Each small group or set of partners will do the following:

1. Read a quote assigned to the group (see list below).
2. Discuss the author's intended meaning.
3. Formulate a response that explains how it is applicable to music education.
4. Present responses to the class.

Quotes

- "If he is indeed wise he does not bid you to enter the house of his wisdom, but rather leads you to the threshold of your own mind" (Kahlil Gibran).
- "School is not easy and it is not for the most part very much fun, but then if you are lucky, you may find a real teacher. Three real teachers in a lifetime is the very best of luck. I have come to believe that a great teacher is a great artist. . . . Teaching might be the greatest of the arts since the medium is the human mind and the spirit" (John Steinbeck).

- "A musician who is only a musician is only half a musician" (Bruno Walter).
- "They know enough who know how to learn" (Henry Adams).
- "Creative minds have always been known to survive any kind of bad training" (Anna Freud).
- "If you don't like the road you're walking, start paving another one" (Dolly Parton).
- "A true leader always keeps an element of surprise up his sleeve, which others cannot grasp, but which keeps his public excited and breathless" (Charles de Gaulle).
- "Don't find fault. Find a remedy" (Henry Ford).
- "The highest reward for a man's toil is not what he gets for it, but what he becomes by it" (John Ruskin).
- "No one is useless in the world who lightens the burden of it for anyone else" (Charles Dickens).
- "You cannot shake hands with a clenched fist" (Indira Gandhi).
- "Tact is the art of making a point without making an enemy" (Howard W. Newton).
- "One of the best ways to persuade others is with your ears" (Dean Rusk).
- "Statistics are no substitute for judgment" (Henry Clay).
- "The best things and best people rise out of their separateness; I'm against a homogenized society because I want the cream to rise" (Robert Frost).
- "It is impossible for a man to be made happy by putting him in a happy place, unless he be first in a happy state" (Benjamin Whichcote).
- "There are only two lasting bequests we can hope to give our children. One of these is roots; the other, wings" (Hodding Carter).
- "The future belongs to those who believe in the beauty of their dreams" (Eleanor Roosevelt).
- "None are so empty as those who are full of themselves" (Benjamin Whichcote).

MODULE 23 REFERENCES

Gagne, E. D., Yekovich, C. W., & Yekovich, F. R. (1993). *The cognitive psychology of school learning* (2nd ed.). New York, NY: HarperCollins College.

Leberman, S., Mcdonald, L., & Doyle, S. (2006). *The transfer of learning: Participants' perspectives of adult education and training.* Burlington, VT: Ashgate.

Body Gestures Playing Bowed String Instruments—Outlining Tonic—Independence in Conducting 2/4—Public-Speaking Skills

I n this module, you will focus on:

- Personal awareness: Continued awareness of body gestures when playing bowed string instruments of the orchestra.
- Personal musicianship: The ability to outline the tonic in *la*-based minor with various pitches functioning as tonic.
- Pre-conducting: Developing independence while conducting the 2/4 pattern.
- Professional knowledge: Improving listening and public-speaking skills.

PERSONAL AWARENESS: FACIAL AND BODY GESTURE AWARENESS IX

This is a continuation from module 23, where you became an instrumental instructor and the class was your group. Because of the number of elements in that component, it was suggested that it be continued to allow ample time for all class members to complete the exercise. As before, the emphasis is on identifying proper and improper instrument holds, bow holds, arm/hand/finger placements, and postures.

Classroom Setup

As in module 23, the seating should be as presented in figure 24.1.

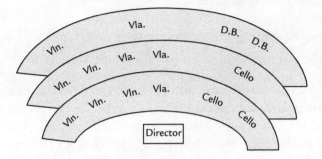

Figure 24.1 Suggested seating arrangement for bowed string instruments, 15 players and director.

Exercise

The same procedure and assessment criteria detailed in module 23 should be used here.

Assignment

Being able to quickly assess instrument and bow holds, arm/hand/finger placements, and postures is a fundamental skill for instrumental music teaching. You should explore assessment criteria for additional bowed string performance procedures.

Observation

As you study various groups of instruments, think about the types of things you might address as a director.

PERSONAL MUSICIANSHIP: INTRODUCTION TO *LA*-BASED MINOR

For this component, the focus is to:

- Outline the tonic in *la*-based minor with various pitches functioning as tonic.

Figure 24.2 provides an example of *do*-based major and *la*-based minor. Note that in *la*-based minor, the solfège syllables remain the same as in the major key. Use of *la*-based minor facilitates the sight-reading process, as there are fewer solfège syllable changes than when singing in *do*-based minor. Another way to think about the process is that in *la*-based minor, you base your solfège syllables on the key *signature* rather than the *key*.

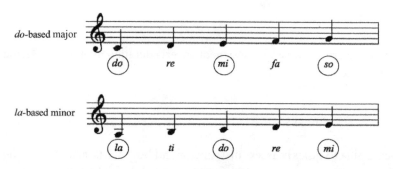

Figure 24.2 *do*-based major and *la*-based minor.

Practice the following steps for outlining the tonic in *la*-based minor on various pitches (suggested pitches for tonic: F, D, G, C, E♭). See figure 24.3 for a notated example.

1. Sing tonic or *la*.
2. Outline the triad (l,-m-d-m-l,)
3. Sing tonic or *la*.
4. Sing cadence (l,-m-l,)

Figure 24.3 Sample of notation for outlining the tonic in *la*-based minor.

PRE-CONDUCTING: DEVELOPING INDEPENDENCE WHILE CONDUCTING THE 2/4 PATTERN

In modules 22 and 23, you began to develop right-hand/arm independence while conducting 4/4 and 3/4 patterns. You should continue to practice both patterns to gain additional independence.

In this exercise, you will begin to develop independence of motion using a 2/4 pattern. Focus on having the 2/4 conducting pattern become automatic, in the sense that you will be able to conduct the pattern while doing other actions. You should monitor the movements suggested.

Classroom Setup

All class members can complete this exercise simultaneously. Students should stand and allow about one arm's length of space around them. An instructor should initiate each activity and each step of any given task so the class is practicing as a unit. As individuals become more proficient in completing the elements in this activity, they should form small groups of three or four individuals and conduct preparatory gestures for others.

Exercise

1. Establish your conducting posture and a tempo of mm = 69–72.
   a. Practice the 2/4 pattern as a group.
   b. Begin conducting the 2/4 pattern at the suggested tempo. The instructor asks one of the following questions/directives, to which you should give a response as you continue conducting. Keep a steady beat. Maintain the flow, consistency, and smoothness of the drop and rebound throughout the exercise. The group should simultaneously respond to each question/directive. Once a question/directive is asked and a response given, another question/directive should be asked and another response given, and so on.
      i. How tall are you?
      ii. What are your mother's and father's names?
      iii. What are the names of your elementary, middle, and high schools?
      iv. Repeat the multiplication table for 2's ($2 \times 2 = 4$, $2 \times 3 = 6$, $2 \times 4 = 8$, ... $2 \times 9 = 18$).

     v. Turn in a circle to your right. Turn in a circle to your left. Stand on your right leg, now your left. Jump up and down five times. Walk forward five steps, and then walk backward six steps.

        Different questions/directives can be created in place of the above questions/directives and/or additional questions/directives provided. Stop and rest once this part of the exercise is completed.

  c. Form groups of two to four people. An instructor has all individuals begin conducting the 2/4 pattern and tells you when to begin.

     i. Each individual, in turn, asks a question or gives a directive to another individual, while conducting the 2/4 pattern.

    ii. After a few rounds of questions/directives, stop and rest. Each individual should, in turn, introduce himself or herself while conducting. For example:

> "Hello, I'm _____. I'm a _____ major with additional interests in _____. My principal performing medium is _____. I want to become a (teacher/performer/conductor, etc.) because _____. I became interested in music when/because _____. Some of my favorite composers are _____."

        The script does not need to be identical to the one above, but the introduction should contain elements of teaching, musical interests, and so on.

   iii. After each round, remember to assess and/or receive feedback on your performance.

Assignment

Continue to practice the 2/4 conducting pattern until it is so natural that you do not have to give it your full attention and it becomes automatic. You can practice this exercise with varying tempi. Should you want to further challenge yourself, try reading while conducting. While you are conversing with friends, try conducting the 4/4, 3/4, and 2/4 patterns.

Observation

Notice how various conductors have developed their ability to conduct the 2/4 pattern while performing a multitude of other tasks.

PROFESSIONAL KNOWLEDGE: LISTENING AND PUBLIC-SPEAKING SKILLS

For this component, the focus is to:

- Conduct a brief interview with a classmate.
- Practice speaking in front of a group.

You have been learning about the importance of body language and non-verbal gestures as effective tools in the classroom. Teachers need to be effective listeners, strong communicators, and able to express their own ideas clearly, both verbally and in writing.

There will be times that require you to make brief introductions for guest speakers in your classroom, guest conductors during a concert, or a new student being welcomed to the class. Effective public-speaking skills are like all other aspects of teaching: they must be practiced. For those who experience nervousness when in front of an audience, the best way to counteract it is to practice talking to smaller groups in a safe, comfortable environment.

Increasing your effectiveness as a public speaker is possible but not without practice. Winston Churchill said the following about public speaking: "It's quite simple. Say what you have to say and when you come to a sentence with a grammatical ending, sit down." Well, speaking to an audience—whether a classroom or an auditorium filled with parents—is not quite as simple as that.

> Yes, great teachers are born and, yes, great teachers are made, but it's rather pointless to try to untangle the exact contribution of each. Every great teacher combines natural talents with skills developed along the way, attentiveness to student learning, and an eagerness to improve. (Timpson & Burgoyne, 2002, p. 41)

The same attributes apply to public speaking. Yes, great public speakers are born, and yes, great public speakers are made, but everyone improves with practice.

In the following activity, you will have the opportunity to practice your listening and public-speaking skills. As you ask your partner questions, be sure to listen intently to his or her responses, while thinking about your nonverbal body language during the communication exchange. As you walk to the front of the class to introduce your partner, think about your posture and facial expressions. Speak clearly and with confidence. Make eye contact with your audience, and glance sparingly at your notes.

Partner/Small-Group Activity

For this communication activity, divide the class into sets of two partners. Each set of partners will perform the following tasks:

1. Each individual asks his or her partner four questions.
2. Brief notes or responses are written on index cards or a half sheet of paper. It is important to keep in mind that you should not read the responses word for word, but rather use the information to frame or formulate your introduction.
3. Following the "interviews," each set of partners practices introducing each other to the class.

Interview Questions

- Why did you decide to become a music educator?
- What area will be your focus for teaching (elementary, secondary, band, etc.)?
- If you had to name one goal for yourself as an educator, what would it be?
- What do you see as your biggest challenge?

MODULE 24 REFERENCE

Timpson, W. M., & Burgoyne, S. (2002). *Teaching and performance: Ideas for energizing your classes*. Madison, WI: Atwood.

Body Gestures in a Full Orchestra Setting—Singing in *la*-Based Minor—Cueing on the Downbeat—Improving Public Speaking

In this module, you will focus on:

- Personal awareness: Developing awareness of body gestures of wind, brass, and bowed string instruments in a full orchestra setting.
- Personal musicianship: Singing a melody in *la*-based minor.
- Pre-conducting: Cueing on the downbeat while conducting the 4/4 pattern.
- Professional knowledge: Improving your public-speaking abilities and effectiveness as a communicator.

PERSONAL AWARENESS: FACIAL AND BODY GESTURE AWARENESS X

In the personal awareness exercises in modules 23 and 24, you've been either an instrumental or a string director. Now you will be a full orchestra director and have the opportunity to assess both winds and strings in one situation.

In this exercise, you will be assessing the following:

- Instrument hold.
- Embouchure.
- Bow hold (upper-body awareness).
- Arm/hand/finger placement (upper-body awareness).
- Posture (upper- and lower-body awareness).

No instruments will be used, but students will mimic playing and holding instruments. The instrument assessment criteria will be the same as detailed in modules 21 and 23.

Classroom Setup

All class members will be participating in this exercise. The classroom arrangement will be discussed at the beginning of the exercise.

Exercise

In this exercise, the focus will be on winds (flute, clarinet, trumpet, and horn) and bowed string instruments (violin, viola, cello, and double bass). It will be assumed that about one-third or one-fourth of the class will be playing winds and two-thirds or three-fourths will be playing a bowed string instrument, depending on class size. In a class of 16 individuals, the instrumentation assignment would be one director; one each of flute, clarinet, trumpet, and horn; four violins; four violas; two cellos; and one double bass. For purposes of this exercise, using a 16-member group, the seating arrangement in figure 25.1.

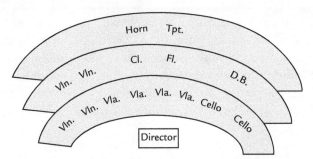

Figure 25.1 Suggested seating arrangement for a full orchestra with 15 players and director.

1. To begin the exercise, the class should be arranged and students assigned to the various instruments as suggested above. One class member serves as the director of the group. When the instructor signals, each class member determines whether he or she wants to transmit a positive or negative embouchure or bow hold, a positive or negative instrument hold, a positive or negative hand/finger placement, and/or a positive or negative posture.

2. There are three trials/assessment periods for each director. For the first trial, it is suggested that only instrument hold and posture be assessed; however, the full orchestra members should display all portions of the instrument hold, posture, embouchure/bow hold, and left-arm/hand/finger placement during each trial. On the second trial, the embouchure/bow hold should be added; and on the third trial, arm/hand/finger placement should be added in order to assess all elements.

3. The instrument poses should be held for a maximum of 15 seconds. The instructor initiates the count, and the individual in front of the class begins his or her scan.

4. At the end of 15 seconds, the instructor calls "time," and everyone returns to a neutral/calm pose.

5. The director is then asked to assess the various factors being considered, positive or negative. Feedback should also be provided for the director. Because of the amount of time it takes to complete and adequately assess each director, it is suggested that at least two sessions be allotted for all individuals to complete this exercise.

6. All class members should have the opportunity to stand in front of the group and complete the exercise.

7. This exercise can be repeated as time permits.

Assignment

The ability to quickly assess a host of physical playing criteria is a fundamental skill for instrumental music teaching, but it requires practice and time. You may have noticed that as instruments and criteria are added, the complexity of assessment becomes exponentially more challenging. As you continue to practice the skills required in this exercise, you will find that your ability to diagnose problems increases significantly.

Observation

As you complete observations in various environments—whether in elementary, middle, or high school or in community or university settings—see how accurately you can assess the factors considered in this exercise. As you improve your skills, add instruments and assessment criteria to your rubrics. As you observe various groups, think about the types of things you might address as a director.

PERSONAL MUSICIANSHIP: SINGING A MELODY IN *la*-BASED MINOR

For this component, the focus is to:

- Review the steps for outlining the tonic in *la*-based minor.
- Transfer the steps for outlining the tonic to sight-reading a *la*-based minor melody.
- Sing a melody with limited pitches (l,-t,-d-r-m-s).

In module 24, you practiced outlining the tonic in *la*-based minor. Notice how the steps for outlining the tonic in *la*-based minor form the foundation for the following steps to sight-singing a melody in *la*-based minor:

1. Sing tonic or *la*.
2. Outline the triad (l,-d-m-d-l,).
3. Sing tonic or *la*.
4. Sing cadence (l,-m-l,).
5. Determine the syllable with which the song begins (it is not always tonic/*la*),
6. Look for familiar patterns (scale-wise, triad outline, *la,-mi* cadence, repeated patterns).
7. Sing through in your head (audiate).
8. Outline tonic or *la*.
9. Perform on solfège.

Practice this sequence for sight-singing the melody in figure 25.2.

Russian Folk Song

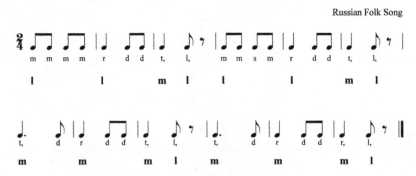

Figure 25.2 "The Birch Tree," stick notation.

PRE-CONDUCTING: CUEING ON THE DOWNBEAT
WHILE CONDUCTING THE 4/4 PATTERN

In this exercise, we will continue exploring the pre-conducting left-hand preparatory gesture for giving a cue on a downbeat while conducting the 4/4 pattern. The cue, as used in a musical setting, is a conductor gesture signaling an entrance for a performer or group of performers. Conductors provide cues through eye contact, facial gestures, head movement, body proximity, right-hand gestures, and so on.

A cue indicates tempo, style, and other features, but for this exercise, you will focus only on the entrance/tempo aspect of cueing.

You will be using both the right and left hands/arms. You should carefully monitor the movements suggested, in a mirror, through electronic feedback, or by having others observe you.

Classroom Setup

All class members can complete any of these exercises simultaneously. Initially, students should stand and allow about one arm's length of space around them. An instructor should initiate each activity. Once individuals become more proficient in completing the elements in this activity, they should form small groups of three or four individuals and conduct the cue gesture for others.

Exercises
Exercise 1

1. Establish your conducting posture, with your right hand/arm slightly above your waist and your left hand/arm at the same height but closer to your body, and a tempo of mm = 69.
   a. As a warm-up, complete rebounds with your right hand (do not conduct the 4/4 pattern at this time), and count by saying, "cue, 2, 3, up, cue, 2, 3, up," and so on.
   b. Your left hand/arm now performs a cue on the downbeat of each sequence of four beats—in this case, when you say "up," the left hand/arm prepares for the cue, and when you say "cue," the left hand/arm gives the cue.
      i. The left-hand/arm cue begins with a preparation motion. The preparatory motion begins with your hand moving up and away from your body to the height of your face (about nose/eye

height) and then stopping. The palm of your hand faces away from you, and your fingers are slightly curved and relaxed. This motion begins when you say "up."

    ii. The left-hand/arm cue is given when you say "cue." The motion for the cue is initiated with a flick of your wrist. Once you have completed the cue motion, your left hand should return to its position.

  c. Practice the cueing motion with the left hand/arm while completing rebounds (not the 4/4 conducting pattern yet) with the right hand/arm. Remember to say "cue, 2, 3, up" to help facilitate this action. After you give your first cue, return the left hand on beat two.

  d. Once you feel confident completing this motion, rest, and then continue to the next exercise.

Exercise 2

1. Reestablish your right- and left-hand/arm conducting position.
2. Establish a tempo of mm = 69, and begin to conduct the 4/4 pattern.
   a. Again, say "cue, 2, 3, up" as you conduct the 4/4 pattern. On the word "cue," you should be in first position, completing the downbeat, and on the word "up," you will be in fourth position, completing the upbeat.
   b. Practice the 4/4 conducting pattern while saying the phrase. Once you are confident with this motion, continue to the next step.
3. Continue to conduct the 4/4 pattern while saying the phrase, and now add the left-hand/arm cue as described in exercise 1.
4. Once you feel confident completing this motion, rest, and then continue to the next exercise.

Exercise 3

1. Reestablish your right- and left-hand/arm conducting position and tempo of mm = 69.
2. Begin to conduct the 4/4 pattern.
   a. Again, say "cue, 2, 3, up" as you conduct the 4/4 pattern. On the word "cue," you should be in first position, completing the downbeat, and on the word "up," you will be in fourth position, completing the upbeat.
3. Continue to conduct the 4/4 pattern while saying the phrase, and now add the left-hand/arm cue; however, you will now move the cue location as described below.

a. On your first downbeat cue, perform the motion with your left hand in front of your face, and then return the left hand to your body position.

b. On your second downbeat cue, move your left hand/arm slightly to the left of your left thigh. Your left hand/arm should be at about the same height as your first cue but farther to the left of your body. Return your left hand to the body after this cue.

c. On your third downbeat cue, move your left hand/arm slightly to the right of your right thigh, and complete the cue. Again, the same cue height should be maintained. Return your left hand to the body after the cue.

d. Your next cue is once again in front of your face, and so on.

4. Continue practicing this motion until you feel comfortable. You may wish to continue saying "cue, 2, 3, up" while completing this exercise, but if doing so does not help facilitate the motion, you may discontinue it.

Assignment

As you begin to feel more at ease with the cue gesture for a downbeat in 4/4 meter, you can practice this exercise at varying tempi. Should you want to further challenge yourself, using the parameters provided in this exercise, try moving your left hand/arm to other positions. For example, (a) face, (b) left of left thigh, (c) extreme left, (d) right of right thigh, and then (e) extreme right, and so on.

Observation

Notice the cue gestures used by your directors and conductors. We will explore cue downbeat motions in the left hand/arm in 3/4 and 2/4 meter in later exercises.

PROFESSIONAL KNOWLEDGE: REMOVING FILLERS AND EMPTY LANGUAGE

For this component, the focus is to:

• Improve your public-speaking abilities and effectiveness as a communicator.

"Speech without filled pauses gives a sense of directness and strength, and what is more, of the speaker's superiority" (Deese, 1984, p. 100). When you speak with individuals and groups, they will form opinions about you based on your ability to communicate, express yourself, and use proper grammar. In addition to creating well-formed sentences, speaking clearly, projecting your voice, and using a good pace and tone, of equal importance is your ability to speak without using fillers or empty language.

Fillers are words used during speech that *fill in* the silences or pauses between words but do not add content to the sentence. Fillers have also been referred to as word tics, verbal viruses, and empty calories in speaking. They often occur when one is trying to think of what to say next, allowing more time to answer a question, or during stressful situations. Over time, language and conversations are becoming more informal, which has resulted in some fillers seeping into most sentences. "While some speakers utter hundreds of 'ums' in an hour's talking, others get away with only a handful" (Christenfeld, 1995, p. 171). When was the last time you had a conversation without using the word "like"?

Use of fillers is not a new problem. In *Urania: A Rhymed Lesson*, published in 1846 by Oliver Wendell Holmes (as cited in Erard, 2008), a Dartmouth College professor wrote a poem in which he criticized the use of "uh" when speaking. Although they are now a common part of everyday speech, fillers can be a distraction during a classroom lecture or at a formal speaking presentation.

Group Activity

For this activity, the class will be seated in chairs in a circle. You will need a timer (watch, phone, electronic device) and a ball or other small object that can be easily tossed within the circle. Appoint one student to be the teacher and one student to be the timer. The entire activity is conducted with class members seated at all times.

1. Hand the ball or small object to the assigned teacher.
2. Ask him or her to tell you everything he or she knows about a certain topic. The topic does not need to be music-related, and sometimes the more unusual the topic, the more enjoyable the activity. Some examples include weather, space, animals, cartoons, TV shows, and so on.
3. The teacher then must attempt to inform the class with an extemporaneous explanation of the topic for 60 seconds without using identified fillers, such as "um," "uh," "like," "you know," and so on.
4. When the teacher reaches the 60-second mark or inadvertently uses a filler, he or she then tosses the ball to another individual and provides the new teacher with another topic. The activity continues.
5. Depending on the size of the class, completion of this activity may require more than one session if all students are to have an opportunity to be the teacher.

Make a conscious effort during the next few days to limit your use of fillers. Listen to conversations between your friends, and determine which fillers are used most often.

MODULE 25 REFERENCES

Christenfeld, N. (1995). Does it hurt to say um? *Journal of Nonverbal Behavior* 19(3): 171–186.

Deese, J. (1984). *Thought into speech: The psychology of language.* Englewood Cliffs, NJ: Prentice-Hall.

Erard, M. (2008). *Um . . .: Slips, stumbles, and verbal blunders, and what they mean.* New York, NY: Anchor.

Continued Body Gesture Awareness—*la*-Based Minor—Cueing on Beat Two—Music Performance Anxiety

I n this module, you will focus on:

- Personal awareness: Continued development of body gesture awareness of wind, brass, and bowed string instruments in a full orchestra setting.
- Personal musicianship: *la*-based minor in standard notation.
- Pre-conducting: Cueing on the second beat while conducting the 4/4 pattern.
- Professional knowledge: Examining basic strategies for coping with music performance anxiety.

PERSONAL AWARENESS: FACIAL AND BODY GESTURE AWARENESS XI

This is a continuation from module 25, where you became the director of a full orchestra and the class was your group. Because of the number of elements in that component, it was suggested that it be continued to allow ample time for all class members to complete the exercise. As before, the emphasis is on identifying proper and improper instrument holds, bow holds, arm/hand/finger placements, embouchures, and postures.

Classroom Setup

See figure 26.1 for the suggested classroom setup.

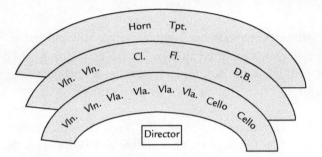

Figure 26.1 Suggested seating arrangement for a full orchestra with 15 players and director.

Exercise

The same procedure and assessment criteria detailed in module 25 should be used here.

Assignment

As you continue developing your awareness and your personal evaluation system, you may notice that your ability to assess an ensemble has become somewhat easier. With continued practice, your diagnostic skills and proficiency will increase significantly.

Observation

As you observe various groups, think about the types of things you might address as a director.

PERSONAL MUSICIANSHIP: *la*-BASED MINOR IN STANDARD NOTATION

For this component, the focus is to:

- Review the steps to sight-reading a melody in *la*-based minor.
- Sing a melody with limited pitches (l,-t,-d-r-m-s) in standard notation.
- Perform single-note accompaniments to a melody using Roman numerals.

You will again be singing the song "The Birch Tree," but notice that this time, the example is written with standard notation (figure 26.2). Clap rhythms within the melody using your preferred rhythm-duration system (numbers, rhythm-duration syllables, Gordon, etc.). Sing the melody with solfège syllables and hand signs, and then practice performing the single-note accompaniment represented by Roman numerals rather than solfège syllables as in the previous component. In the first three measures, you will sing the Roman numeral i on the *la*-based tonic for the key signature (E) for the duration of two beats. In measure 4, you will sing V on the pitch designated by the numeral—in this case B—for one beat and then return to i on the pitch E for one beat. Find a partner or a small group for performing the combined melody and single-note accompaniment.

Figure 26.2 "The Birch Tree," standard notation.

PRE-CONDUCTING: CUEING ON THE SECOND BEAT WHILE CONDUCTING THE 4/4 PATTERN

In this exercise, we will continue exploring the left-hand cue gesture and will focus on the gesture for a cue provided on the second beat in 4/4 meter. You will be using both right and left hands/arms. You should carefully monitor the movements suggested.

Classroom Setup

All class members can complete any of these exercises simultaneously. Initially, students should stand and allow about one arm's length of space around them. An instructor should initiate each activity. Once individuals become more proficient in completing the elements in this activity, they should form small groups of three or four individuals and conduct the cue gesture for others.

Exercises
Exercise 1

1. Establish your right- and left-hand/arm conducting posture and a tempo of mm = 69.
   a. As a warm-up, complete rebounds with your right hand (do not conduct the 4/4 pattern at this time), and count by saying "up, cue, 3, 4, up, cue, 3, 4," and so on.
   b. Add the left hand/arm, and perform a cue on the second beat of each sequence of four beats—in this case, when you say "up," the left hand/arm prepares for the cue on the downbeat, and when you say "cue," the left hand/arm gives the cue on beat two. On beat three, the hand returns to its neutral position.
   c. Practice the cueing motion with the left hand/arm while completing rebounds (not the 4/4 conducting pattern yet) with the right hand/arm. Remember to say "up, cue, 3, 4" to help facilitate this action.
   d. Once you feel confident completing this motion, rest, and then continue to the next exercise.

Exercise 2

1. Reestablish your right- and left-hand/arm conducting position and a tempo of mm = 69.
2. Begin to conduct the 4/4 pattern.
   a. Again, say "up, cue, 3, 4" as you conduct. On the word "cue," you should be in second position (completing the second beat in a 4/4 measure), and on the word "up," you will be in first position (completing the downbeat).
   b. Practice the 4/4 conducting pattern while saying the phrase. Once you feel confident with this motion, continue to the next step.
3. Continue to conduct the 4/4 pattern while saying the phrase, and now add the left-hand/arm cue as described in exercise 1.
4. Once you feel confident completing this motion, rest before continuing to the next exercise.

Exercise 3

1. Reestablish your right- and left-hand/arm conducting position and a tempo of mm = 69.
2. Begin to conduct the 4/4 pattern.
   a. Again, say "up, cue, 3, 4" as you conduct.
3. Continue to conduct the 4/4 pattern while saying the phrase, and now add the left-hand/arm cue; however, you will now move the cue location as described below.
   a. On your first cue, perform the motion with your left hand in front of your face, and then return the left hand to your body position.
   b. On your second cue, move your left hand/arm slightly to the left of your left thigh. Your left hand/arm should be at about the same height as your first cue. Return your left hand to the body after this cue.
   c. On your third cue, move your left hand/arm slightly to the right of your right thigh, and complete the cue. Again, the same cue height should be maintained. Return your left hand/arm to the body position after the cue.
   d. Your next cue is once again in front of your face, and so on.
4. Continue practicing this motion until you feel comfortable. You may wish to continue saying "up, cue, 3, 4" while completing this exercise, but if doing so does not help facilitate the motion, you may discontinue it.

Assignment

As you begin to feel more at ease with the cue gesture for the second beat in 4/4 meter, you can practice this exercise at varying tempi. Should you want to further challenge yourself, using the parameters provided in this exercise, try moving your left hand/arm to other positions. For example, (a) face, (b) left of left thigh, (c) extreme left, (d) right of right thigh, and then (e) extreme right, and so on.

Observation

Notice the cue gestures used by your directors and conductors. We will explore cue motions in the left hand/arm further in 4/4 and also in 3/4 and 2/4 meter in later exercises.

PROFESSIONAL KNOWLEDGE: MUSIC PERFORMANCE ANXIETY

For this component, the focus is to:

- Examine basic strategies for coping with music performance anxiety.

Music performance anxiety is "the experience of persisting, distressful apprehension about and/or actual impairment of performance skills in a public context, to a degree unwarranted given the individual's musical aptitude, training, and level of preparation" (Salmon, 1990, p. 3).

Many of us feel nervous and slightly anxious before performing music. You've likely been told that being a little nervous is necessary for a good performance and/or that all people have stage fright, and it's just normal.

Music performance anxiety is more than just being "a little nervous" but rather such strong physical and/or psychological reactions that your performance level is negatively affected or impeded. As many as 25 percent of musicians consider music performance anxiety a barrier to their careers (Steptoe, 2001).

How can music teachers recognize students who are suffering from music performance anxiety? Signs include the following:

- Sweaty and cold hands.
- An upset stomach or uneasy feeling in the stomach ("butterflies").
- Dry mouth.
- Rapid breathing, hyperventilation.
- Shaky hands, knees, and/or voice.
- Changes in vision.

Some music teachers do not address performance anxiety with their students in an ensemble or classroom setting. This results in some students thinking that everyone feels the same way and that stress and anxiousness are a normal part of music performance. Students need to be provided with techniques for coping with anxiety so they don't feel they have to suffer in silent terror. It is important to remember that teachers can't eliminate students' music performance anxiety. However, implementing relaxation exercises within rehearsals and before performances can prove beneficial for all students, whether or not they suffer from anxiety.

Deep breathing and meditation are common strategies for releasing tension and removing stress. Slow, deep breathing can offset the body's natural fight-or-flight reaction to stressful situations. Visualization techniques are also useful. Picture yourself giving a successful performance, rather than imagining yourself failing. Healthy habits, such as adequate sleep, proper diet, and avoidance of caffeine and alcohol, can reduce stress levels. Preparation is the key in gaining self-confidence and knowing you've done your best to be successful. Be realistic in your expectations. Rather than focusing on a perfect performance—which very few individuals can accomplish, even professional musicians—focus on doing your personal best.

Discussion

1. With a partner or a small group, identify physical and psychological risk factors in making music.
2. List personal strategies you have used or observed for overcoming performance anxiety.

MODULE 26 REFERENCES

Salmon, P. G. (1990). A psychological perspective on music performance anxiety: A review of literature. *Medical Problems of Performing Artists, 5*(1), 2–11.
Steptoe, A. (1989). Stress, coping, and stage fright in professional musicians. *Journal of Research in Music Education, 17,* 3–11.

Proximity and Gestures—Breath Management—Cueing on Beat Three—Avoiding Performance Injury

I n this module, you will focus on:

- Personal awareness: Proximity and gestures.
- Personal musicianship: Breath management and posture.
- Pre-conducting: Cueing on the third beat while conducting the 4/4 pattern.
- Professional knowledge: Avoiding performance injury.

PERSONAL AWARENESS: PROXIMITY AND GESTURES I

In this exercise, you will continue to combine skills learned in earlier modules. As directors and teachers, we send nonverbal messages. Some of your gestures will be meant to be corrective in nature, while others are signs of approval. Your gestures are often sent from different distances (proximity). Defined by Hall (1990), the proximity levels were detailed in the "Eye to Eye" exercise in module 2: intimate distance (6 to 18 inches apart), personal distance (1.5 to 4 feetapart), social distance (4 to 12 feet apart), and public distance 12 to 25 feetapart).

Here and in modules 28 and 29, you will be asked to combine your skills of identifying individual gestures while initiating your own gestures (facial and/or body) and changing your proximity within the classroom.

There are several components to each of these exercises. The fundamentals involved in this first set are as follows:

Teacher/director

1. The teacher/director (the individual in front of the class) must be able to convey two types of facial expressions convincingly:
   a. Disapproval.
   b. Approval.
2. The teacher/director will be required to send the disapproval and approval messages at various proximity distances (intimate, personal, social, and public).
3. The teacher/director will be required to:
   a. Identify members of the class who are being inattentive.
   b. Convey the facial disapproval expression.
   c. Attempt to "contact" the individuals who are being inattentive by changing proximity distances.
   d. Signal a facial gesture of approval once the students are again attentive.

Selected class members

1. Class members will be selected by the instructor to be inattentive (as if texting or reading email and not paying attention).
2. The instructor will also direct the selected class members to respond to the teacher/director's facial expression only when the teacher/director has reached a certain proximity level (intimate, personal, social, or public). The class member must then ascertain whether that proximity was reached and respond by being attentive when the teacher/director reaches that proximity.
3. Class members, other than those chosen, will convey attentive behavior gestures.

Instructor

1. Using a whiteboard, smart board, projected screen image, or other means, the instructor will identify the individuals who are to convey inattentive behavior.

2. The instructor will also indicate the distance point (intimate, personal, social, or public) at which the inattentive student should respond to the teacher/director's facial message. For example, the instructor might write:

    John—Social

    Mary—Personal

3. The instructor should ensure that the teacher/director is not aware of the individuals selected or the distances at which they are to respond.

All class members

1. All class members should practice their inattentive and attentive gestures in addition to their facial gestures of disapproval and approval.

Classroom Setup

The classroom should be arranged in three rows with five columns. If your class contains fewer than 15 individuals, position empty chairs in the rows/columns and randomly fill the other positions. If you have a larger class, add more rows. Ample room should be left between rows and chairs for the teacher/director's proximity movement. Students should sit with their feet flat on the floor, shoulders' width apart, with hands crossed or on top of each other and placed on the lap or desktop, in a relaxed but elevated posture (no slumping).

Exercises
Exercise 1

1. One class member is selected to be inattentive. The instructor indicates the proximity level at which this person should respond to the teacher/director.
2. One individual comes to the front of the class as teacher/director and is not informed of the individual who was directed to be inattentive or of the distance at which that individual is to respond to the teacher/director's facial gesture once identified.
3. Once the teacher/director and the inattentive student are selected:
   a. The teacher/director is asked to close his or her eyes. At this point, the inattentive student conveys inattentiveness and is aware of the proximity level at which he or she is to respond.

b. All other individuals express attentiveness.
c. The teacher/director is then directed to open his or her eyes and must then:
   i. Identify the inattentive student.
   ii. Initiate a facial gesture of disapproval directed at that student.
   iii. Continue to change proximity until the student responds—the response being attentiveness—at which point the teacher/director responds by conveying a facial gesture of approval.
4. There is no imposed time limit on this exercise; however, the instructor should use his or her discretion regarding the time each teacher/director is allowed before inviting another individual to be teacher/director.
5. All class members should have the opportunity to stand in front of the group as teacher/director.

Exercise 2

1. Two members of the class are now selected to be inattentive. The instructor again indicates the proximity level at which these people should respond to the teacher/director.
2. Follow the same procedure outlined in exercise 1.

Exercise 3

1. As time allows, three or more members of the class are invited to be inattentive and told the proximity level at which a positive response is to be given to the teacher/director.
2. Follow the same procedure outlined in exercise 1.

Assignment

Discuss the exercise you completed with your colleagues in class. How did they feel about your actions and gestures? Discuss how you and they might expand your expressions and use them in actual classroom or rehearsal situations. Practice using nonverbal facial gestures at different distances. How do people respond?

Observation

Note the facial gestures of individuals in groups who are not talking. At what distances do they convey various expressions? Do some expressions generally occur primarily at an intimate or personal level?

PERSONAL MUSICIANSHIP: BREATH MANAGEMENT

For this component, the focus is to:

- Identify the interdependency of breath and posture.
- Sing a melody in *la*-based minor with limited pitches (m,-s,-l,-t,-d-r-m) in stick notation.
- Perform single-note accompaniments to a melody using solfège syllables.

"Proper breath management is the foundation of good singing technique, and the beginning of proper breath usage is correct posture development" (Phillips, 2004, p. 230). Breathing forms the foundation for singing, yet defining breath management can be problematic. When you manage something, you are controlling it, which is why you commonly hear the term *breath control* when discussing singing techniques. Singing requires more energy than speaking; therefore, it makes sense that your breathing for singing will be different from when you are having a normal conversation with friends. A car needs gasoline to run the engine, your body needs food for energy, and your singing needs breath management for a consistent vocal tone.

Before singing the melody in figure 27.1, utilizing the sequential steps from earlier modules, focus on your posture. With a partner or a small group, provide feedback on the ability to stand and/or sit using a posture conducive for singing.

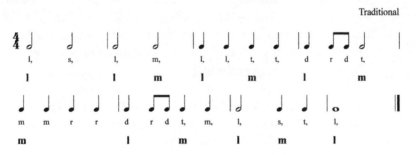

Figure 27.1 "Rose Red," stick notation.

PRE-CONDUCTING: CUEING ON THE THIRD
BEAT WHILE CONDUCTING THE 4/4 PATTERN

In this exercise, you will continue exploring the left-hand cue gesture and will focus on the gesture for a cue provided on the third beat in 4/4 meter. You will be using both right and left hands/arms. You should carefully monitor the movements suggested.

Classroom Setup

All class members can complete any of these exercises simultaneously. Initially, students should stand and allow about one arm's length of space around them. An instructor should initiate each activity. Once individuals become more proficient in completing the elements in this activity, they should form small groups of three or four individuals and conduct the cue gesture for others.

Exercises
Exercise 1

1. Establish your conducting posture and a tempo of mm = 69.

   a. As a warm-up, complete rebounds with your right hand (do not conduct the 4/4 pattern at this time), and count by saying "1, up, cue, 4, 1, up, cue, 4," and so on.
   b. Add the left hand/arm, and perform a cue on the third beat of each sequence of four beats—in this case, when you say "up," the left hand/arm prepares for the cue on beat two, and when you say "cue," the left hand/arm gives the cue on beat three. On beat four, the hand returns to its neutral position.
   c. Practice the cueing motion with the left hand/arm while completing rebounds (not the 4/4 conducting pattern yet) with the right hand/arm. Remember to say "1, up, cue, 4" to help facilitate this action.
   d. Once you feel confident completing this motion, rest, and then continue to the next exercise.

Exercise 2

1. Reestablish your right- and left-hand/arm conducting position and a tempo of mm = 69.

2. Begin to conduct the 4/4 pattern.
   a. Again, say "1, up, cue, 4" as you conduct. On the word "cue," you should be in third position (completing the third beat in a 4/4 measure), and on the word "up," you will be in second position (completing the second beat).
   b. Practice the 4/4 conducting pattern while saying the phrase. Once you feel confident with this motion, continue to the next step.
3. Continue to conduct the 4/4 pattern while saying the phrase, and now add the left-hand/arm cue as described in exercise 1.
4. Once you feel confident completing this motion, rest before continuing to the next exercise.

Exercise 3

1. Reestablish your right- and left-hand/arm conducting position and a tempo of mm = 69.
2. Begin to conduct the 4/4 pattern.
   a. Again, say "1, up, cue, 4" as you conduct.
3. Continue to conduct the 4/4 pattern while saying the phrase, and now add the left-hand/arm cue; however, you now move the cue location as described below.
   a. On your first cue, perform the motion with your left hand in front of your face, and then return the left hand to your body position.
   b. On your second cue, move your left hand/arm slightly to the left of your left thigh. Your left hand/arm should be at about the same height as your first cue. Return your left hand to the body after this cue.
   c. On your third cue, move your left hand/arm slightly to the right of your right thigh, and complete the cue. Again, the same cue height should be maintained. Return your left hand/arm to the body position after the cue.
   d. Your next cue is once again in front of your face, and so on.
4. Continue practicing this motion until you feel comfortable with it. You may wish to continue saying "1, up, cue, 4" while completing this exercise, but if doing so does not help facilitate the motion, you may discontinue it.

Assignment

As you begin to feel more at ease with the cue gesture for the third beat in 4/4 meter, you can practice this exercise at varying tempi. Should you want to further challenge yourself, using the parameters provided in this exercise, try moving your left hand/arm to other positions. For example, (a) face, (b) left of left thigh, (c) extreme left, (d) right of right thigh, and then (e) extreme right, and so on.

Observation

Notice the cue gestures used by your directors and conductors. We will explore cue motions in the left hand/arm in 3/4 and 2/4 meter in later exercises.

PROFESSIONAL KNOWLEDGE: AVOIDING PERFORMANCE INJURY

For this component, the focus is to:

• Examine strategies for avoiding performance injuries.

In module 26, you were encouraged not to dismiss the existence of performance anxiety or stage fright and its effects on the students in your classroom. In this module we will address another issue not often discussed in music education preparation classes or within the rehearsal setting: performance injuries.

Stature "may impose limits on musicians' technique by determining how they must adapt with their own physical limitations to the instrument's requirements" (Brandfonbrener & Lederman, 2002, p. 1012). Instruments were "not designed with body ergonomics in mind" and are "basically non-anatomical or contrary" to the body (Winberg and Salus, 1990, pp. 11–12). Your classrooms will be filled with students of various body sizes and physical limitations regarding coordination and dexterity. Yet instrument sizes remain uniform, with the exception of string instruments, but even those size modifications don't match every child or compensate for the unnatural holding of the instrument and the bow. Therefore, musical instruments require students to make physical adjustments in order to perform. For example, young flute players often have difficulty stretching the left arm across the body while balancing the weight of the instrument. Young trombone players often become contortionists in attempts to reach beyond fifth position.

Musicians of all ages are vulnerable to performance injuries, yet do we provide our students with strategies for avoiding injury? An athlete would not consider playing a game or running in a marathon without long-term training and knowledge regarding the importance of warm-ups and stretching exercises. Athletes also "listen" to their bodies for cues that they should rest and allow the body muscles to recover and avoid pushing past the safety point, and causing physical harm.

"Perhaps, the first step for teachers is to give their students permission to acknowledge discomfort or pain and then to provide solutions to alleviate and/or decrease the level of such discomfort during rehearsals" (Cooper, Hamann, & Frost, 2012, p. 75). Students must feel empowered to inform their teachers when playing feels physically uncomfortable.

The second step involves teacher awareness of strategies for avoiding injury and alleviating pain when and if it occurs. Basic issues to consider are proper posture, breathing exercises, and warm-ups—both gross motor (arms, legs, back, etc.) and fine motor (wrists and fingers). Consider planning stretching breaks during your rehearsals; stretching breaks allows time for the body to recover and avoids mental fatigue. "[T]he most distinguishing feature of all diseases and injuries related to music is that they are preventable" (Chesky, Kondraske, Henoch, Hipple, & Rubin, 2002, p. 1035). Remembering that students in your classrooms are musical athletes will promote an environment that includes healthy training of the body.

Discussion

1. With a partner or a small group, identify physical risk factors when playing various instruments.
2. List strategies to incorporate within rehearsal settings for avoiding performance injuries.

MODULE 27 REFERENCES

Brandfonbrener, A. G., & Lederman, R. J. (2002). Performing arts medicine. In R. Colwell & C. Richardson (Eds.), *The new handbook of research on music teaching and learning* (pp. 1009–1022). New York, NY: Oxford University Press.

Chesky, K., Kondraske, G. V., Henoch, M., Hipple, J., & Rubin, B. (2002). Musicians' health. In R. Colwell & C. Richardson (Eds.), *The new handbook of research on music teaching and learning* (pp. 1023–1039). New York, NY: Oxford University Press.

Cooper, S., Hamann, D., & Frost, R. (2012). The effects of stretching exercises during rehearsals on string students' self-reported perceptions of discomfort. *Update: Applications of Research in Music Education, 30*(2), 71–76.

Hall, E. T. (1990). *The hidden dimension.* New York, NY: Anchor.

Phillips, K. H. (2004). *Directing the choral music program.* New York, NY: Oxford University Press.

Winberg, J. S., & Salus, M. F. (1990). *Stretching for strings.* Reston, VA: American String Teachers Association.

Gesture Identification—Hydration—Cueing on Beat Four—Classroom Management

In this module, you will focus on:

- Personal awareness: Extending your gesture identification and response while changing proximity within the classroom.
- Personal musicianship: The importance of hydration for basic body health and singing.
- Pre-conducting: Cueing on the fourth beat while conducting the 4/4 pattern.
- Professional knowledge: Classroom management in the music classroom.

PERSONAL AWARENESS: PROXIMITY AND GESTURES II

In module 27, you were asked to combine your skills of identifying individual gestures while initiating your own gestures (facial and/or body) and changing your proximity within the classroom. Here you will extend your gesture identification and response while once again changing your proximity within the classroom.

There are several components to each of these exercises. The fundamentals involved are as follows:

Teacher/director

1. The teacher/director (the individual in front of the class) must be able to convey four types of facial expressions:
   a. Disapproval.
   b. Approval.
   c. Questioning. (For example, an individual might raise his or her eyebrows while the forehead is somewhat flat, the eyes open, the mouth closed and perhaps a bit tense, as if saying, "Do you understand? Do you have a question?")
   d. Understanding. (For example, an individual might have a relaxed forehead, with the eyebrows relaxed or slightly raised, the eyes somewhat open, and the mouth closed but relaxed and perhaps slightly lifted at the corners, all accompanied by a nod of the head, as if saying, "Great, I'm glad I addressed your question appropriately.")
2. The teacher/director will be required to send the disapproval/approval or questioning/understanding messages at various proximity distances (intimate, personal, social, and public).
3. The teacher/director will be required to:
   a. Identify members of the class who are being inattentive or inquisitive (those who appear to have a question).
   b. Convey the appropriate facial expression (disapproval for inattentive behavior, questioning for inquisitive expressions).
   c. Attempt to "contact" the individuals who are being inattentive or inquisitive by changing proximity distances.
   d. Signal a facial gesture of approval or understanding once the students are again attentive.

Selected class members

1. Class members will be selected by the instructor to be inattentive (as if texting or reading email and not paying attention) or inquisitive (as if needing further understanding for clarification).
2. The instructor will also direct the selected class members to respond to the teacher/director's facial expression only when the teacher/director has reached a certain proximity level (intimate, personal, social, or public). The class members will then respond by being attentive or no longer inquisitive.
3. Class members, other than those chosen, will convey attentive behavior gestures.

Instructor

1. Using a whiteboard, smart board, projected screen image, or other means, the instructor will identify the individuals who are to convey inattentive or inquisitive behavior.
2. The instructor will also indicate the distance point (intimate, personal, social, or public) at which the inattentive and inquisitive students should respond to the teacher/director's facial message. For example, the instructor might write:
   > John—Inattentive—Social
   > Mary—Inquisitive—Personal
3. The instructor should ensure that the teacher/director is not aware of either the individuals selected or the distances at which they are to respond.

All class members

1. All class members should practice the following gestures: inattentive, inquisitive, attentive, disapproval, approval, questioning, and understanding.

Classroom Setup

The classroom should be arranged in three rows with five columns. If your class contains fewer than 15 individuals, place empty chairs in the rows/columns and randomly fill the other positions. If you have a larger class, add more rows. Ample room should be left between rows and chairs for the teacher/director's proximity movement. Students should sit with their feet flat on the floor, shoulders' width apart, with hands crossed or on top of each other and placed on the lap or desktop, in a relaxed but upright posture (no slumping).

Exercises
Exercise 1

1. One class member is selected to be inattentive and one to be inquisitive. The instructor indicates the proximity level at which each person should respond to the teacher/director.

2. One individual comes to the front of the class as teacher/director and is not informed of the individuals who were directed to be inattentive and inquisitive or of the distance at which the individuals are to respond to the teacher/director's facial gesture once identified.
3. Once the the teacher/director and the inattentive and inquisitive students are selected:
   a. The teacher/director is asked to close his or her eyes. At this point, the inattentive student conveys inattentiveness, and the inquisitive student conveys inquisitiveness.
   b. All other individuals express attentiveness.
   c. The teacher/director is then directed to open his or her eyes and must then:
      i. Identify the inattentive student and the inquisitive student.
      ii. Initiate a facial gesture of disapproval or questioning directed as appropriate at each student.
      iii. Continue to change proximity until one and then the other student respond—the response being attentiveness—at which point the teacher/director responds by conveying a facial gesture of approval or understanding.
4. There is no imposed time limit on this exercise; however, the instructor should use his or her discretion regarding the time each teacher/director is allowed before inviting another individual to be teacher/director.
5. All class members should have the opportunity to stand in front of the group as teacher/director.

Exercise 2

1. Four members of the class are now selected, two to be inattentive and two to be questioning. The instructor again indicates the proximity level at which these people should respond to the teacher/director.
2. Follow the same procedure outlined in exercise 1.

Exercise 3

1. As time allows, five, six, or more members of the class are invited to be inattentive or questioning and told the proximity level at which a positive response is to be given to the teacher/director.
2. Follow the same procedure outlined in exercise 1.

Assignment

Discuss the exercise you completed with your colleagues in class. How did they feel about your actions and gestures? What other gestures does a teacher/director commonly use? Discuss how you and they might expand expressions and how or when they might be used in actual classroom or rehearsal situations.

Observation

Note the facial gestures of individuals in groups who are not talking. At what distances do they convey various expressions? Do some expressions generally occur primarily at an intimate or personal level?

PERSONAL MUSICIANSHIP: HYDRATION

For this component, the focus is to:

- Identify your hydration needs.
- Sing a melody in *la*-based minor with limited pitches (m,-s,-l,-t,-d-r-m) in standard notation.
- Perform single-note accompaniments to a melody using Roman numerals.

You have brains in your head. You have feet in your shoes.
You can steer yourself any direction you choose.
You're on your own. And you know what you know.
And YOU are the one who'll decide where to go.
(Dr. Seuss, 1990)

When you're going for a long walk or hike, it is likely you will remember to bring water on your journey, because you've been taught that dehydration and its symptoms can range from slight discomfort to death. Water is crucial for basic body needs and healthy singing. Your vocal folds need moisture to move easily, and your brain needs water to function efficiently. Water accounts for a significant amount of one's body weight.

The following basic suggestions will aid in maintaining hydration and vocal health:

- Drink plenty of water.
- Eat a variety of fruits and vegetables.
- Stay conscious of dry environments, both indoor and outdoor.
- Remember that exercise drains your body of fluids.
- Avoid caffeine and alcohol, as they work as drying agents in the body.

Many of the concepts in the personal musicianship components of this book focus on suggestions for alignment, posture, breathing, and now hydration. You are in control of your own path and "can steer yourself any direction you choose." Choose at least one of the elements discussed in this or earlier components, and keep a journal recording personal progress and improvement in that area.

Sing the melody in figure 28.1, utilizing the sequential steps from previous modules.

Figure 28.1 "Rose Red," standard notation.

PRE-CONDUCTING: CUEING ON THE FOURTH BEAT WHILE CONDUCTING THE 4/4 PATTERN

In this exercise, you will continue exploring the left-hand cue gesture and will focus on the gesture for a cue provided provided on the fourth beat in 4/4 meter. You will be using both right and left hands/arms. You should carefully monitor the movements suggested.

Classroom Setup

All class members can complete any of these exercises simultaneously. Initially, students should stand and allow about one arm's length of space around them. An instructor should initiate each activity. Once individuals become more proficient in completing the elements in this activity, they should form small groups of three or four individuals and conduct the cue gesture for others.

Exercises
Exercise 1

1. Establish your conducting posture and a tempo of mm = 69.
   a. As a warm-up, complete rebounds with your right hand (do not conduct the 4/4 pattern at this time), and count by saying "1, 2, up, cue, 1, 2, up, cue" and so on.
   b. Add the left hand/arm, and perform a cue on the fourth beat of each sequence of four beats—in this case, when you say "up," the left hand/arm prepares for the cue on beat three, when you say "cue," the left hand/arm gives the cue on beat four. On beat one, your left hand returns to its neutral position.
   c. Practice the cueing motion with the left hand/arm while completing rebounds (not the 4/4 conducting pattern yet) with the right hand/arm. Remember to say "1, 2, up, cue" to help facilitate this action.
   d. Once you feel confident completing this motion, rest, and then continue to the next exercise.

Exercise 2

1. Reestablish your conducting position and a tempo of mm = 69.
2. Begin to conduct the 4/4 pattern.

a. Again, say "1, 2, up, cue" as you conduct. On the word "up," you should be in third position, and on the word "cue," you should be in fourth position.

b. Practice the 4/4 conducting pattern while saying the phrase. Once you feel confident with this motion, add the left hand/arm cue.

3. Once you feel confident completing this motion, rest before continuing to the next exercise.

Exercise 3

1. Reestablish your right- and left-hand/arm conducting position and a tempo of mm = 69.
2. Begin to conduct the 4/4 pattern.
   a. Again, say "1, 2, up, cue" as you conduct.
3. Continue to conduct the 4/4 pattern while saying the phrase, and now add the left-hand/arm cue; however, you now move the cue location as described below.
   a. On your first cue, perform the motion with your left hand in front of your face.
   b. On your second cue, move your left hand/arm slightly to the left of your left thigh.
   c. On your third cue, move your left hand/arm slightly to the right of your right thigh, and complete the cue.
   d. Your next cue is once again in front of your face, and so on.
4. Continue practicing this motion until you feel comfortable with it. You may wish to continue saying "1, 2, up, cue" while completing this exercise, but if doing so does not help facilitate the motion, you may discontinue it.

Assignment

As you begin to feel more at ease with the cue gesture for the fourth beat in 4/4 meter, you can practice this exercise with varying tempi. Should you want to further challenge yourself, using the parameters provided in this exercise, try moving your left hand/arm to other positions. For example, (a) face, (b) left of left thigh, (c) extreme left, (d) right of right thigh, and then (e) extreme right, and so on.

Observation

Notice the cue gestures used by your directors and conductors. We will explore cue motions in the left hand/arm in 3/4 and 2/4 meter in later exercises.

PROFESSIONAL KNOWLEDGE: CLASSROOM MANAGEMENT I

For this component, the focus is to:

• Begin examining classroom management in the music classroom.

According to the "Glossary of Education Reform" (http://edglossary.org/classroom-management), "Classroom management refers to the wide variety of skills and techniques that teachers use to keep students organized, orderly, focused, attentive, on task, and academically productive during a class." Effective teachers tend to have strong classroom-management skills, while more inexperienced teachers may struggle with management issues. As with all other skills you develop in regard to musicianship and teaching abilities, you can become more effective at classroom management with practice.

The term *management* has many synonyms. By examining the various word choices, one can gain a greater understanding of the magnitude of the term. Synonyms include *organization, running, administration, supervision, controlling, care, charge, governance, guidance, discipline, handling, oversight, stewardship, regulation,* and more. It is therefore not surprising that classroom management remains a concern for preservice, novices, and experienced teachers. It affects all aspects of the teaching and learning process within the classroom.

Why do we need to "manage" students? You can be the most knowledgeable person in your subject area, but if you can't control your class, you can't communicate that knowledge to your students. Classroom management is not a separate entity in your teaching or classroom, but rather it is connected with all other aspects of your teaching.

In earlier modules, you learned about the importance of formulating goals and objectives and then planning lessons that serve as road maps to reach those goals. Lesson planning and the ability to deliver music instruction are essential, key factors for classroom management. Students need to know the purpose of what you are asking them to do. Students need to know what they're expected to learn. Many classroom behavior problems and disruptions occur because of student frustration, boredom, and/or failure caused by poor sequencing or developmentally inappropriate material. See figure 28.2.

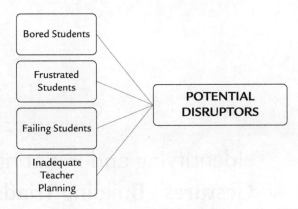

Figure 28.2 Potential classroom disruptors.

A successful teacher is a successful manager—a manager of students, classroom environment, curriculum, teaching materials, and instructional delivery. The time and effort spent in developing effective lessons greatly affect the quality of student behaviors and interactions.

Discussion

1. With a partner or a small group, discuss areas of concern regarding management.
2. List strategies you've observed used by teachers whom you consider effective managers.

MODULE 28 REFERENCE

Dr. Seuss. (1990). *Oh, the places you'll go*. New York, NY: Random House.

Identifying and Initiating Gestures—Building Triads in *la*-Based Minor—Cueing on the Downbeat in 3/4—Positive Management Techniques

In this module, you will focus on:

- Personal awareness: Identifying and initiating gestures while varying your proximity in the classroom.
- Personal musicianship: Building triads with solfège in *la*-based minor.
- Pre-conducting: Cueing on the downbeat while conducting the 3/4 pattern.
- Professional knowledge: Continued classroom-management examination with an emphasis on positive management techniques.

PERSONAL AWARENESS: PROXIMITY AND GESTURES III

In modules 27 and 28, you were asked to combine your skills of identifying individual gestures while initiating your own gestures (facial and/or body) and changing your proximity within the classroom. Here, instead of a facial gesture, you will be asked to provide a physical gesture and a physical response using your fingers/hands/arms while once again changing your proximity within the classroom.

The components of these exercises are as follows:

Teacher/director

1. The teacher/director (the individual in front of the class) must be able to convey two types of physical gestures using fingers/hands/arms:
   a. Disapproval, or "Please cease your current activity." This could be achieved by raising the hand and moving the index finger sideways, as if to say "No, I don't want you doing what you are doing." Another example could be holding the hand up, palm forward, with fingers pointing up, as if indicating "Stop what you are doing."
   b. Approval, or "Thank you for changing your action(s)." This might be the thumbs-up sign or the OK sign, where the thumb and index finger touch and form a circle.
2. The teacher/director will be required to make the disapproval and approval physical gestures at various proximity distances (intimate, personal, social, and public).
3. The teacher/director will be required to:
   a. Identify the members of the class who are being inattentive.
   b. Convey the appropriate physical gesture.
   c. Attempt to "contact" the individuals who are being inattentive by changing proximity distances.
   d. Signal a physical gesture of approval once the students are again attentive.

Selected class members

1. Class members will be selected by the instructor to be inattentive (as if texting or reading email and not paying attention).
2. The instructor will also direct the selected class members to respond to the teacher/director's physical gesture only when the teacher/director has reached a certain proximity level (intimate, personal, social, or public), at which point the class members will then respond by being attentive.
3. Class members, other than those chosen, will convey attentive behavior gestures.

Instructor

1. The instructor will identify the individuals who are to convey inattentive behavior.

2. The instructor will also indicate the distance point (intimate, personal, social, or public) at which the inattentive students should respond to the teacher/director's gesture. For example, the instructor might indicate:
   John—Social
   Mary—Personal
3. The instructor should ensure that the teacher/director is not aware of either the individuals selected or the distances at which they are to respond.

All class members

1. All class members should practice their inattentive, attentive, disapproval, and approval physical gestures.

Classroom Setup

The classroom should be arranged in three rows with five columns. If your class contains fewer than 15 individuals, place empty chairs in the rows/columns and randomly fill the other positions. If you have a larger class, add more rows. Ample room should be left between rows and chairs for the teacher/director's proximity movement. Students should sit with their feet flat on the floor, shoulders' width apart, with hands crossed or on top of each other and placed on the lap or desktop, in a relaxed but upright posture (no slumping).

Exercises
Exercise 1

1. One class member is selected to be inattentive. The instructor indicates the proximity level at which this person should respond to the teacher/director.
2. One individual comes to the front of the class as teacher/director and is not informed of the individual who was directed to be inattentive or of the distance at which the individual is to respond to the teacher/director's gesture once identified.
3. Once the teacher/director and the inattentive student are selected:
   a. The teacher/director is asked to close his or her eyes. At this point, the inattentive student conveys inattentiveness (behavior such as texting, emailing, being otherwise distracted, etc.).
   b. All other individuals express attentiveness.

    c. The teacher/director is then directed to open his or her eyes and must then:

       i. Identify the inattentive student.

      ii. Initiate a physical gesture of disapproval, as deemed appropriate.

     iii. Continue to change proximity until the student responds—the response being attentiveness—at which point the teacher/director responds by conveying a physical gesture of approval.

4. There is no imposed time limit on this exercise; however, the instructor should use his or her discretion regarding the time each teacher/director is allowed before inviting another individual to be teacher/director.

5. All class members should have the opportunity to stand in front of the group as teacher/director.

Exercise 2

1. Two class members are now selected to be inattentive. The instructor again indicates the proximity level at which these people should respond to the teacher/director.

2. Follow the same procedure outlined in exercise 1.

Exercise 3

1. As time allows, three, four, or more members of the class are invited to be inattentive and told the proximity level at which a positive response is to be given to the teacher/director.

2. Follow the same procedure outlined in exercise 1.

Assignment

Discuss the use of teacher/director-initiated physical gestures to get desired responses. Discuss how you felt when physical gestures were used to get desired responses in class. Think about other possible physical gestures that could be used in various situations by a teacher/director to elicit appropriate student responses. Discuss when such gestures might be used in actual classroom or rehearsal situations.

Observation

Note the physical gestures of individuals in groups. At what distances do they use various physical gestures? What physical gestures are most often used?

PERSONAL MUSICIANSHIP: BUILDING TRIADS WITH SOLFÈGE IN *la*-BASED MINOR

For this component, the focus is to:

- Review building triads with solfège syllables.
- Practice singing and outlining various triads using solfège.
- Sing a melody with limited pitches (l,-t,-d-r-m) in stick notation.
- Perform one-note accompaniments to a melody using solfège syllables.

You have been singing one-note accompaniments with your melodies to promote independent part singing. Before applying accompaniments using chords in *la*-based minor, what follows is a brief review of building triads using solfège syllables.

A triad is a chord made up of three notes with the distance of a third separating them. Figure 29.1 outlines triads used when singing a melody that is *la*-centered, or what your ear will identify as a minor. Select a pitch for *la* (e.g., middle C), and practice singing each column of triads with solfège and hand signs. You might be more successful singing all the triads that create major triads (e.g., triads built on *do, fa,* and *so*) before moving to the minor triads. Eventually, you should be able to sequence through these triads with ease; therefore, repeated practice is recommended.

Sing the melody in figure 29.2, utilizing the sequential steps from previous modules.

i	ii	III	iv	v	VI	VII
mi	fa	so	la	ti	do	re
do	re	mi	fa	so	la	ti
la	ti	do	re	mi	fa	so

Figure 29.1 Solfège and chords, *la*-based (minor).

Latvian Folk Song

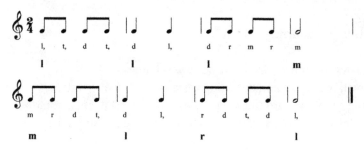

Figure 29.2 "Aija, Anzit, Aija," stick notation.

PRE-CONDUCTING: CUEING ON THE DOWNBEAT
WHILE CONDUCTING THE 3/4 PATTERN

In these exercises, you will explore the left-hand cue gestures in 3/4 meter. You will begin with the gesture for a cue provided on the downbeat. You will be using both right- and left-hands/arms. You should carefully monitor the movements suggested.

Classroom Setup

All class members can complete any of these exercises simultaneously. Initially, students should stand and allow about one arm's length of space around them. An instructor should initiate each activity. Once individuals become more proficient in completing the elements in this activity, they should form small groups of three or four individuals and conduct the cue gesture for others.

Exercises
Exercise 1

1. Establish your conducting posture and a tempo of mm = 69.
   a. As a warm-up, complete rebounds with your right hand (do not conduct the 3/4 pattern at this time). You may not wish to say the phrase "up and cue"; however, should you wish to do so, you would say "cue, 2, up," and so on.
   b. Add the left hand/arm, and perform a cue on the downbeat of each sequence of three beats—in this case, if you say "up," the left hand/arm prepares for the cue on beat three, and if you say "cue," the left hand/arm gives the cue on the downbeat. On beat two, your hand returns to its neutral position.
   c. Practice the cueing motion with the left hand/arm while completing rebounds (not conducting the 3/4 pattern yet) with the right hand/arm.
   d. Once you feel confident completing this motion, rest, and then continue to the next exercise.

Exercise 2

1. Reestablish your conducting position and a tempo of mm = 69.
2. Conduct the 3/4 pattern, and add the left-hand/arm cue.
3. Once you feel confident completing this motion, rest before continuing to the next exercise.

Exercise 3

1. Reestablish your conducting position and a tempo of mm = 69.
2. Continue to conduct the 3/4 pattern and the left-hand/arm cue; however, now move the cue to various positions—in front of your face, to the left of your left thigh, and to the right of your right thigh.
3. Continue practicing this motion until you feel comfortable.

Assignment

As you begin to feel more at ease with the cue gesture for the downbeat in 3/4 meter, you can practice this exercise at varying tempi. Should you want to further challenge yourself, using the parameters provided in this exercise, try moving your left hand/arm to other positions. For example, (a) face, (b) left of left thigh, (c) extreme left, (d) right of right thigh, and then (e) extreme right, and so on.

Observation

Notice the cue gestures used by your directors and conductors. We will continue exploring cue motions in the left hand/arm in 3/4 and 2/4 meter in later exercises.

PROFESSIONAL KNOWLEDGE: CLASSROOM MANAGEMENT II

For this component, the focus is to:

• Continue examining classroom management with an emphasis on positive management techniques.

If you think you can't be manipulated by students, you are destined for struggle and failure. Students are the best manipulators. They've spent their entire lives learning to manipulate peers and adults. From the time they could walk, talk, and have opinions, children have been learning how to get what they want and to avoid what they don't like.

Do music classes have fewer management problems, or are music classes more prone to behavior problems? The answer . . . is yes. Fortunately, most students enjoy music classes, and by secondary school (grades 7–12), they have elected to participate in music. They are in your class because they chose to be there and have a high interest in the subject content. Another benefit for music teachers is that their students are kept physically and mentally busy, which leaves less time for disruptions and interruptions.

On the other hand, music classes can be prone to behavior problems. The music class environment often lacks the concreteness or structure of some other academic subjects. Students spend a majority of their time making sounds or noise with instruments. When the music making stops, some tend to continue making sounds or noise, either with their instrument or by talking. The large number of students involved in performing ensembles can make management problematic. Students may sometimes experience a sense of invisibility and think you can't see them or hear them, and they are more willing to test the limits. This sense of invisibility will prompt some students to act out purposely in order to get your attention and to feel recognized within the classroom.

The beginning of the school year is the preferred time to start successful management programs, but it is possible to make changes throughout the year. The main thing to remember is that if the strategies aren't working, you need to be open to making changes. There are numerous articles and books available on positive management techniques. Figure 29.3 provides only a select few strategies.

Figure 29.3 Positive management techniques.

Class members, depending on the age group, should have a chance either to help make and/or thoroughly discuss guidelines for class conduct. Although time-consuming, it gives them a sense of ownership as they create input for class rules. There are numerous articles and books available on how to create classroom rules. Here are a few of the most common suggestions:

- Keep them simple.
- Don't have too many.
- Make them specific.
- Write them down.
- Post them in the classroom.
- Make sure they are understood by teacher and students.
- Review them when needed.
- Enforce them in a consistent and fair manner.
- Clearly define the consequences of breaking them.

Remember, as with all the other skills you are developing in regard to your musicianship and teaching abilities, you can become effective at classroom management with practice and conscious effort.

Discussion

1. With a partner or a small group, brainstorm procedural strategies for the following basic items that are common initiators of classroom-management problems:
   a. Coming to class late.
   b. Going to the restroom.
   c. Getting a drink during class.
   d. Going to the office.
   e. Going to the lockers.
   f. Needing to sharpen a pencil.
   g. Leaving the classroom when dismissed.
2. Have you observed classroom-management issues this week? If yes, what were they, and what were the steps the teacher took to defuse them? If no, what were the proactive techniques the teacher used to avoid problems?

Facial and Physical Gestures—Voice-Leading Patterns—Cueing on Beat Two in 3/4—Implementing Classroom Management

I n this module, you will focus on:

- Personal awareness: Combining your facial and physical gesture deliveries while changing your proximity within the classroom.
- Personal musicianship: Voice-leading patterns in *la*-based minor.
- Pre-conducting: Cueing on the second beat while conducting the 3/4 pattern.
- Professional knowledge: Implementing appropriate classroom-management strategies.

PERSONAL AWARENESS: PROXIMITY AND GESTURES IV

In modules 27, 28, and 29, you identified the gestures of others and then initiated facial or physical gestures while changing your proximity within the classroom. You will now combine your facial and physical (fingers/hands/arms) gesture deliveries while changing your proximity within the classroom.

The components of these exercises are as follows:

Teacher/director

1. The teacher/director (the individual in front of the class) must be able to convey two types of facial expressions:
   a. Disapproval.
   b. Approval.

   And two types of physical gestures using fingers/hands/arms:

   c. Disapproval, or "Please cease your current activity."
   d. Approval, or "Thank you for changing your action(s)."

2. The teacher/director will be required to make the appropriate disapproval and approval facial and physical gestures at various proximity distances (intimate, personal, social, and public).
3. The teacher/director will be required to:
   a. Identify the members of the class who are being inattentive.
   b. Convey the appropriate facial and physical gestures.
   c. Attempt to "contact" the individuals who are being inattentive by changing proximity distances.
   d. Signal both a facial and a physical gesture of approval once the students are again attentive.

Selected class members

1. Class members will be selected by the instructor to be inattentive (as if texting or reading email and not paying attention).
2. The instructor will also direct the selected class members to respond to the teacher/director's physical gesture only when the teacher/instructor has reached the prescribed proximity (intimate, personal, social, or public), at which point the class members will then respond by being attentive.
3. Class members, other than those chosen, will convey attentive behavior gestures.

Instructor

1. The instructor will identify the individuals who are to convey inattentive behavior.
2. The instructor will also indicate the distance point (intimate, personal, social, or public) at which the inattentive students should respond to the teacher/director's gesture.

3. The instructor should ensure that the teacher/director is not aware of either the individuals selected or the distances at which they are to respond.

All class members

1. All class members should practice their inattentive, attentive, disapproval, and approval facial and physical gestures.

Classroom Setup

The classroom should be arranged in three rows with five columns. If your class contains fewer than 15 individuals, place empty chairs in the rows/columns and randomly fill the other positions. If you have a larger class, add more rows. Ample room should be left between rows and chairs for the teacher/director's proximity movement. Students should sit with their feet flat on the floor, shoulders' width apart, with hands crossed or on top of each other and placed on the lap or desktop, in a relaxed but upright posture (no slumping).

Exercises
Exercise 1

1. One class member is selected to be inattentive. The instructor indicates the proximity level at which this person should respond to the teacher/director.
2. One individual comes to the front of the class as teacher/director and is not informed of the individual who was directed to be inattentive or of the distance at which the individual is to respond to the teacher/director's facial/physical gestures once identified.
3. Once the teacher/director and the inattentive student are selected:
   a. The teacher/director is asked to close his or her eyes. At this point, the inattentive student conveys inattentiveness.
   b. All other individuals express attentiveness.
   c. The teacher/director is then directed to open his or her eyes and must then:
      i. Identify the inattentive student.
      ii. Initiate both a facial and a physical gesture of disapproval, as deemed appropriate.

     iii. Continue to change proximity until the student responds—the response being attentiveness—at which point the teacher/director responds by conveying both a facial and a physical gesture of approval.

4. There is no imposed time limit on this exercise; however, the instructor should use his or her discretion regarding the time each teacher/director is allowed before inviting another individual to be teacher/director.
5. All class members should have the opportunity to stand in front of the group as teacher/director.

Exercise 2

1. Two class members are now selected to be inattentive. The instructor again indicates the proximity level at which these people should respond to the teacher/director.
2. Follow the same procedure outlined in exercise 1.

Exercise 3

1. As time allows, three, four, or more members of the class are invited to be inattentive and told the proximity level at which a positive response is to be given to the teacher/director.
2. Follow the same procedure outlined in exercise 1.

Assignment

Discuss the use of teacher/director-initiated physical gestures combined with facial gestures to get desired responses. Discuss how you felt when both facial and physical gestures were combined to get desired responses in class. Were the combined gestures more influential than if only a facial or only a physical gesture was used? Think about other possible facial and physical gesture combinations that a teacher/director could use to elicit appropriate student responses. Discuss when such gestures might be used in actual classroom or rehearsal situations.

Observation

Note the combined facial and physical gestures of individuals use in groups. At what distances do they use various facial and physical gestures? What facial and physical gesture combinations are most often used?

PERSONAL MUSICIANSHIP: VOICE-LEADING PATTERNS IN *la*-BASED MINOR

For this component, the focus is to:

- Review the definition of a triad.
- Sing a melody with limited pitches (l,-t,-d-r-m) in standard notation.
- Perform accompaniments to a melody using solfège syllables.

In this module you will review triad building using solfège syllables. Additionally, you will practice applying different inversions of triads to create appropriate voice-leading patterns when singing in *la*-based minor. Turn to a partner, and define *triad*.

The exercise in this component requires using three-chord accompaniments (*la*, *re*, and *mi*; i, iv, and V). Using the three syllables *la*, *re*, and *mi* to build triads will result in the following triads: *la, do, mi; re, fa, la*; and *mi, si, ti*. Root-position chords do not promote smooth voice leading and result in large awkward leaps. Inverting the triads (chord inversions) will result in smooth voice leading. Refer to figure 30.1, and notice how inverting the triads promotes accessible part singing.

Figure 30.1 Three-chord accompaniments in inverted positions, *la*-based.

Sing the melody in figure 30.2, and add chordal accompaniment that includes appropriate voice leading. (This will require at least four people to perform all parts, three singing triads and one singing the melody.)

Latvian Folk Song

Figure 30.2 "Aija, Anzit, Aija, standard notation.

PRE-CONDUCTING: CUEING ON THE SECOND
BEAT WHILE CONDUCTING THE 3/4 PATTERN

In these exercises, you will continue to explore the left-hand cue gestures in 3/4 meter. In particular, we will introduce the pre-conducting gesture for a cue provided on the second beat. You should carefully monitor the movements suggested.

Classroom Setup

All class members can complete any of these exercises simultaneously. Initially, students should stand and allow about one arm's length of space around them. An instructor should initiate each activity. Once individuals become more proficient in completing the elements in this activity, they should form small groups of three or four individuals and conduct the cue gesture for others.

Exercises
Exercise 1

1. Establish your conducting posture and a tempo of mm = 69.
   a. As a warm-up, complete rebounds with your right hand (do not conduct the 3/4 pattern at this time). Should you wish to use the words "up" and "cue" to prepare your left hand, you would say "up, cue, 3," and so on.
   b. Practice the cueing motion with the left hand/arm while completing rebounds (not the 3/4 conducting pattern yet) with the right hand/arm.
   c. Once you feel confident completing this motion, rest, and then continue to the next exercise.

Exercise 2

1. Reestablish your conducting posture and a tempo of mm = 69.
2. Conduct the 3/4 pattern, and add the left-hand/arm cue.
3. Once you feel confident completing this motion, rest before continuing to the next exercise.

Exercise 3

1. Reestablish your conducting posture and a tempo of mm = 69.
2. Continue to conduct the 3/4 pattern and the left-hand/arm cue; however, now move the cue to various positions—in front of your face, to the left of your left thigh, and to the right of your right thigh.
3. Continue practicing this motion until you feel comfortable.

Assignment

As you begin to feel more at ease with the cue gesture for the second beat in 3/4 meter, you can practice this exercise at varying tempi. Should you want to further challenge yourself, using the parameters provided in this exercise, try moving your left hand/arm to other positions. For example, (a) face, (b) left of left thigh, (c) extreme left, (d) right of right thigh, and then (e) extreme right, and so on.

Observation

Notice the cue gestures used by your directors and conductors. We will continue exploring cue motions in the left hand/arm in 3/4 and 2/4 meter in later exercises.

PROFESSIONAL KNOWLEDGE:
CLASSROOM MANAGEMENT III

For this component, the focus is to:

• Practice implementing appropriate classroom-management strategies.

The professional knowledge components in modules 28 and 29 focused on classroom management. You will now have an opportunity to synthesize and apply the material presented in those modules to various behavior-management scenarios. As you prepare for your class presentation, refer back to those components as needed for ideas and strategies to implement in your demonstration.

Some behavior problems are serious enough to mandate immediate and appropriate disciplinary actions. Behavior problems that result in severe consequences—usually addressed at the administrative level (principal, assistant principal, counselor, etc.)—include bullying, inappropriate touching, sexual harassment, racial profiling, and so on. If one of these occurs in your classroom, it is your responsibility to report it to a higher authority. Most school districts have specific and detailed policies for these severe actions; therefore, it is important for teachers to know district policy. Ignorance is not an excuse.

Classroom Setup

Divide the class into four groups. Allow as much room as possible between groups.

Class Activity

1. Assign each group one behavior-management scenario from this list:
   a. You have two students who are constant talkers. Their talking is disrupting your teaching and the learning of those around them.
   b. You have a student who will not participate. He or she will not do anything. This individual never participates, only gives you a blank stare or pretends not to notice you trying to get his or her attention.
   c. You have a student who constantly questions your teaching ability. He or she constantly tries to undermine your authority.
   d. You have a student who will not stay in his or her seat or assigned area.

2. Allow each group approximately five minutes to prepare its presentation.
3. Group tasks include:
    a. Deciding on an effective management technique to address the given behavior-management scenario.
    b. Deciding on a less effective (or totally incorrect) management technique to address the given behavior-management scenario.
    c. Assigning roles for the group members. Who will be students? Who will be the effective teacher? Who will be the less effective teacher?
    d. Practicing the role-playing performance.
    e. Presenting to the class both the effective and the ineffective management technique. (It is the group members' option to present the effective technique first or the ineffective technique first.)
4. During the role-playing performances, the groups not presenting should do the following:
    a. Identify the two different approaches or strategies the presenting group used to address the behavior problem.
    b. Determine the most effective technique, and provide a rationale for why it was selected as most effective.
    c. Determine other appropriate options that could have been used to address the problem.

SUGGESTED READINGS

Canter, L. (2010). *Assertive discipline: Positive behavior management for today's classrooms* (4th ed.). Bloomington, IN: Solution Tree Press.
Stiefel, B. (2013). *Winning over your toughest music class K–6.* Franklin, TN: Melody Mountain.

Nonverbal Music Directives—Diction—Cueing on Beat Three in 3/4—Adult Learners

I n this module, you will focus on:

- Personal awareness: Nonverbal music directives.
- Personal musicianship: Diction in relation to vocal production.
- Pre-conducting: Cueing on the third beat while conducting the 3/4 pattern.
- Professional knowledge: Teaching music to adult learners.

PERSONAL AWARENESS: NONVERBAL MUSIC DIRECTIVES I

In an article published in 2010, Alan Gumm talked about the "speechless rehearsal." In essence, what he and many others have found is that the spoken word takes valuable time away from the rehearsal situation and is relatively inefficient in conveying a directive or delivering a message. The idea behind Gumm's article was that as teachers and directors, we use many nonverbal messages in our daily lives, so why not incorporate those same nonverbal directives into music rehearsals?

In this exercise, you and your colleagues will rediscover and practice nonverbal directives that can be used in musical rehearsal situations. How many times does a teacher/director tell his or her group to repeat something? Some of your directors have invented their own verbal directives, such as saying "again" or using a facial gesture that means "repeat" or "again." A director may use a physical gesture such as moving a hand in a circular motion to indicate "again/repeat/let's do that again."

What gestures can be used to indicate "begin," "get ready," "again," "repeat/again," "play in tune/listen carefully," "more air support," "louder/softer," "up bow/down bow," "first finger," and so forth? In this exercise, you will think of gestures, both facial and physical, that are or could be used in rehearsals to replace verbal directives. Once you identify such gestures, you will practice them in a small group and then move to another group and repeat the process to discover additional/new gestures to practice. Just think of the words we could eliminate and the time we could save in rehearsals if we incorporated gestures rather than words for commonly used directives.

Classroom Setup

In this exercise, you will be working primarily in small groups; therefore, the classroom setup should facilitate small-group discussion and interaction and also allow for physical practice within the group setting. Members will move from one group to another. Class members should have some way to record notes, easily transportable, to share among colleagues as they rotate through various small groups.

Exercise

1. The instructor divides the class into groups of three or four individuals. Once the groups are selected:
   a. Each group is allotted one or two minutes to rediscover and list/record three rehearsal gestures used to convey messages in place of verbal messages.
   b. Once the gestures are identified, each group member practices the gesture.
   c. The groups are reformed by having only one individual from each group move to a new group. That individual then shares the gestures from the first group with his or her new group, and vice versa. Each gesture that is new to the individuals in the reformed group should be practiced.

    d. The reformed groups then rediscover and list/record three additional, new rehearsal gestures and practice performing those gestures, given a time limit of one or two minutes.

    e. The groups are reformed one more time, and they share and record gestures, create three additional gestures, and practice all gestures.

2. When all the groups have finished, the instructor may wish to record all responses for later distribution to the class.

3. As time permits, all rediscovered gestures should be discussed. Were there gestures that were not rediscovered? Are there actions for which no gestures currently exist?

Assignment

Think about the gestures rediscovered in your groups and those that exist but were not rediscovered. Could you use these gestures in a rehearsal without verbal directives? Think about actions you might need to conduct a 10-minute "speechless rehearsal," along with the gestures you might use to convey those actions. List those actions, and bring them to the next class session for discussion and presentation.

Observation

Note the combined facial and physical gestures that teachers and directors use in classes and rehearsals.

PERSONAL MUSICIANSHIP: DICTION

For this component, the focus is to:

- Discuss diction in relation to vocal production.
- Sing a melody with limited pitches (m,-si,-l, -t, -d -r -m) in stick notation.
- Perform chordal accompaniments to a melody using solfège syllables.

Diction is the enunciation of words when speaking or singing. Common synonyms include *articulation* and *pronunciation*. During singing, one must form vowels and consonants in a precise manner so the audience can clearly understand the song text. In module 20, you practiced using your articulators (lips, teeth, tongue) by saying various tongue-twisters. Here the focus will be on distinguishing between voiced and unvoiced consonants.

A voiced consonant uses the vocal folds to make the sound, whereas an unvoiced consonant does not. Pronounce the consonant *d* by saying "day" four times. Notice how you feel the vibration in your throat. Now pronounce the consonant *t* by saying "tea" four times. The *t* is an unvoiced consonant and does not contain the resonance of the voiced consonant *d*. In some sources, you might also see the term *liquid consonants*, which are those on which you can sustain a pitch during the formation, such as *m*. See figure 31.1 for a list of select consonants.

Consonants		
Voiced	Unvoiced	"Liquid"
b	p	l
d	t	m
g	c / k / ck	n
v	f	"ng" (e.g., sing)
z	s	
r	h	

Figure 31.1 Consonant categories.

Attention to diction and the correct pronunciations and placements within the rhythmic context of the music will promote a unified sound within an ensemble. The way you form your consonants and vowels can also cause fluctuations in your pitch, resulting in tones being flat or sharp.

Sing the melody in figure 31.2, and add chordal accompaniment that includes appropriate voice leading. (This will require at least four people to perform all parts, three singing triads and one singing the melody.) Focus on creating a unified sound with voiced, unvoiced, and liquid consonants.

Folk Song

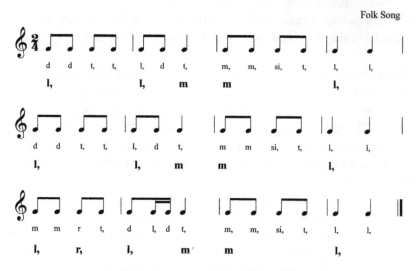

Figure 31.2 "Thanksgiving," stick notation.

PRE-CONDUCTING: CUEING ON THE THIRD
BEAT WHILE CONDUCTING THE 3/4 PATTERN

In these exercises, we will complete the left-hand gestures for a cue provided on the third beat in 3/4 meter. You will be using both right and left hands/arms. You should carefully monitor the movements suggested.

Classroom Setup

All class members can complete any of these exercises simultaneously. Students should stand and allow one arm's length of space around them. An instructor should initiate each activity. Once individuals become more proficient in completing the elements in this activity, they should form small groups of three or four individuals and conduct the cue gesture for others.

Exercises
Exercise 1

1. Establish your conducting posture and a tempo of mm = 69.
   a. As a warm-up, complete rebounds with your right hand (do not conduct the 3/4 pattern at this time). Should you wish to use the words "up" and "cue" to prepare your left hand, you would say "1, up, cue," and so on.
   b. Practice the cueing motion with the left hand/arm on the third beat while completing rebounds (not the 3/4 conducting pattern yet) with the right hand/arm.
   c. Once you feel confident completing this motion, rest, and continue to the next exercise.

Exercise 2

1. Reestablish your conducting position and a tempo of mm = 69.
2. Conduct the 3/4 pattern, and add the left-hand/arm cue.
3. Once you feel confident completing this motion, rest before continuing to the next exercise.

Exercise 3

1. Reestablish your conducting position and a tempo of mm = 69.
2. Continue to conduct the 3/4 pattern and the left-hand/arm cue; however, now move the cue to various positions—in front of your face, to
   the left of your left thigh, to the right of your right thigh, and in front of
   your face. Repeat.
3. Continue practicing this motion until you feel comfortable.

Assignment

As you begin to feel more at ease with the cue gesture for the third beat
in 3/4 meter, you can practice this exercise at varying tempi. Should you
want to further challenge yourself, using the parameters provided in this
exercise, try moving your left hand/arm to other positions. For example,
(a) face, (b) left of left thigh, (c) extreme left, (d) right of right thigh, and
then (e) extreme right, and so on.

Observation

Notice the cue gestures used by your directors and conductors. We will
explore cue motions in the left hand/arm in 2/4 meter in later exercises.

PROFESSIONAL KNOWLEDGE: TEACHING MUSIC TO ADULT LEARNERS

For this component, the focus is to:

• Discuss the characteristics of working with adult learners.

It is likely that during your teaching career, you will encounter teaching experiences with adults. It may involve leading a workshop with other music teachers in your school district, instructing an adult in a private lesson, or directing a church or community choir, band, or orchestra.

If you instruct adults in the same way as you approach teaching children, neither you nor the adults will be satisfied with the outcome. In modules 7 and 8, you learned how young children and adolescents differ physically, emotionally, and developmentally in their learning. Adults also have different needs during their learning and music making.

The integrated framework that describes adult teaching is *andragogy*, whereas the theoretical framework for teaching children is *pedagogy* (Knowles, Holton, & Swanson, 2011, p. 57). Andragogy was introduced to American educational systems in 1967. "Although introduced more than 50 years ago—in comparison to theorists examining children's learning pathways—the field of andragogy is relatively young. Whereas learning is didactic (the teacher conveys the knowledge) when instructing children, adult learning is more problem-based and collaborative" (McDonough, 2013, p. 346). Adults need to be treated as equals or partners in learning and can be expected to take ownership of their learning. They like to work at their own pace. Adults may be more inhibited than children when trying to learn new concepts, and they worry about making mistakes, not "sounding good."

Figure 31.3 is a diagram that presents differences in learning between children and adults. Please note that this is not an exhaustive list.

Learning Traits and Characteristics

Adults	Children
More inhibited	Less inhibited
Learner sets the pace	Teacher sets the pace
Longer attention spans	Shorter attention spans
Individual personality traits dominate	Maturation factors dominate
High interest in the theoretical aspects	Construct their learning through the concrete rather than abstract (theoretical)
Less capacity for memorization	High capacity for memorization
High capacity for logic, rationalizations, and objectivity	High capacity for imagination (thinking "outside the box")

Figure 31.3 Comparing learning characteristics of children and adults.

Discussion

1. With a partner or a small group, discuss your perception of how you might feel about teaching adults.
2. Share any experiences you may have had with teaching adults.
3. Discuss how learning in college classrooms has been the same as and/or different from your high school experiences.

MODULE 31 REFERENCES

Gumm, A. J. (2010). The speechless rehearsal. *Choral Journal, 2*, 16–21.

Knowles, M. S., Holton, E. F., & Swanson, R. A. (2011). *The adult learner: The definitive classic in adult education and human resource development* (7th ed.). New York, NY: Elsevier.

McDonough, D. (2013). Similarities and differences between adult and child learners as participants in the natural learning process. *Psychology, 4*, 345–348.

Speechless Lessons—Pure Vowels—Cueing on the Downbeat in 2/4—Analogies and Metaphors

I n this module you will focus on:

- Personal awareness: The directives, actions, and tasks needed to teach a speechless lesson.
- Personal musicianship: Pure vowels and their effect on tone color.
- Pre-conducting: Cueing on the downbeat while conducting the 2/4 pattern.
- Professional knowledge: Enhancing awareness of the effectiveness of analogies and metaphors in the classroom.

PERSONAL AWARENESS: NONVERBAL MUSIC DIRECTIVES II

In module 31, you explored gestures used to convey directives/actions/tasks nonverbally. In essence, you've begun to consider the elements needed to create a "speechless rehearsal." In this exercise, you and your colleagues will discuss the directives/actions/tasks needed to begin and conduct a 10-minute rehearsal, create or repurpose nonverbal directives that can be used to convey those directives/actions/tasks, and practice those gestures.

Classroom Setup

In this exercise, you will be directing class discussion, eventually working in small groups. The classroom setup should facilitate group discussion and interaction and allow for physical practice within small-group settings.

Exercise

1. In module 31, you were assigned to think about the directions/actions/tasks needed to begin and conduct a 10-minute rehearsal. Each person in the class now shares one directive/action/task with the class. This is repeated until the class cannot provide any new tasks. The instructor records and displays all ideas.
2. The class lists gestures that could be used to convey each directive/action/task. This may involve using gestures rediscovered in module 31 or creating new gestures.
3. As each rediscovered or newly created gesture is presented, all students practice the gesture.
4. After each gesture has been reviewed and practiced, form small groups of four or five individuals.
5. Each group selects one individual to be the director. That individual begins a speechless rehearsal. A mutually agreed-upon task is devised. For example, the group could sing a triad. Using only nonverbal directives, the director needs to:
   a. Inform the group of the triad quality (major, minor, diminished, augmented).
   b. Provide the beginning pitch for the root of the chord.
   c. Indicate which individuals sing the root, third, and fifth of the chord.
   d. Start the group, ensuring that they begin together, are singing the correct pitches for the chord indicated, and end together.
6. Once the director has successfully instructed the group to complete the task, another individual from the group acts as director. Repeat the process until all group members have practiced completing the task.
7. If time permits, the small groups can be combined, with each individual performing the task in front of a larger group.

Assignment

Think about and discuss the actions and gestures you and your classmates used to indicate various actions and to elicit different responses. How did each director effect change? Were some directors more successful than others? If so, why?

Observation

Watch various individuals in rehearsal and classroom situations. Imagine yourself in front of those groups, and think about the nonverbal actions you might perform in place of verbal directives.

PERSONAL MUSICIANSHIP: PURE VOWELS

For this component, the focus is to:

- Discuss pure vowels and their effect on tone color.
- Sing a melody with limited pitches (m,-si,-l,-t,-d-r-m) in standard notation.
- Perform chordal accompaniments to a melody using Roman numerals and solfège syllables.

When you look up a term in a dictionary, you will encounter International Phonetic Alphabet (IPA) symbols that represent all the various sounds. This uniform system is intended to help you correctly pronounce the word in question. In module 31, we focused on the different types of consonants and how to articulate them. This component focuses on enunciation, the formation of vowels. There are entire courses that focus on the nuances of diction, and your degree plan may require such a course for graduation. The components in this book are intended as an introduction to enunciation, with the intent to get you thinking about the ways in which you form words, consonants, and vowels when singing.

Vowel formation is crucial to singing, as vowels are used to sustain tones. Where you place your tongue inside your mouth changes the sound and color of the vowels and therefore changes the resonance of your singing tone. A pure vowel—also known as a monophthong—is "a vowel that has a single perceived auditory quality" (*New Oxford American Dictionary*). The vowel sounds the same at both beginning and end, in contrast to a diphthong, which has two sounds. ("I," as in "I am singing," is a diphthong with two vowel sounds, "a" and "e"). There are 12 pure vowels in the English language (see figure 32.1 for the list). Practice each vowel by speaking the suggested word next to the IPA symbol and then singing the word on a sustained pitch of your choice. (The emphasis is on the vowel within the word. Speaking the word that contains the IPA sound is merely a way to "hear" the IPA vowel.)

IPA	Word Sample	IPA	Word Sample
[i]	see	[ʊ]	foot
[I]	hid	[O]	moan
[e]	pay	[ɔ]	lawn
[ɛ]	red	[ʌ]	shut
[a]	pot	[æ]	bat
[u]	soon	[ə]	*ago*, so*fa*

Figure 32.1 Pure vowels.

Sing the melody in figure 32.2, and add chordal accompaniment that includes appropriate voice leading. (This will require at least four people to perform all parts, three singing triads and one singing the melody.) As you enunciate your vowels within the designated solfège syllables, think about your tongue placement. Also, note that each solfège syllable uses a pure vowel sound or monophthong.

Figure 32.2 "Thanksgiving," standard notation.

PRE-CONDUCTING: CUEING ON THE DOWNBEAT
WHILE CONDUCTING THE 2/4 PATTERN

In these exercises, we will introduce the left-hand cue on the downbeat in 2/4 meter. You will be using both right and left hands/arms. You should carefully monitor the movements suggested.

Classroom Setup

All class members can complete any of these exercises simultaneously. Initially, students should stand and allow about one arm's length of space around them. An instructor should initiate each activity. Once individuals become more proficient in completing the elements in this activity, they should form small groups of three or four individuals and conduct the cue gesture for others.

Exercises
Exercise 1

1. Establish your conducting posture and a tempo of mm = 69.
   a. As a warm-up, complete rebounds with your right hand (do not conduct the 2/4 pattern at this time). If you wish, you can say the phrase "up, cue." "Up" is said on the second beat, "cue" on the downbeat. After each cueing motion, the left hand returns to your body. This requires you to add one measure of rebounds without any left-hand cuing action.
   b. Your left hand/arm now performs a cue on the downbeat.
   c. Practice the cueing motion with the left hand/arm while completing rebounds (not the 2/4 conducting pattern yet) with the right hand/arm.
   d. Once you feel confident completing this motion, rest, and continue to the next exercise.

Exercise 2

1. Reestablish your conducting position and a tempo of mm = 69.
   a. Practice the 2/4 conducting pattern. Once you feel confident with this motion, continue to the next step.

2. Continue to conduct the 2/4 pattern, and add the left-hand/arm cue. Remember to add a measure of conducting the 2/4 pattern without any left-hand motion between cues.
3. Once you feel confident completing this motion, rest before continuing to the next exercise.

Exercise 3

1. Reestablish your conducting position and a tempo of mm = 69.
2. Continue to conduct the 2/4 pattern and the left-hand/arm cue; however, now move the cue to various positions—in front of your face, to the left of your left thigh, to the right of your right thigh, and in front of your face. Repeat.
3. Continue practicing this motion until you feel comfortable.

Assignment

As you begin to feel more at ease with the cue gesture for the downbeat in 2/4 meter, you can practice this exercise at varying tempi. Should you want to further challenge yourself, using the parameters provided in this exercise, try moving your left hand/arm to other positions. For example, (a) face, (b) left of left thigh, (c) extreme left, (d) right of right thigh, and then (e) extreme right, and so on.

Observation

Notice the cue gestures used by your directors and conductors. We will explore cue motions in the left hand/arm in 2/4 meter in later exercises.

PROFESSIONAL KNOWLEDGE: ANALOGIES AND METAPHORS FOR LEARNING

For this component, the focus is to:

• Enhance awareness of the effectiveness of analogies and metaphors in the classroom.

Before we delve into the usefulness of analogies and metaphors in the classroom, defining each term is necessary for clarification. An *analogy* is a comparison based on similarities between concepts or objects (e.g., gardening and teaching both require patience). A *metaphor* is a term or phrase used in a symbolic manner to represent a connection, either implicit or implied, between two dissimilar things. The word has Greek origins and means "to transfer." One of the most famous metaphors is William Shakespeare's "All the world's a stage, and all the men and women merely players."

"Metaphors can be powerful emotional tools that provide a shift in perception, give a new outlook on an old topic, or organize new information into understandable categories" (Noe, 2007, p. 30). Metaphors encourage new perceptions and can assist students in making learning transfers. "Research indicates metaphor creation can provide useful insight into our student audience and can also serve as a strategy for encouraging student reflection" (Bozik, 2002, 150). Noe (2007) believes that metaphors can inspire, motivate, and clarify. "Metaphors give meaning laced with opinion and personal connections" (p. 30). An effective teacher can provide students with an analogy and then extend student learning through metaphors. Let's look at our analogy of gardening and teaching and change it into a metaphor:

• Analogy: Gardening and teaching both require patience.
     Two dissimilar professions contain a common connection: the need for patience.
• Metaphor: If you cultivate a strong learning foundation and plant the seeds of music early, you will reap the bounty of musically literate, lifelong learners.
     It presents the terms *cultivate, plant, reap,* and *bounty* as a transfer from gardening to learning.
     In the original sense, you have to prepare the soil and tend to the garden before harvesting a crop.
     In the metaphorical sense, it is a symbolic representation of the planning, diligence, and work required to promote an abundance of lifelong learners.

Why do metaphors serve as a useful teaching tool? Using metaphors can intrigue students' imagination. Conductors often use metaphors during an ensemble rehearsal to assist instrumentalists and/or vocalists in creating a visual imagery that will promote a certain articulation or sound. "Metaphor is important because it provides us with a way of moving from known ideas and familiar concepts to new and unknown ones. Whenever we find our current repertoire of concepts inadequate for expression, we can merge and reorganize concepts in new ways through metaphor in order to explore different and startling perspectives" (Way, 1994, p. 8). Asking students to formulate and/or understand metaphors requires them to analyze, synthesize, and apply past knowledge—it is critical thinking or higher-order thinking at its best. Critical thinking requires students to reflect on a topic or problem by evaluating relevant information, interpreting that information, and then reaching solutions or reasonable conclusions. Students who demonstrate their ability at critical thinking will be able to approach abstract and theoretical topics with success.

Discussion

1. With a partner or a small group, determine what is mean by Shakespeare's metaphor "All the world's a stage . . ."
2. Recall or create two or three analogies that present similarities between music and another topic or discipline.
3. Recall or create one metaphor that transfers a symbolic message for music, musicians, and/or music educators.

MODULE 32 REFERENCES

Bozik, M. (2002). The college student as learner: Insight gained through metaphor analysis. *College Student Journal, 36*(1), 142–151.

Noe, L. R. (2007). What's it like? Making meaning with metaphors. *Young Children, 62*(4), 30–31.

Way, E. C. (1994). *Knowledge representation and metaphor.* Oxford, UK: Intellect Books.

Speech Comprehension and Projection—Warming Up on Pure Vowels—Cueing on Beat Two in 2/4—Traits of an Effective Teacher

In this module, you will focus on:

- Personal awareness: Speech comprehension, projection, and dynamics.
- Personal musicianship: A warm-up for pure vowels.
- Pre-conducting: Conducting a cue on the second beat in a 2/4 pattern.
- Professional knowledge: Exploring the personal and professional traits that form an effective teacher.

PERSONAL AWARENESS: VOCAL EXERCISES I— SPEECH COMPREHENSION—PROJECTION AND DYNAMICS

Excellent vocal presentation and speech comprehension skills are indispensable. Here and in the next five modules, you are going to explore some of the basic elements of effective vocal presentation. In module 38, you will combine those fundamentals into a culminating exercise: a two-minute presentation or speech. Each skill or combination of analogous elements will be divided into units to allow for separate practice, but keep in mind that effective vocal presentation involves the use of all components simultaneously. The skills to be explored are:

1. Projection and dynamics.
2. Enunciation and articulation.
3. Pauses.
4. Rate of speech.
5. Vocal emotion.
6. Vocal inflection (accent and pitch).

The first set of skills to be explored is projection and dynamics. Effective vocal projection is essential if you want to be heard. Equally important is effective use of dynamics; it is one of the many fundamentals used to keep individuals interested in what you are saying. For example, one way to get the attention of the audience is to suddenly speak very quietly.

In order to use dynamics efficiently, project effectively, and prevent vocal fatigue, you need to ensure that your throat muscles are relaxed, you are breathing properly, and you are effectively using your breath to project. The exercises in this component, along with those in the personal musicianship component, will help you develop your vocal projection techniques.

Classroom Setup

For these exercises, the classroom setup should facilitate individual investigation.

Exercises
Exercise 1: Breathing

1. Stand using an elevated posture, making sure your shoulders are relaxed. Let your stomach muscles relax.
2. Place one hand on your stomach and one hand on your side. Take a few deep breaths through your nose, exhaling through your mouth. Feel your stomach moving during the process.
3. Breathe in through your nose, and exhale through your mouth while making a hard, quick "huh" sound. You should feel your stomach muscles contract. Repeat several times.

4. Next, take a deep breath through your nose, and keep your mouth closed. When you exhale, use your out breath to make your lips vibrate (lip fluttering) without vocalizing. (Do not exhale through your nose.)
5. Repeat the lip-fluttering exercise several times, and note how your facial muscles have begun to relax.
6. Now practice saying "Hello, my name is _____," and notice that your voice is stronger, has more clarity, and has better projection when you breathe abdominally.

Exercise 2: Throat-Muscle Relaxation

Relaxing your throat muscles is important to prevent vocal injury and reduce vocal fatigue.

1. While standing, place your hand lightly on your throat muscles, and speak in a normal tone. Note any tenseness in your throat muscles or your jaw.
2. Yawn while opening your mouth widely. (It is important not to overextend the jaw, so open only as widely as is comfortable.) Repeat the yawn, and as you finish, vocalize "hummmm." Hold the "mmm" for several seconds while dropping your jaw as far as possible without stress.
3. Yawn again, and as you finish, move your jaw from side to side while continuing to hum. Maintain a relaxed jaw.
4. Repeat the yawning and humming three more times.
5. You should notice that your throat muscles have loosened and are more relaxed than when you started the exercises.

Exercise 3: Resonance

You may have become aware of resonators in your head while performing the previous exercises. As your vocal cords produce sound, the sound resonates through your chest, throat, and head as it exits your mouth.

1. Hold your nose, and repeat the following phrase as forcefully as possible: "Many mighty men making much money in the moonlight."
2. Let go of your nose, and say the phrase again. You should notice a difference in the projection of your voice.
3. Another way to improve vocal resonance is to hum.

a. Choose a comfortable pitch, and hum, keeping your tongue relaxed.
b. Now, lower the pitch slightly, and hum again. Note how your chest feels. Continue to hum until you feel the resonance in your chest. If needed, lower the pitch to achieve this feeling.
c. Hum at your original comfortable pitch level, once again keeping your tongue relaxed. Now, raise the pitch, and note how your head feels. Open your jaws slightly while keeping your lips closed. Hum until you feel a slight vibration in your tongue and lips and behind and above your mouth.
d. Continue to hum, and attempt to increase the vibrations.
e. Repeat this part of the exercise.
f. Breathe frequently, and stop if you become lightheaded.
4. Another humming exercise to promote resonation:
a. With your lips closed, begin to hum.
b. As you hum, make chewing movements, as if eating.
c. While gently moving your hands to your nose and cheeks and then to your neck and throat, feel the vibrations resulting from the humming.

Exercise 4: Volume

1. Breathe deeply through your nose, and during exhalation through the mouth, produce a hissing sound. Practice this three times.
2. Now, produce the sound "mmm-mmmm" during your exhale, and vary your voice's volume. Begin at a *piano* (*p*) level, and crescendo to a *forte* (*f*) level. Repeat, beginning *f* and going to *p*. Repeat again, going from *p* to *f* and back to *p*.
3. Repeat the exercise using the vowel "ah."
4. Now, try the exercise using numbers (see figure 33.1). Your volume level should increase as the number size increases.

1 2 3 4 5 6 7 8 9

9 8 7 6 5 4 3 2 1

1 2 3 4 5 6 7 8 9 10

1 2 3 4 5 6 7 8 9 10

1 2 3 4 5 6 7 8 9

Figure 33.1 Number pattern for volume exercise.

Assignment

Practice the various exercises in this component to improve your vocal projection.

Observation

Listen to various individuals in rehearsal and classroom situations. Are they easily heard? Are they using vocal dynamics effectively?

PERSONAL MUSICIANSHIP: A WARM-UP FOR PURE VOWELS

For this component, the focus is to:

- Review the definition of pure vowels.
- Perform a warm-up that uses pure vowels.
- Sing a melody with limited pitches (m,-l,-t,-d-r-m-f-s-l) in stick notation.
- Perform chordal accompaniments to a melody using solfège syllables.

In module 32, you learned the difference between pure vowels and diphthongs. Turn to a partner, and explain the difference and provide an example for each.

As a class or in small groups, perform the warm-up in figure 33.2. Sequence through all the pure vowels, stressing the accuracy of each during singing. Strive for a resonant tone. Listen to the singers in your group, and identify which vowels are more difficult to sing with a unified sound.

Figure 33.2 Warm-up for pure vowels.

Sing the melody in figure 33.3, and add chordal accompaniment that includes appropriate voice leading. (This will require at least four people to perform all parts, three singing triads and one singing the melody.) As you enunciate your vowels within the designated solfège syllables, think about forming pure vowels.

Folk Song from Spain
(Basque)

Figure 33.3 "Aldapeko (Blackbird's Song)," stick notation.

PRE-CONDUCTING: CUEING ON THE SECOND BEAT WHILE CONDUCTING THE 2/4 PATTERN

In these exercises, you will explore a left-hand cue on the second beat in 2/4 meter. You will be using both right and left hands/arms. You should carefully monitor the movements suggested.

Classroom Setup

All class members can complete any of these activities simultaneously. Initially, students should stand and allow about one arm's length of space around them. An instructor should initiate each activity. Once individuals become more proficient in completing the elements in this activity, they should form small groups of three or four individuals and conduct the cue gesture for others.

Exercises
Exercise 1

1. Establish your conducting posture and a tempo of mm = 69.
   a. As a warm-up, complete rebounds with your right hand (do not conduct the 2/4 pattern at this time). If desired, you can say the phrase "up, cue." "Up" is said on the downbeat, "cue" on the second beat.
   b. Practice the cueing motion with the left hand/arm on the second beat while completing rebounds (not the 2/4 conducting pattern yet) with the right hand/arm. After each cueing motion the left hand should return to your body. This will require you to add one measure of rebounds without any left-hand cuing action.
   c. Once you feel confident completing this motion, rest, and continue to the next exercise.

Exercise 2

1. Reestablish your conducting position and a tempo of mm = 69.
   a. Practice the 2/4 conducting pattern. Once you feel confident with this motion, add the left-hand/arm cue on the second beat.
   b. Remember to add a measure of conducting the 2/4 pattern without any left-hand motion between cues.
2. Once you feel comfortable completing this motion, rest before continuing to the next exercise.

Exercise 3

1. Reestablish your conducting position and a tempo of mm = 69.
2. Conduct the 2/4 pattern, and add the left hand/arm cue, first with your left hand in front of your face, then to the left of your left thigh, next to the right of your right thigh, and finally again in front of your face, and so on.
3. Continue practicing this motion until you feel comfortable.

Assignment

As you begin to feel more at ease with the cue gesture for the upbeat, or second beat, in 2/4 meter, you can practice this exercise with varying tempi. Should you want to further challenge yourself, using the parameters provided in this exercise, try moving your left hand/arm to other positions. For example, (a) face, (b) left of left thigh, (c) extreme left, (d) right of right thigh, and then (e) extreme right, and so on.

Observation

Notice the cue gestures used by your directors and conductors.

PROFESSIONAL KNOWLEDGE: EFFECTIVE TEACHING I

For this component, the focus is to:

- Begin exploring the personal and professional traits that form an effective teacher.

"While parents possess the original key to their offspring's experience, teachers have a spare key. They, too, can open or close the minds and hearts of children"(Ginott, 1975, p. 7). A parent serves as a child's first teacher. When children enter the school system, at the average age of five, they soon find themselves spending a majority of their waking hours surrounded by teachers and adults other than their parents. Think about the statement "Parents send us their very best children." It's not as if they have the "second-string players" at home and are only sending their "first-string players" to school. Parents are sending their best children and are expecting teachers to recognize their children as wonderful, unique, important, and valuable. Parents are placing their children's care and education in your hands. Are you up to the job? Will you be an effective teacher?

We have all had average, good, and great teachers throughout our education. What makes a great teacher? What makes an effective teacher? *Effective* is defined as "successful in producing a desired or intended result" (*New Oxford American Dictionary*). The desired result for music educators is to encourage lifelong learning and participation in music. Timpson and Burgoyne (2002) isolated the qualities of energy, creativity, and spontaneity as the most important personal traits. Katz (1993) noted that effectiveness as a teacher stems from a combination of knowledge, skills, and personal characteristics; therefore, it is important to take the time to identify and reflect on the personal and professional traits needed to be an effective teacher.

Small-Group Activity

Divide the class into small groups of two or three students to answer these questions:

1. Approximately how many teachers have you had since birth?
2. Were they all "good" teachers? Why or why not?
3. What traits determine a "good" teacher? (To answer this question, divide your responses into two categories: personal traits and professional traits.)

4. Do you think the same traits would work for each teacher? Why or why not?
5. If time allows, share your responses with another group.

Assignment

In your next class session, give an oral presentation to the class on the topic of effective teaching. Read a recent article from a music journal that discusses effective teaching. Summarize the article in writing. Include your reason for choosing the article, what you learned by reading it, points you agreed or disagreed with and why, and so on. Be prepared to turn in your written paper and to make a brief verbal presentation of your article in class. (Do not read from your paper.)

MODULE 33 REFERENCES

Ginott, H.G., (1975), Teacher and child: A book for parents and teachers, New York, NY: Macmillan.

Katz, L. G. (1993). *Dispositions: Definitions and implications for early childhood practices.* Champaign-Urbana, IL: ERIC Clearinghouse on Elementary and Early Childhood Education.

Timpson, W. M., & Burgoyne, S. (2002). *Teaching and performance: Ideas for energizing your classes.* Madison, WI: Atwood.

Speech Comprehension—Mental Imagery—Indicating Crescendos and Diminuendos in 4/4—Examining Effective Teacher Traits

I n this module, you will focus on:

- Personal awareness: Speech comprehension, enunciation, and articulation.
- Personal musicianship: Using mental imagery during singing.
- Pre-conducting: Indicating crescendos and diminuendos while conducting the 4/4 pattern.
- Professional knowledge: Continuing to examine the personal and professional traits of an effective teacher.

PERSONAL AWARENESS: VOCAL EXERCISES II— SPEECH COMPREHENSION—ENUNCIATION AND ARTICULATION

In module 33, you explored and enhanced your projection capabilities and awareness of the use of dynamics when speaking. Two other projection components are enunciation and articulation. They are similar and relate to the art of speaking clearly and distinctly. Words become slurred without clear enunciation or proper pronunciation of each syllable. Your listener will have a difficult time hearing and understanding you. The better your enunciation and articulation, the easier you'll be heard and better understood.

Dropping g's is one of the most common examples of poor enunciation. Say the following words aloud: "going," "walking," "jogging," "thinking," "striking," and "selling." If you said "go-in'," "walk-in'," "jog-gin'," and so on, you're a g dropper.

Pronouncing words in isolation is very different from normal speaking. Say these sentences aloud:

> "I'm going to have to rethink that thought."
> "Waiting to hear back from the principal is very nerve-wracking and stressful."
> "Before starting my career, I looked at a lot of different career opportunities."
> "There's more to learning than just reading, writing, and arithmetic."

Did you enunciate each syllable of each word? The exercise in this component will help you become more aware of your enunciation and articulation.

Before beginning the following exercise, there are a few things to keep in mind when enhancing your articulation and enunciation:

1. *Open your mouth.* In order to enunciate properly, you need to open your mouth. One way to practice this is to read aloud with vocal variety, adding color and liveliness to your voice as you do so, pronouncing each vowel and consonant distinctly, as if you were reading a book to a child.
2. *Posture.* Ensuring that you have an elevated posture when speaking is important for breathing. Proper posture supports proper airflow from your lungs, past your vocal cords, and out through your mouth. Also important is the direction your body and head face. When you are speaking, look up and at your audience. If you use notes, do not speak when checking your notes; wait until you look up before speaking.
3. *Focus your voice.* When you are speaking, focus on a point that is farther away, rather than closer to you. When you practice speaking, begin with something close to you (e.g., a person or a chair). Gradually begin to focus on a person or chair farther and farther away, while ensuring that you are projecting and focused. As you do so, remember to open your mouth and maintain your posture. You will notice your articulation and enunciation will improve when you are focusing, opening your mouth, and maintaining an elevated posture.
4. *Warm up before speaking.* To warm up properly, use the exercises in the personal awareness component of module 33.

Classroom Setup

For this exercise, the classroom setup should facilitate individual investigation.

Exercise: Enunciation and Articulation

1. Repeat the following, making sure you are opening your mouth widely and closing your mouth with ease:
   fah, fah, fah, fah, blah, blah, blah, blah
2. Say the following, making sure your jaw is loose:
   she, sah, kah,
   she, fah, rah, pah, kah,
   she, fah, rah, wah, kah,
   she, fah, rah, bah, kah
   she, fah, rah, dah, kah
   she, fah, rah
Repeat this until you feel your jaw become increasingly freer.
3. Focus on your lips, making them as active as possible while repeating the following:
   wah wah wah, bah bah bah, wah wah wah, bah bah bah,
   wah bah wah, wah bah wah, wah bah wah
4. Now, again focusing on the mouth, jaw, and lips, note movement in your cheeks as you repeat the following letters:
   lll, ldl, www, ldl, wlwd, bdld, dwlb
5. To focus, add awareness of your tongue placement, especially the tip of your tongue, as you repeat the following:
   Lah lee loo lee.
   The tip of the tongue, the teeth, and the lips.
   Tea Time Tiny Tim.
   We'll weather the weather, whatever the weather, whether we like
      it or not.
6. Once you have practiced the exercise above, practice tongue-twisters. Make sure to enunciate and articulate clearly while slowly saying each tongue-twister. You can either make up a tongue-twister for different letters of the alphabet, such as the following, or go to a website such as http://plays.about.com/od/actvities/a/enunciation.htm for such material:
   A. Around arid areas arachnids arrive in an array of activity.
   B. Big black bugs bit big black beans and beamed broadly.
   C. Connie cooked a cup of coffee correctly in a copper cup.

D. Deviant dogs dove deeply dictating devotion to divergent dimensions.
R. Racy Robert reeled recklessly revoking rational reasoning while raising ridiculous reservations.
S. Suzy sauntered seemingly slowly sensing shallow seashells sinking in sand.
T. Tom Tunes treaded tenuously toward the towering temple.

Assignment

Practice the various exercises above, and see if your vocal enunciation and articulation improve.

Observation

Listen to various individuals in rehearsal and classroom situations. Are they easily understood? Are they using effective enunciation and articulation?

PERSONAL MUSICIANSHIP: MENTAL IMAGERY AND SINGING

For this component, the focus is to:

- Discuss using mental imagery during singing.
- Sing a melody with limited pitches (m,-l,-t,-d-r-m-f-s-l) in standard notation.
- Perform chordal accompaniments to a melody using Roman numerals and solfège syllables.

We will focus here on creating a mental image of your singing. How do you want your singing to sound? How can you explain this to others? What type of singing style do you prefer? Why? When do you feel the most expressive during singing?

Imagery is language that causes people to create a visual image in their minds. Why do you think imagery can be effective when discussing singing and during singing? With a partner, take turns singing the imagery warm-up in figure 34.1. Alternate between who provides the statement and who sings the response. Depending on which statement your partner selects, you can choose to sing "Oh, no" or "Oh, yes."

Oh,   no.
Oh,   yes.

You wanted to go to the dance, but you have a flat tire.

Your sports team won the championship.

You woke up with the flu.

You have to attend a funeral for a closer friend.

You won a free trip to Disneyland.

Figure 34.1 Imagery warm-up.

Did you sing the responses the same each time? Likely, you did not. Did you sing the "Oh, yes" response always the same way? What about the "Oh, no" response? If you answered no to some or all of those questions, now the goal is to determine *why* you sang differently. How did you physically change your sound, your tone color, your dynamics, and so on. As you become more aware of how you can change your voice and create mental images of how you want your voice to sound, you've started down the path toward expressive singing.

Sing the melody in figure 34.2, and add chordal accompaniment that includes appropriate voice leading. (This will require at least four people to perform all parts, three singing triads and one singing the melody.) As you sing, create different mental images to make your singing more expressive.

Figure 34.2 "Aldapeko (Blackbird's Song)," standard notation.

PRE-CONDUCTING: INDICATING CRESCENDOS AND DIMINUENDOS WHILE CONDUCTING THE 4/4 PATTERN

In the pre-conducting component of module 7, a pre-conducting left-hand motion for dynamic contrasts was introduced. Here we will begin to combine dynamic-contrast movements with conducting patterns, specifically with the 4/4 pattern. You should carefully monitor the movements suggested through self-observation and feedback from other individuals.

Classroom Setup

All class members can complete any of these exercises simultaneously. Students should stand and allow about one arm's length of space around them. An instructor should initiate each exercise and each step so the class practices as a unit.

Exercises
Exercise 1

1. Establish your conducting posture and a tempo of mm = 69.
2. Begin conducting the 4/4 pattern. Perform the pre-conducting dynamic-contrast motion with the left hand.
3. As a review of the dynamic-contrasts exercise presented in module 7, the left hand/arm begins its motion starting on the right shoulder.
   a. Place your left hand/arm on your right shoulder, with the palm on the shoulder joint. The hand/arm stays at shoulder height throughout this exercise; however, you move your left hand/arm across and away from your body during the movement.
   b. The beginning and ending left-hand/arm position is at the right shoulder.
   c. Move your left hand/arm away from your right shoulder and to your left. The palm of your hand should be facing toward you.
   d. Halfway through this movement, your left hand/arm is slightly below and in front of your chin, and your arm is extended about halfway.
   e. At the end of the movement, your left hand/arm is directly in front of your left shoulder as you extend across your body, and the arm is also extended but has a very slight bend at the elbow. When you are at this point, turn your hand so that the palm faces away from you.

   f. Thus far, the left-arm movement would generally be perceived as a motion requesting an increase in dynamic level (a crescendo) until the palm turns away from the body.

   g. The left-arm return movement follows the same path, and your left hand resumes its position on the right shoulder joint. The palm faces away from you until it reaches the right shoulder, at which point it is again turned, and the palm is placed on the right shoulder.

   h. The return portion of the movement would generally be perceived as a motion requesting a decrease in dynamic level (a diminuendo).

4. Conducting a 4/4 pattern, use two beats at mm = 69 to attain your left-hand/arm position in front of the left shoulder (a crescendo indication) and two beats to return to the right shoulder (a diminuendo indication). The left-hand/arm movements should be fluid and graceful and the right-hand/arm rebound appropriately completed. Remember to keep your left-hand/arm movement at shoulder height throughout the exercise.

5. This will be referred to as crescendo and diminuendo pattern A in future exercises.

Exercise 2

1. Reestablish your conducting posture and a tempo of mm = 69.
2. Begin conducting the 4/4 pattern.
3. For this exercise, the beginning location of the left hand/arm is slightly above the waist and somewhat in line with your left hip. The palm of the left hand faces down/toward the floor. The movement of your left hand/arm is as follows.

   a. The left hand/arm (palm up) moves in a circular motion such that the left hand/arm will extend forward and up to the height of the left shoulder (a crescendo indication) and then return to the beginning position. The palm of the left hand begins facing the floor (a diminuendo indication).

   b. The resultant arc or circle formed should be completed so it is flowing, graceful, and without pause.

2. Conduct the 4/4 pattern, then practice these crescendo and diminuendo indications. Use two beats, at mm = 69, to attain your left-shoulder position height and two beats to return to the conducting position.

3. This will be referred to as crescendo and diminuendo pattern B in future exercises.

Exercise 3

1. Once you have successfully completed exercises 1 and 2, combine the left-hand movements while conducting the 4/4 pattern with the right hand.
   a. Begin with the left hand/arm on the right shoulder, extending for two beats until the left hand/arm is in front of the left shoulder. The palm of your hand will be facing you (a crescendo indication).
   b. Now, instead of returning to the right shoulder, move your hand down to your left hip. The palm of your hand will now be facing away from you (a diminuendo indication).
   c. Reverse these motions, beginning with your left hand at hip level, moving to left shoulder height, and returning to the right shoulder position.
3. Practice these combinations several times until you feel comfortable. Whether these exact motions are used in future conducting classes is not important. The process of developing the independence needed to perform these and future motions is the main purpose.
4. This will be referred to as crescendo and diminuendo pattern C in future exercises.
5. Perform all these exercises individually and in small groups.

Assignment

Try these exercises using different tempi and varying the number of beats used to attain the crescendo and diminuendo positions while conducting the 4/4 pattern.

Observation

Notice the movements your directors and conductors use when indicating crescendos or diminuendos.

PROFESSIONAL KNOWLEDGE: EFFECTIVE TEACHING II

For this component, the focus is to:

- Continue examining the personal and professional traits of an effective teacher.

In this continuation of the professional knowledge component of module 33, you will give your oral presentation to the class on the topic of effective teaching. (See the criteria in module 33.)

Pauses in Speech—Vocal Health—Indicating Crescendos and Diminuendos in 3/4—Importance of Personal Resilience

I n this module, you will focus on:

- Personal awareness: The use of pauses in speech.
- Personal musicianship: The importance of warm-ups and periodic breaks for vocal health.
- Pre-conducting: Indicating crescendos and diminuendos while conducting the 3/4 pattern.
- Professional knowledge: Examining the personal and professional traits of an effective teacher with an emphasis on the importance of personal resilience.

PERSONAL AWARENESS: VOCAL EXERCISES III—SPEECH COMPREHENSION—PAUSES

You've explored vocal projection, dynamics, articulation, and enunciation. Now you will investigate the use of pauses in speech. Many individuals speak too quickly for optimal audience comprehension. Additionally, some speakers fly over important materials without informing the listener that such materials are important.

One tool for enhancing audience comprehension is the use of pauses or emphases through phrasing. A pause can range from a slight hesitation to a longer break and/or silence between words and phrases. Oral speech is composed of phrases and sentences, which provide listeners with clarity and understanding. Failure to pause for commas, hyphens, question marks, or even periods causes words and phrases to blur together. Pauses facilitate listeners' fact assimilation and alert them to important materials, allowing ample time to register and record information.

Before you begin the exercises, make sure to warm up, maintain an elevated posture to ensure proper breathing, focus your voice, open your mouth, and articulate and enunciate.

Classroom Setup

For these exercises, the classroom setup should facilitate individual investigation and small-group work.

Exercises: Pauses
Exercise 1

Your goal is to monitor your speaking fluency and intelligibility by inserting pauses to enhance listeners' understanding and comprehension.

Practice the four versions of the phrase "Stop Don't Go." Insert a pause when you see an asterisk (*). Once you have practiced the four versions of the phrase as presented, experiment with changing the duration of each pause, make some longer or shorter than others. Notice how the command changes as you change the pause location and duration. After you have practiced this example individually, form small groups of three or four and practice for one another.

> Version 1.
>   Stop Don't Go
> Version 2.
>   Stop * Don't Go
> Version 3.
>   Stop Don't * Go
> Version 4.
>   Stop * Don't * Go

Try the following phrases, varying the location and duration of the pauses.

Version 1.
   Brass and Woodwinds *
   Find Letter B *
   And Count Forward *
   Six Measures *
Version 2.
   Brass * and Woodwinds *
   Find Letter * B *
   And * Count Forward *
   Six * Measures
Version 3.
   Brass * and * Woodwinds *
   Find * Letter B *
   And Count * Forward *
   Six Measures

Notice how each version creates a different emphasis. You may wish to create your own version of this musical directive or create a new one. After you have practiced this example individually, form small groups of three or four and practice for one another.

Exercise 2

In this exercise, you will focus on listener comprehension. You will be in small groups of three or four. Listeners comprehend what you are saying and give feedback about the appropriateness of the presentation.

The task is to tell your group how to do something in five steps (e.g., how to change a string on the violin, how to change a pad on a woodwind, how to make a sandwich, how to brush your teeth, how to tie your shoes, etc.). Members of the group jot down the five steps on a piece of paper. When the presenter finishes, the listeners repeat the five steps described. Did the listeners comprehend all five steps? If not, why? Did anyone have different steps from those presented? If so, why? Did the presenter speak too quickly, not incorporate enough pauses, not wait long enough between pauses, and so on?

Exercise 3

Oral reading is a good way to practice using pauses when speaking. You may have noticed that individuals such as politicians use pauses for emphasis and comprehension.

Abraham Lincoln gave the Gettysburg Address in the open, on a hill-side. Clarity and careful attention to the rate of speech and pauses were paramount. In your small groups, have each person read the opening lines of the Gettysburg Address as if he or she were Lincoln standing on a hill. The asterisks (*) indicate appropriate places for pauses. Practice using these pauses, and as time allows, insert additional pauses as deemed appropriate. Try varying the length of the pauses.

Four score *
and seven years ago*
our fathers *
brought forth * upon this continent*
a new nation,*
conceived * in liberty, *
and dedicated * to the proposition *
that * all * men *
are created equal.

Should you like to recite the complete Gettysburg Address, the so-called Bliss Copy, one of several versions written by Lincoln but believed to be the final rendition, is found in Basler (2013).

Assignment

Practice the various exercises above, and see how your vocal presentations change.

Observation

Listen to various individuals in rehearsal and classroom situations. Are they easily understood? Are they using effective pauses?

PERSONAL MUSICIANSHIP: VOCAL HEALTH

For this component, the focus is to:

- Discuss the importance of warm-ups and periodic breaks for vocal health.
- Sing a melody with limited pitches (d-r-m-f-s-l-t-d') in stick notation.
- Perform accompaniments to a melody using solfège syllables.

Your lesson plan is ready, but is your voice? As a musician, you will be using your voice constantly in rehearsals and classrooms. You will use your voice for singing, modeling, lecturing, and talking. Earlier, you learned about the importance of hydration. The focus here is to recognize the need for warming up the voice, avoiding muscle discomfort, and taking breaks during rehearsals and individual practice sessions.

Athletes have systematic ways of warming up their muscles and bodies. Singers should also engage in systematic warm-ups that are gentle and focused. Similarly, athletes recognize the importance of breaks during practice and for constant hydration during a workout. Singers also should take periodic breaks during singing practice and remember the importance of hydrating. Athletes recognize the need to stop an activity that is causing pain. If your voice or throat feels uncomfortable during singing, don't continue. Avoid long durations of loud singing and yelling, which will irritate and can even permanently damage vocal cords. Your voice is part of your teacher persona and a crucial communication tool; maintaining its health is of utmost importance.

Sing the melody in figure 35.1, and add chordal accompaniment that includes appropriate voice leading. (This will require at least four people to perform all parts, three singing triads and one singing the melody.)

Folk Song from Switzerland

Figure 35.1 "Das Langwieser Lied," stick notation.

PRE-CONDUCTING: INDICATING CRESCENDOS AND DIMINUENDOS WHILE CONDUCTING THE 3/4 PATTERN

In this component, we will combine dynamic-contrast movements, the crescendo and the diminuendo, here with the 3/4 pattern. You should carefully monitor the movements suggested through self-observation and feedback from other individuals.

Classroom Setup

All class members can complete any of these exercises simultaneously. Students should stand and allow about one arm's length of space around them. An instructor should initiate each exercise and each step so the class practices as a unit.

Exercises
Exercise 1

1. Establish your conducting posture and a tempo of mm = 69.
2. Begin conducting the 3/4 pattern. Perform the crescendo and diminuendo pattern A with your left hand. (To review the crescendo and diminuendo patterns A, B, and C, see module 34.)
3. Use three beats at mm = 69 to move your left hand/arm out and to the front of the left shoulder and three beats to return to the right shoulder. The left-hand/arm movements should be fluid and graceful and the right-hand/arm rebound appropriately completed. Remember to keep your left-hand/arm movement at shoulder height throughout the exercise.

Exercise 2

1. Reestablish your conducting posture and a tempo of mm = 69.
2. Begin conducting the 3/4 pattern. Perform the crescendo and diminuendo pattern B.
3. When performing this exercise, make sure both hands are relaxed. You will note that your hands/fingers will be slightly curved and the fingers slightly spread when in a relaxed position.

Exercise 3

1. Reestablish your conducting posture and a tempo of mm = 69.
2. Begin conducting the 3/4 pattern. Perform the crescendo and diminuendo pattern C.
3. The idea of these exercises is to help develop the hand/arm independence needed for similar movements within conducting classes.
4. Perform all these exercises individually and in small groups.

Assignment

Try these exercises using different tempi and varying the number of beats
used to attain the crescendo and diminuendo positions while conducting
the 3/4 pattern.

Observation

Notice the movements your directors and conductors use when indicating crescendos or diminuendos.

PROFESSIONAL KNOWLEDGE:
EFFECTIVE TEACHING III

For this component, the focus is to:

• Continue examining the personal and professional traits of an effective teacher, with an emphasis on the importance of personal resilience.

Resilient is defined as "able to withstand or recover quickly from difficult conditions" (*New Oxford American Dictionary*). Effective teachers are resilient and able to overcome adversity. "If schools are to help create a happy present and sustainable future for children, their teachers should be confident, emotionally intelligent, flexible, healthy, optimistic, positive people" (Barnes, 2013, p. 74). How will you maintain optimism, stay emotionally healthy, and foster your own resilience in a career that is at times as problematic and demanding as it is enjoyable and fulfilling?

There are numerous books and articles on how to foster resilience in children, but that isn't the case regarding fostering reliance in teachers. How do we strengthen the human spirit of teachers? What is needed in the teacher's tool kit to promote resilience?

The term *resilience* is often used in mental-health fields. Resilient individuals are able to bounce back from adversity and are also more likely to be able to manage emotions, communicate effectively, solve problems, accept responsibility, set goals, and sustain personal needs. It is important for you to acknowledge and sustain your own needs. That may sound unusual in a career that expects that students' needs are always placed before teachers' needs, yet when teachers are happy, healthy, and personally fulfilled, they are more likely to be more effective in the classroom and able to promote resilience in others.

Andrew Fuller, an Australian psychologist, explains resilience using the analogy of bungee jumping:

> Resilience is the happy knack of being able to bungy jump through the pitfalls of life. It is the ability to rebound or spring back after adversity or hard times. It is as if the person has an elasticised rope around their middle so that when they meet pitfalls in their lives they are able to bounce back out of them. (Fuller, 2001, p. 2).

Resilient people have a sense of connectedness to and empathy with others. So it makes sense that effective teachers are resilient, as they are the ones who demonstrate the capacity to connect with personal and professional communities, to empathize with others within their personal and professional communities, and to promote resilience in others.

By surviving passages of doubt and depression on the vocational journey, I have become clear about one thing: self-care is never a selfish act—it is simply good stewardship of the only gift I have, the gift I was put on the earth to offer to others. Anytime we can listen to true self and give it the care it requires, we do so not only for ourselves but for the many others whose lives we touch. (Palmer, 2000, pp. 30–31)

Care for yourself. Engage in activities that bring you fulfillment. Be a good steward of yourself.

Discussion

1. What activities do you engage in to relax?
2. When do you feel the most fulfilled?
3. What are some coping mechanisms you use, or have seen used by others, to release stress or to cope during adversity?

MODULE 35 REFERENCES

Barnes, J. M. (2013). What sustains a fulfilling life in education? *Journal of Education and Training Studies, 1*(2), 74–88.

Basler, R. P. (Ed.). (2013). *Collected works of Abraham Lincoln.* http://quod.lib.umich.edu/l/lincoln/

Fuller, A. (2001). A blueprint for the development of social competencies in schools. http://www.dhs.vic.gov.au/__data/assets/pdf_file/0008/589886/andrew-fuller-blueprint-for-developing-scoial-competencies.pdf

Palmer, P. J. (2000). *Let your life speak: Listening for the voice of vocation.* San Francisco, CA: Jossey-Bass.

Varying Speaking Tempi—Body Warm-Up Sequence—Indicating Crescendos and Diminuendos in 2/4—Legal Issues in the Classroom

In this module, you will focus on:

- Personal awareness: Varying speaking tempi.
- Personal musicianship: The importance of creating a consistent body warm-up sequence.
- Pre-conducting: Indicating crescendos and diminuendos while conducting the 2/4 pattern.
- Professional knowledge: An introduction to the legal issues affecting students and teachers.

PERSONAL AWARENESS: VOCAL EXERCISES IV—SPEECH COMPREHENSION—RATE OF SPEECH

You've explored vocal projection and dynamics, articulation and enunciation, and the use of pauses. You will now experiment with the fourth element of speech comprehension: rate of speech.

You've most likely had the experience of listening to an instructor who speaks too slowly or too quickly. Using the wrong rate of speech or a continuous rate of speech without variation results in inattentive and/or strained listeners who become easily bored and tired.

Different rates of speaking project different characteristics. Your emotional state can affect your rate of speech. When you are excited, joyful, or happy, you most likely will speak faster than your normal rate; similarly, when you are sad or reflective, you will tend to talk more slowly. When you speak slowly, you project an image of calmness, formality, or acceptance; however, if you speak too slowly, you project an image of dullness, listlessness, apathy, laziness, or even lack of intelligence. Speaking quickly projects a sense of animation, enthusiasm, excitement, and informality, while speaking too quickly projects nervousness, tension, anxiety, or even a flighty personality.

When a varied rate of speech is used, your presentations will be more interesting and thought-provoking. When you have an important phrase or a series of significant commands, you will want to slow your rate of speech, providing emphasis and weight to those words and phrases.

You will be using exercises to help enhance your awareness of your rate of speech by controlling the speed at which you speak. Before beginning the exercises, make sure to warm up, maintain an elevated posture to ensure proper breathing, focus your voice, open your mouth, and articulate and enunciate.

Classroom Setup

For this exercise, the classroom setup should facilitate individual investigation.

Exercise

You will once again be reading the opening lines from the Gettysburg Address. You will be practicing speaking at a markedly slower rate than normal. Most individuals speak too quickly to be easily understood in a classroom setting; therefore, becoming aware of a speech rate slightly slower than your normal rate is the goal of this exercise.

Using a metronome marking of mm = 60, all class members should read the passage simultaneously, allowing one beat for speaking each syllable. For example, the words "our fathers" would be said in four beats: "ou-r-fa-thers." Stretch out both the vowel and the consonant sounds, blending each word together smoothly. Vowels and nasal and continuant consonants should be spoken as follows: the word "no," for example, would be said "nnnnoooo," and "yes" would be said "yyy-eeesss" For consonants such as *p, b, t, d, k,* and *g,* release the consonant, and extend the sound using a breathy pronunciation/aspiration following the release of the consonant. For example, the word "pet" would sound something like "phhheeet." Using the opening words of the Gettysburg Address, you would say "Fooouur scooooore aaaaannd seeeeev eeeeen," and so on. Use normal intonation and intensity during the recitation.

An instructor begins this exercise by establishing the beat for speaking each syllable (mm = 60) and then starting the group.

Note that a syllable division, where appropriate, is indicated by a slash mark (/).

Four score and sev/en years a/go
ou/r fa/thers brought forth up/on this con/ti/nenta new na/tion,
con/ceived in lib/er/ty, and ded/i/cat/ed to the prop/o/si/tion
that all men are cre/ated e/qual.

After you and your class members have mastered this very slow rate of speech, try the address at a moderately slow rate. The metronome marking should now be set at mm = 120. Each syllable will be spoken at a rate of approximately two syllables per second.

After successfully speaking the address at mm = 120, try for a slightly faster rate. Your goal is for a speech pattern that sounds natural but is slightly slower than your customary speaking rate. An appropriate target would be about three syllables per second or mm = 176–184.

You have most likely noticed that forcing yourself to speak each syllable using a metronome, simultaneously in a group, is rather artificial. Now, individually or in small groups, repeat the exercise using your natural speech rhythm. Do this at a slower-than-normal speaking rate. Vary your rate of speech for different phrases, ensuring that important words or phrases are spoken more slowly than others.

Assignment

Practice the various exercises above using a different script.

Observation

Listen to various individuals in rehearsal and classroom situations. Are they easily understood? Are they speaking too quickly or too slowly and/ or varying their speech rate?

PERSONAL MUSICIANSHIP: BODY WARM-UP SEQUENCE

For this component, the focus is to:

- Discuss the importance of creating a consistent body warm-up sequence.
- Sing a melody with limited pitches (d-r-m-f-s-l-t-d') in standard notation.
- Perform chordal accompaniments to a melody using Roman numerals and solfège syllables.

In previous modules, you practiced various vocal warm-ups. Here the focus will be on creating a consistent body warm-up sequence for starting your class. The main purpose of a sequence is to provide students with a specified set of events or activities that will lead to a desired outcome; in this case, the desired outcome is a relaxed body, ready for healthy vocal production.

The following five-step sequence should be used only as a basic foundation; you will undoubtedly find many ways to incorporate these basic steps into your own unique approach. The following movements are designed specifically to reduce stress in the large muscles of the body.

1. Shoulder roll: Incorporate both forward and backward rolls.
2. Shoulder scrunch: Squeeze your shoulders together, raising them toward your head. Squeeze for five seconds, and then release. Repeat for a minimum of three repetitions.
3. Abdominal stretch: Keeping feet and legs stationary, rotate your hips to allow your body to slowly turn from one side to the other. Rotate one direction, and hold, before rotating to the other side. It is important to not force the stretch; therefore, the first few rotations may not extend as far as later ones.
4. Rib-cage raise: Extend both arms upward as if trying to touch the ceiling. As you slowly let your arms lower to the sides of your body, concentrate on maintaining a raised rib cage.
5. Shoulder-blade touch: Gently squeeze your shoulder blades together as if you are trying to touch them together. Obviously, they can't touch, but the process promotes proper neck and head posture.

Sing the melody in figure 36.1, and add chordal accompaniment that includes appropriate voice leading. (This will require at least four people to perform all parts, three singing triads and one singing the melody.)

Concentrate on singing with a raised rib cage. If necessary, repeat the rib-cage raise exercise before singing.

Folk Song from Switzerland

Figure 36.1 "Das Langwieser Lied," standard notation.

PRE-CONDUCTING: INDICATING CRESCENDOS AND DIMINUENDOS WHILE CONDUCTING THE 2/4 PATTERN

In this component, we will continue to combine dynamic-contrast movements, the crescendo and the diminuendo, here with the 2/4 pattern. You carefully should monitor the movements suggested through self-observation and feedback from other individuals.

Classroom Setup

All class members can complete any of these exercises simultaneously. Students should stand and allow about one arm's length of space around them. An instructor should initiate each exercise and each step so the class practices as a unit.

Exercises
Exercise 1

1. Establish your conducting posture and a tempo of mm = 69.
2. Begin conducting the 2/4 pattern. Perform the crescendo and diminuendo pattern A with your left hand. (To review the crescendo and diminuendo patterns A, B, and C, see module 34.)
3. Use two beats to attain your left-hand/arm position in front of the left shoulder and two beats to return to the right shoulder. The left-hand/arm movements should be fluid and graceful. Remember to keep your left-hand/arm movement at shoulder height throughout the exercise.

Exercise 2

1. Reestablish your conducting posture and a tempo of mm = 69.
2. Begin conducting the 2/4 pattern. Perform the crescendo and diminuendo pattern B.
3. Use two beats to attain your left-shoulder position height and two beats to return to the conducting position.

Exercise 3

1. Reestablish your conducting posture and a tempo of mm = 69.
2. Begin conducting the 2/4 pattern. Perform the crescendo and diminuendo pattern C with your left hand.
3. Perform all these exercises individually and in small groups.

Assignment

Try these exercises using different tempi and varying the number of beats
used to attain the crescendo and diminuendo positions while conducting
the 2/4 pattern.

Observation

Notice the movements your directors and conductors use to indicate crescendos or diminuendos.

PROFESSIONAL KNOWLEDGE: LEGAL ISSUES I

For this component, the focus is to:

• Introduce the legal issues affecting students and teachers.

It's likely, at this point on your career path, that you haven't thought about the legal issues surrounding the education field. Yet legalities remain a constant part of a teacher's life, both in and out of the classroom. Students and teachers both have responsibilities and rights, but as you will see in figure 36.2, teachers have many more legal factors and issues that have an impact on their careers. "[B]ecause of the sensitive role you play as a nurturer of young people, as a teacher you are expected to reflect standards of personal behavior that are higher than those expected of average citizens" (Savage, Savage, & Armstrong, 2006, p. 395).

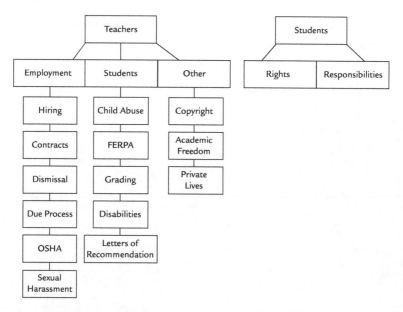

Figure 36.2 Selected legal issues affecting teachers and students.

Legal issues are complex and constantly changing. Just as in all other parts of your pathway to professional teaching, knowing your rights and responsibilities and those of your students will involve constant diligence and scrutiny. Don't find yourself traveling along a slippery slope in regard to a legal issue, as ignorance never serves as an effective defense. See figure 36.2 for selected legal issues affecting teachers and students.

Discussion

1. Choose at least five of the legal factors affecting students and teachers noted in figure 36.2.
2. For each factor, list items that you believe are addressed or must be followed under the law.
3. As time allows, list other factors you think could be added to the figure.

Assignment

1. Select one of the legal issues listed in figure 36.2 to examine or research.
2. Submit a typed document that includes the following:
   a. Summary of your findings.
   b. References.
   c. Two items that you believe are the most crucial for you and your classmates to know or understand.
   d. Two items for which you still have questions.
3. Prepare an oral presentation that includes the following:
   a. A brief overview of your findings.
   b. Identification of items you believe are most crucial.
   c. At least one item for which you still have questions or need further clarification.

MODULE 36 REFERENCE

Savage, T. V., Savage, M. K., & Armstrong, D. G. (2006). *Teaching in the secondary school.* Upper Saddle River, NJ: Pearson.

Vocal Emotion—Diaphragmatic Action—Cutoff Gesture in 4/4—Legal Issues II

I n this module, you will focus on:

- Personal awareness: Vocal emotion in speech.
- Personal musicianship: The importance of connecting diaphragmatic action with breath and sound.
- Pre-conducting: Performing a cutoff gesture while conducting the 4/4 pattern.
- Professional knowledge: More about the legal issues affecting students and teachers.

PERSONAL AWARENESS: VOCAL EXERCISES V— SPEECH COMPREHENSION—VOCAL EMOTION

Here you will explore a fifth basic component of speech comprehension: vocal emotion. Exploring emotional ranges of your voice can change the character of a classroom presentation and transform a seemingly uninteresting delivery into an exciting one.

Before beginning the exercises, make sure to warm up, maintain an elevated posture to ensure proper breathing, focus your voice, open your mouth, and articulate and enunciate.

Classroom Setup

You will be practicing these exercises in pairs. The classroom should be set up to facilitate this interaction.

Exercises
Exercise 1

Two statements are used for this exercise:

Yes, it is.
No, it isn't.

Each individual in each pair should choose to say "Yes, it is" or "No, it isn't." Each pair conveys the eight emotions, in the order listed below, by saying only either "Yes, it is" or "No, it isn't." Each individual makes his or her statement three times with one emotion, before continuing with another emotion. One individual begins by saying "Yes, it is," and the partner responds, "No, it isn't," with the selected emotional emphasis. The instructor tells the pairs when to begin the exercise using the first emotion, happiness. After each pair has made both statements three times, the instructor stops the group and announces the next emotion, which would be sadness. This procedure will be repeated until all emotions have been completed. As time permits, individuals can switch partners and repeat the exercise. The emotions, in order, are as follows:

1. Happiness
2. Sadness
3. Excitement
4. Fearfulness
5. Inquisitiveness
6. Surprise
7. Bashfulness
8. Anger

Exercise 2

Again in pairs, one individual reads a statement/question from the list below. The other individual responds by saying the same statement/question with a different emotion, as if answering or questioning the first person. Using the same statement/question, switch roles. One partner now says the statement/question, and the other responds with yet another different emotion from that of the first partner. Continue this procedure until all statements/questions have been explored. If time permits, switch partners and begin the exercise again.

> Over here
> I need that
> Let go
> What are you doing
> What are you talking about
> Don't do that
> Do you understand
> I don't think that's a good idea
> Give me the new one
> No
> Try it again
> Listen to me
> All right
> Stop right there
> Wow, that's huge

Review the various ways each statement/question can be spoken and the way you normally would say each one. The next time you say a statement/question, allow yourself the choice to speak it outside of your natural inclination. Eventually, you will see that this can yield very interesting results.

Assignment

Practice saying phrases and words with different emotional emphasis. Try to vary commonly spoken phrases and words.

Observation

Listen to various individuals in rehearsal and classroom situations. Do they vary their emotional range?

PERSONAL MUSICIANSHIP:
CONNECTING THE BREATH I

For this component, the focus is to:

- Discuss the importance of connecting diaphragmatic action with breath and sound.
- Sing a melody with limited pitches (s,-t,-d-r-m-f-s) in stick notation.
- Perform chordal accompaniments to a melody using solfège syllables.

Review and perform the body warm-up sequence from module 36. Now that you are relaxed and have released your body from stress and tension, let's focus on connecting diaphragmatic action with breath and sound.

The diaphragm is "a dome-shaped, muscular partition separating the thorax from the abdomen in mammals. It plays a major role in breathing, as its contraction increases the volume of the thorax and so inflates the lungs" (*New Oxford American Dictionary*).

Place one hand on your chest and the other hand on your stomach. Breathe in deeply through your nose (see the "Smell the Flowers" activity in module 21), and feel your stomach move. The stomach motion indicates that you are engaging the diaphragm. Now, place both hands on your stomach, and perform full-bodied chuckles, using "ho-ho-ho," the kind of chuckles associated with Santa Claus.

Sing the melody in figure 37.1, and add chordal accompaniment that includes appropriate voice leading. (This will require at least four people to perform all parts, three singing triads and one singing the melody.) Focus on coordinating your breath and sound.

Irish Folk Song

Figure 37.1 "Aéire Cinn Bó Rúin," stick notation.

PRE-CONDUCTING: PERFORMING CUTOFF GESTURE A WHILE CONDUCTING THE 4/4 PATTERN

This exercise is an extension of the one in module 8 where you developed cutoff indications in the left hand/arm using gesture A. Now you will conduct the 4/4 pattern while performing this cutoff. You should carefully monitor the movements suggested through self-observation and feedback from other individuals.

Classroom Setup

All class members can complete this exercise simultaneously. Students should stand and allow about one arm's length of space around them. An instructor should initiate each exercise and each step so the class practices as a unit.

Exercise

1. Establish your conducting posture and a tempo of mm = 52.
2. Perform a cutoff on the downbeat in the 4/4 pattern using cutoff gesture A. Conduct two measures of the 4/4 pattern, and on the fourth beat of the second measure, initiate the left-hand cutoff motion, and complete the cutoff on the downbeat.
3. Next, perform the cutoff on the second beat in the 4/4 pattern using cutoff gesture A. Conduct one measure of the 4/4 pattern, and on the downbeat of the second measure, initiate the left-hand cutoff motion, and complete the cutoff on the second beat.
4. Now, perform the cutoff on the third beat in the 4/4 pattern using cutoff gesture A. Conduct one measure of the 4/4 pattern, and on the second beat of the second measure, initiate the left-hand cut-off motion, and complete the cutoff on beat three.
5. Finally, perform the cutoff on the fourth beat in the 4/4 pattern using cutoff gesture A. Conduct one measure of the 4/4 pattern, and on the third beat of the second measure, initiate the left-hand cutoff motion, and complete the cutoff on beat four.

Assignment

Once you feel secure completing the cutoff on different beats in 4/4 meter at this tempo, try performing the cutoff at different tempi.

Observation

Notice the movements your directors and conductors use when indicating cutoffs.

PROFESSIONAL KNOWLEDGE: LEGAL ISSUES II

For this component, the focus is to:

- Continue examining the legal issues affecting students and teachers.

This is a continuation of the professional knowledge component of module 36. In this class session, you will give your oral presentation to the class on one legal issue affecting either teachers or students. (Criteria were provided in module 36.)

Vocal Inflection—Diaphragmatic Action—Cutoff Gesture in 4/4—Collegiality

I n this module, you will focus on:

- Personal awareness: Vocal inflection, accent, and pitch.
- Personal musicianship: Connecting diaphragmatic action with breath and sound.
- Pre-conducting: Performing a cutoff gesture while conducting the 4/4 pattern.
- Professional knowledge: The importance of collegiality within the profession.

PERSONAL AWARENESS: VOCAL EXERCISES VI— SPEECH COMPREHENSION—VOCAL INFLECTION (ACCENT AND PITCH)

Here you will focus on vocal inflection, accent, and pitch. Inflection is the way we change our vocal tone and emphasis within a sentence, and it incorporates accent and pitch. Inflection can dramatically change the meanings of the words you say and can increase your ability to effectively and dynamically communicate with others. Changes of accents or alterations of pitch may be subtle, but such changes have the power to change the meanings of words, phrases, and sentences and to capture your audience's attention.

Inflection, the process of varying your tone throughout a speech—whether raising your voice slightly to indicate a question or lowering it to end a declarative sentence—will help keep your audience alert. There are four kinds of inflection generally discussed:

1. *Level* inflection occurs when there is no change in pitch within the word. Level inflection most often conveys a sense of lack of interest or indecision.
2. *Upward* inflection involves a change in pitch from lower to higher, generally on a vowel, and indicates a question, insincerity, surprise, or even suspense.
3. *Downward* inflection, going from higher to lower pitch, indicates confidence, finality, power, and certainty.
4. *Double* or *circumflex* inflection occurs when there is either a rising and falling or a falling and rising in pitch within a word or vowel. Such pitch changes generally indicate that we haven't finished speaking, even though we may be taking a pause. Or they can indicate a contrast, such as saying, "It's not up, it's down" or "No, amazing."

Classroom Setup

You will be practicing these exercises in small groups of three or four. The classroom setup should facilitate this interaction.

Exercises
Exercise 1

In turns within each group, each individual says the following words, first with level inflection, then with upward inflection, and finally with downward infection.

Okay
Maybe
Fine

Identify and briefly discuss how the connotation of a word changes with inflection.

Next, each individual within each group says the following words, first with upward inflection and then with downward inflection.

No
Really
Done
Wow
Go

Again, briefly discuss how the connotation of a word changes with inflection.

Most people use rising and falling (double or circumflex) inflections fairly well but generally don't make them broad enough. Now, exaggerate the pitch change on the following words, say them in as many different ways as possible, and incorporate all types of inflection.

No! No!! No!!!
No? No?? No???
Why! Why!! Why!!!
Why? Why?? Why???

Again, briefly discuss how the connotation of a word changes with inflection.

Exercise 2

In turns within each group, each individual reads the following statements/questions, first as you naturally interpret it, then differently by changing the inflection on one or more of the words. End punctuation has been removed purposefully:

Over here
I need that
Let go
What are you doing
What are you talking about
Don't do that
Do you understand

I don't think that's a good idea
Please give me the new one
Try it again
Listen to me
Stop right there
Wow, that's huge
If not you, who
I guess someone did it

Changing inflection in a sentence affects the power of the statement. Lowering inflection at the end of a sentence conveys strength and believability, while incorporating upward inflections in the middle of a sentence can enhance audience interest.

In turns within each group, each individual reads the following phrases, changing inflection (upward, downward, or double/circumflex) on the word or words in italics. Again, end punctuation has been removed purposefully.

Bill isn't here right now
Bill isn't here right now
Bill *isn't* here right now
Bill isn't *here* right now
Bill isn't here *right* now
Bill isn't here right *now*
Bill isn't here *right* now
Bill *isn't here* right now
Bill *isn't here right now*
Bill isn't *here right* now
Bill isn't here right *now*

If time allows, experiment further with inflection using the statement "I didn't say I paid those bills" or one of your own.

Assignment

Practice the various exercises and/or create new words/phrases/statements/questions to use incorporating different inflections.

Observation

Listen to various individuals in rehearsal and classroom situations. Do they use vocal inflection effectively? After observing others, do you have ideas about how you could improve vocal inflection in your own presentations?

PERSONAL MUSICIANSHIP:
CONNECTING THE BREATH II

For this component, the focus is to:

- Continue practicing connecting diaphragmatic action with breath and sound.
- Sing a melody with limited pitches (s,-t,-d-r-m-f-s) in standard notation.
- Perform chordal accompaniments to a melody using Roman numerals and solfège syllables.

In the module 37, you practiced a warm-up intended to promote diaphragmatic breathing. We will now extend that exercise by incorporating additional vowels.

Place one hand on your chest and the other hand on your stomach. Breathe in deeply through your nose (see the "Smell the Flowers" activity in module 21), and feel your stomach move. As you have learned, the stomach motion indicates that you are engaging the diaphragm. Place both hands on your stomach, and perform full-bodied chuckles, using "ho-ho-ho." Now, begin changing the "ho-ho-ho" to include other vowels, such as "ha-ha-ha," "he-he-he," and so on.

Sing the melody in figure 38.1, and add chordal accompaniment that includes appropriate voice leading. (This will require at least four people to perform all parts, three singing triads and one singing the melody.) Concentrate on using diaphragmatic breathing to support a full-bodied sound.

Irish Folk Song

Figure 38.1 "Aéire Cinn Bó Rúin," standard notation.

PRE-CONDUCTING: PERFORMING CUTOFF GESTURE B WHILE CONDUCTING THE 4/4 PATTERN

This exercise is an extension of the one in module 8 where you developed cutoff indications in the left hand/arm using gesture B without conducting. Now you will conduct the 4/4 pattern while performing this cutoff. You should carefully monitor the movements suggested through self-observation and feedback from other individuals.

Classroom Setup

All class members can complete this exercise simultaneously. Students should stand and allow about one arm's length of space around them. An instructor should initiate each exercise and each step so the class practices as a unit.

Exercise

1. Establish your conducting posture and a tempo of mm = 52.
2. Perform a cutoff on the downbeat in the 4/4 pattern using cutoff gesture B. Conduct two measures of the 4/4 pattern, and on the fourth beat of the second measure, initiate the left-hand cutoff motion, and complete the cutoff on the downbeat.
3. Next, perform the cutoff on the second beat in the 4/4 pattern using cutoff gesture B. Conduct one measure of the 4/4 pattern, and on the downbeat of the second measure, initiate the left-hand cutoff motion, and complete the cutoff on the second beat.
4. Now, perform the cutoff on the third beat in the 4/4 pattern using cutoff gesture B. Conduct one measure of the 4/4 pattern, and on the second beat of the second measure, initiate the left-hand cutoff motion, and complete the cutoff on beat three.
5. Finally, perform the cutoff on the fourth beat in the 4/4 pattern using cutoff gesture B. Conduct one measure of the 4/4 pattern, and on the third beat of the second measure, initiate the left-hand cutoff motion, and complete the cutoff on beat four.

Assignment

Once you feel secure completing the cutoff on different beats in 4/4 meter at this tempo, try performing the cutoff at different tempi.

Observation

Notice the movements your directors and conductors use when indicating cutoffs.

PROFESSIONAL KNOWLEDGE: COLLEGIALITY

For this component, the focus is to:

• Highlight the importance of collegiality within the profession.

In module 2, you examined the importance of forming a community of learners. Here the focus will be on the importance of collegiality in your teaching career. *Collegial* means "relating to or involving shared responsibility, as among a group of colleagues" (*New Oxford American Dictionary*). Colleagues are those individuals with whom you work within your profession. As a member of the community, it is your obligation to participate in school activities and share responsibility for school tasks (e.g., social events, field trips, fundraising, etc.).

"Relationships among educators within a school range from vigorously healthy to dangerously competitive. Strengthen those relationships, and you improve professional practice" (Barth, 2006, p. 8). Barth (2006) noted that positive relationships among the adults in a school influence the school environment and student achievement, whereas relationships that are extremely competitive, destructive, and negative create an environment that reflects those same behaviors. Barth divided professional relationships into four categories: parallel play, adversarial relationships, congenial relationships, and collegial relationships. In order to understand a collegial relationship, we will first briefly touch on the other three categories.

Parallel play is a term associated with Mildred Parten's (1932, 1933) stages of play. She used it to describe how young children play within proximity of one another—or parallel to one another—but do not interact. It's likely that in your past educational experiences, you can think of some teachers who seemed to live in their classrooms. Day after day, they taught *next to* the other teachers in the building rather than teaching *with* them. There was no sense of teamwork, shared interests, or cross-curricular projects.

Adversarial relationships are sometimes blatant, with teachers openly criticizing and showing animosity for one another. There are also adversarial relationships that are more stealthy. They may consist of lunchroom, parking-lot, or grocery-store encounters in which a furtive comment about another teacher may slide into the conversation, such as "Well, if I had a child in this school, I sure wouldn't want him/her in Mr. or Ms. _____'s class."

At this point, you may be thinking that teachers are being portrayed through a rather dismal lens. Luckily, there are schools where individuals work together and enjoy the camaraderie of engaging in an important and fulfilling teaching career. Barth (2006) defines *congenial relationships* as those in which individuals are willing to help one another in a variety of circumstances. This could involve giving someone a ride home when his or her car is being repaired, offering to cover playground duty for a teacher who isn't feeling well, and so on. It can even be as simplistic as bringing an extra cup of coffee in the morning to give to another teacher. It is definitely more enjoyable to go to work when the environment is congenial. The other benefit is that congenial relationships form the foundation for collegiality.

A *collegial relationship* is more elusive and harder to establish. Let's use the analogy of a sports team to assist in our understanding of the difference between congenial and collegial. A professional sports team is filled with great players, and each player has a specific specialty. The coach's role is to get those great players to play together for a common goal, winning the game. Teaching also has great players, each with his or her own specialty (music, math, English, etc.). When those teachers combine energies and work together toward a common goal, they move from congenial to collegial. Barth (2006) provides examples of indicators that teachers are playing together. These indicators may include sharing knowledge and expertise, conversing about teaching, observing one another's classroom, and celebrating professional accomplishments. Roberts (2009) identifies similar indicators and notes, "Collegiality is fostered when teachers believe that their colleagues are interested in their opinions on instructional issues" (p. 55).

You can make the choice to be collegial with your fellow workers. You can also serve as a role model and foster collegial relationships among students in your classroom and rehearsal settings. Sometimes one hears the question "Can't we all just get along?" Let's take it one step further and, in addition to getting along, let's promote working together for a common goal, ensuring that all students are learning and growing in our classrooms.

Discussion

1. How can you promote a collegial environment with your current peers?
2. Provide an instance where you noted a congenial and/or collegial atmosphere in one of your ensemble rehearsals.
3. What choices will you make if you find yourself teaching in an adversarial environment?
4. What teachers have you observed in the past few weeks engaging in collegial conversation or dialogue? Why would you define it as collegial?

MODULE 38 REFERENCES

Barth, R. S. (2006). Improving relationships within the schoolhouse. *Educational Leadership, 63*(6), 8–13.

Parten, M. (1932). Social participation among preschool children. *Journal of Abnormal and Social Psychology, 27*, 243–269.

Parten, M. (1933). Social play among preschool children. *Journal of Abnormal and Social Psychology, 28*, 136–147.

Roberts, S. M. (2009). *Schools as professional learning communities: Collaborative activities and strategies for professional development.* Thousand Oaks, CA: Corwin.

Combining Verbal and Nonverbal Elements—Moving toward Artistry—Cutoff Gesture in 4/4—Formulating a Philosophy of Music

In this module, you will focus on:

- Personal awareness: Combining verbal and nonverbal elements in a two-minute speech.
- Personal musicianship: Moving toward artistry.
- Pre-conducting: Performing a cutoff gesture while conducting the 4/4 pattern.
- Professional knowledge: Formulating your philosophy of music.

PERSONAL AWARENESS: COMBINING VERBAL AND NONVERBAL—THE TWO-MINUTE SPEECH

Here you will have the opportunity to combine all the verbal and nonverbal elements you've experienced in the personal awareness component exercises. These exercises included body stance, eye contact, walking, facial expression, visual scanning, combining visual and facial gestures, facial and body gesture awareness, proximity and nonverbal gestures, nonverbal music directives, vocal projection and dynamic use, vocal enunciation and articulation, use of pauses, rate of speech, vocal emotion, and vocal inflection.

You will now present a two-minute speech in which you use all these elements during your delivery. You must plan your two-minute speech carefully and choreograph the nonverbal elements such as gestures, proximity, movement, and so on, along with your verbal presentation elements such as inflection, projection, enunciation and articulation, and so on.

The following is a template of a two-minute speech that can be modified as deemed appropriate. You may also construct your own speech; however, remember to keep it to a two-minute maximum. The speech template assumes that you are new to a school or program and are introducing yourself to a meeting of students and parents, who are members of your musical organization. It is assumed that you will have your two-minute speech memorized and that you will not need a microphone, lectern, notes, or any other equipment or materials that would impede your gesturing, movement about the room, and so on. In the template are "asides," which appear in brackets and which indicate the possibility of a movement, gesture, vocal inflection, and so on. Suggested keywords are italicized as possible indicators for an action. And while there are "specified suggestions," consider them suggestions only, not requirements for action. When planning your speech, remember to choreograph your movements with gestures and to practice inflection, dynamic variation, speech rate changes, and so on.

Two-Minute Speech Template

Welcome! [pause and begin scanning the audience immediately after the word "welcome," continuing the scanning until the end of the next sentence]

Thank you for attending (orchestra, choir, band, etc.) *night.*

I [make a gesture indicating self]

am your new [use vocal inflection on the word "new," followed by a pause]

musical director, [slow your speech rate, and enunciate/articulate very clearly at this point so all clearly hear and understand your name]

Mr./Mrs./Ms./Dr. _____.

It is a pleasure [use vocal inflection and facial expression on the word "pleasure," followed by a brief pause] *seeing all* [on the word "seeing," begin an eye scan, and on the word "all," use a casual two-handed sideways gesture, as if conducting a crescendo; a brief pause may be needed after the word "all" to complete the gesture]

of you here tonight. [a smiling, open facial gesture could be used after the word "tonight"]

Each of you [take a brief pause, and begin a change of proximity by moving toward the audience, looking at them while making eye contact and gesturing with an open backhand "bounce" movement, as you move in front of the audience; this action continues through the end of the sentence and longer if needed to move across the audience]

is about to embark and continue on a renewed [pause, and change inflection on the word "renewed"; begin a slow eye scan of the group, making direct eye contact of individuals as you begin this phrase; the eye scan should continue until the statement is finished with the words "learning adventure this year," below]

and possibly new [pause, and change inflection on the word "new"; continue the eye scan]

learning adventure this year. [a longer pause after the word "year" will help set off the next statement; the eye scan of the audience should conclude when finishing this phrase]

If you are a member of the (orchestra, choir, band, etc.), [pause after the organization is identified; a gesture using the back of the hand that "pans" the audience, combined with eye contact and a change of body proximity (turning toward the audience as if you were panning with your body), could be completed after the word "you"]

you will, in addition to all of the wonderful concerts you perform this year, have what is perhaps a once-in-a-lifetime adventure. [to be said with brief pauses after each of the commas; practice different inflections and emphases for this phrase, but place a strong emphasis on the word "perhaps," followed by a pause and then a slowing of tempo, with great clarity, inflection, and emphasis on the words that follow, "a once-in-a-lifetime adventure"; practice using facial, hand/arm, and/or body gestures that you deem appropriate while saying this phrase]

And that once-in-a-lifetime adventure? [use animated facial expression, making certain you are ending with a strong questioning tone; after the word "adventure," stop speaking, and perform a slow scan of the audience]

We've all been invited— [emphasis and a long pause after the word "all," followed by a clear, slow articulation of the words "been invited"; pause for the dash]

yes, all of the groups— [lower your dynamic level as much as possible (*pp*) and still be heard beginning on the word "yes," and maintain that dynamic throughout this phrase; pause for the comma; emphasis on the word "all," with good clarity, diction, articulation, and separation on the words "of the groups," followed by a pause for the dash; a change of proximity and facial expression can be used during this phrase]

we've all been invited to perform at the presidential inaugural celebration at the White House! [having started as quietly as possible on the previous phrase, begin to crescendo to the end of the phrase, ending on as loud a dynamic as you feel comfortable performing on the words "White House"; emphasis should again be placed on the word "all," with a slowing of tempo initiated as you crescendo and clearly articulate each word that follows; practice different inflections and pacing between/within words; pause after the exclamation point]

And this isn't all! [place emphasis and inflection on the word "this," followed by a brief pause and then great emphasis on the word "isn't" (which should be said slowly) and equally strong emphasis, followed by a long pause after the word "all"]

The trip, the hotels, the food, the museum tickets . . . [complete a brief pause with emphasis after the words "trip," "hotels," "food," and a grand pause after the word "tickets"; a scan of the audience should be completed as this phrase is spoken]

everything . . . [the word "everything" should be said slowly, with strong emphasis and inflection and a pause after the word]

is being completely funded by an anonymous supporter! [the words "completely" and "funded" should both be spoken slowly, with great emphasis, clear articulation, and excellent projection]

Yes, everything! [place emphasis on the word "yes," and follow it with a slight pause; insert a long pause with emphasis after "everything!"]

And (orchestra, band, choir, etc.) parents, [pause after the comma]

if you've ever wanted to get in front of a group and conduct, [place heavy emphasis on the word "ever"; slowly and clearly say "wanted to get," followed by a brief pause; slowly and clearly say "in front of a group," followed by another pause, followed by the word "and," with another pause before saying "conduct"; follow the word "conduct" with a long pause, and insert a conducting 4/4 pattern as a gesture during the pause] *this may be your chance to do so.* [place heavy emphasis on the word "this," followed by a moderate pause; group the words "may be your chance," followed by another pause, and the words "to do so" should be separated and spoken slowly; experiment with different vocal inflections on these two word groups; an eye scan of the audience would also be appropriate]

Several lucky winners will have the opportunity to [place emphasis on the word "several," followed by a brief pause; group the words "lucky winners" with heavy vocal inflection on both words; group the words "will have," followed by a slight pause, and then group the words "the opportunity to," followed by a slight pause]

conduct, one of our ensembles, [you could gesture a conducting pattern throughout this phrase; pause after each comma; begin to increase your volume (crescendo) starting with the word "conduct" and ending on the words "in concert!" below]

in concert! ["in concert" should be said with great excitement and enthusiasm, with significant separation between the two words; finish the crescendo]

So, as you have heard, [pauses after each comma]

a wonderful and exciting musical year has been planned. [emphasis on the words "wonderful" and "exciting," with a pause after each of those two words; group the words "musical year" and "has been planned"; decrease the speech rate significantly on the words "has been planned"]

I hope you will enjoy the (orchestral, band, choral, etc.) activities [gesture to the audience, and initiate an eye scan as you begin this sentence; pause slightly after each grouping of words presented]

as much as I [continue gesturing to the audience and completing your eye scan; again, pause slightly after this grouping of words; add any vocal inflection you feel appropriate]

will enjoy bringing them to you. [finish gesturing, scanning the audience; pause after finishing the sentence; add any vocal inflection you feel appropriate]

It is an honor being your new (orchestra, band, choir, etc.) director. [pause after the word "honor"; group the words "being your new" and "(orchestra, band, choir, etc.) director"]

Thank you! [separate the two words with heavy inflection and clarity, adding appropriate facial and body gestures]

Here is the two-minute speech template without asides but presented with suggested grouping/phrasing.

Welcome!
Thank you for attending (orchestra, choir, band, etc.) night.
I
am your new
musical director,
Mr./Mrs./Ms./Dr. _____.
It is a pleasure
seeing all
of you here tonight.
Each of you
is about to embark and continue on a renewed
and possibly new
learning adventure this year.
If you are a member of the (orchestra or choir or band, etc.),
you will, in addition to all of the wonderful concerts you perform this
     year, have, what is perhaps a once-in-a-lifetime adventure.
And that once-in-a-lifetime adventure?
We've all been invited—
yes, all of the groups—
we've all been invited to perform at the presidential inaugural celebra-
     tion at the White House!
And this isn't all!
The trip, the hotels, the food, the museum tickets . . .
everything . . .
is being completely funded by an anonymous supporter!
Yes, everything!
And (orchestra, band, choir, etc.) parents,
if you've ever wanted to get in front of a group and conduct,
this may be your chance to do so.
Several lucky winners will have the opportunity to
conduct, one of our ensembles,
in concert!
So, as you have heard,
a wonderful and exciting musical year has been planned.
I hope you will enjoy the (orchestral, band, choral, etc.) activities
as much as I
will enjoy bringing them to you.
It is an honor being your new (orchestra, band, choir, etc.) director.
Thank you!

PERSONAL MUSICIANSHIP: MOVING TOWARD ARTISTRY I

For this component, the focus is to:

- Define artistry.
- Sing a melody with limited pitches (t,-d-r-m-f-s-l-t-d') in stick notation.
- Perform chordal accompaniments to a melody using solfège syllables.

Artistry is defined as "creative skill or ability" (*New Oxford American Dictionary*). Throughout your music career, you will constantly hone your creative skills and musical abilities. Teaching, although it is a learned craft, is also an art form. Consider yourself a "teaching artist," and with artistry in mind, engage in the following small-group activity.

Small-Group Activity

1. Divide the class into groups of four or five students.
2. Each group determines one suggestion for performing the melody in figure 39.1 with "artistry." It might help to think of the melody as one of your performance pieces for an upcoming concert. Are there dynamic changes to incorporate? Tempo variances, stylistic suggestions, etc.?
3. Perform the melody using the suggestion posed by one group. Then perform the melody using the suggestion posed by another group. (Each time the melody is performed, you will only incorporate one artistic suggestion.)

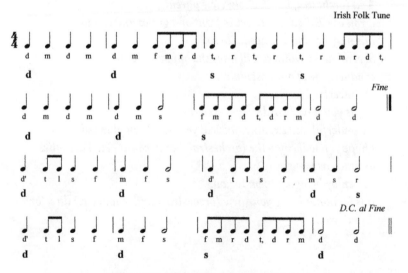

Figure 39.1 "Galway Piper," stick notation.

PRE-CONDUCTING: PERFORMING CUTOFF GESTURE C WHILE CONDUCTING THE 4/4 PATTERN

This exercise is an extension of the one in module 8 where you developed cutoff indications in the left hand/arm using gesture C without conducting. Now you will conduct the 4/4 pattern while performing this cutoff. You should carefully monitor the movements suggested through self-observation and feedback from other individuals.

Classroom Setup

All class members can complete this exercise simultaneously. Students should stand and allow about one arm's length of space around them. An instructor should initiate each exercise and each step so the class practices as a unit.

Exercise

1. Establish your conducting posture and a tempo of mm = 52.
2. Perform a cutoff on the downbeat in the 4/4 pattern using cutoff gesture C. Conduct two measures of the 4/4 pattern, and on the fourth beat of the second measure, initiate the left-hand cutoff motion, and complete the cutoff on the downbeat.
3. Next, perform the cutoff on the second beat in the 4/4 pattern using cutoff gesture C. Conduct one measure of the 4/4 pattern, and on the downbeat of the second measure, initiate the left-hand cutoff motion, and complete the cutoff on the second beat.
4. Now, perform the cutoff on the third beat in the 4/4 pattern using cutoff gesture C. Conduct one measure of the 4/4 pattern, and on the second beat of the second measure, initiate the left-hand cutoff motion, and complete the cutoff on the beat three.
5. Finally, perform the cutoff on the fourth beat in the 4/4 pattern using cutoff gesture C. Conduct one measure of the 4/4 pattern, and on the third beat of the second measure, initiate the left-hand cutoff motion, and complete the cutoff on beat four.

Assignment

Once you feel secure completing the cutoff on different beats in 4/4 meter at this tempo, try performing the cutoff at different tempi.

Observation

Notice the movements your directors and conductors use when indicating cutoffs.

PROFESSIONAL KNOWLEDGE: FORMULATING YOUR PHILOSOPHY OF MUSIC

For this component, the focus is to:

- Begin formulating your philosophy of music.

Philosophy can be defined in different ways: one is as "the study of the theoretical basis of a particular branch of knowledge or experience" (e.g., the philosophy of music); another is as "a theory or attitude held by a person or organization that acts as a guiding principle for behavior" (e.g., "I believe all individuals should have the opportunity to study music") (*Oxford New American Dictionary*).

This textbook has been designed to encourage your personal, musical, and professional growth. In addition, the modules have been preparing you to write your philosophy of music. In module 22, you practiced advocating for music education, and in module 23, you were asked to make meaningful transfers to music and music education using quotes on topics other than music. We all function by an inner philosophy, although it may not always be a conscious process. Our beliefs, values, personal backgrounds, and interest in music are the philosophy by which we function.

Writer and philosopher Iris Murdoch expressed the belief that philosophy, in a sense, always is attempting "to return to the beginning" (quoted in Broackes, 2014, p. 82). She suggested that examining your philosophy provides a time for you to reflect on what you value and hold dear; and if you have veered from your pathway, the reflection will provide an opportunity to return to your intended route.

Why are you asked to formulate a philosophy of music? It demonstrates your understanding of music's role in the development of individuals. The ability to articulate your philosophy of music is yet one more preparation for entering the teaching profession. The journey toward your music philosophy begins with reflection. What do you value, and why do you value it? Be assured, this is not an easy journey and the answers may be difficult to articulate. "Philosophy can be a maddening process for people who want complete answers" (Allsup, 2010, p. 56).

The following questions might help you begin framing your ideas:

1. Why is music important? What is its role/value in society?
2. Why is education important? What is its role/value in society?
3. Why is music education important? What is its role/value in society?

Your philosophy should reflect your experience as a musician and your thinking as a teacher. Remember, your philosophy is developing, is in a constant state of flux, and is a lifelong process. It should be revisited, and often, throughout your professional career.

Discussion

1. When did you know you wanted to major in music?
2. Think of your most effective music teacher.
   a. How did he or she demonstrate a personal philosophy of music education in the classroom?
   b. What did he or she value about music education and learning? How do you know?
3. Why do you think music education should be taught in the public schools?
4. Do you think all public school students should take music classes or only those who are interested?

Assignment

Bring your philosophy of music to the next class session, typed up on no more than one or two pages. Distilling your philosophy to one page of approximately four paragraphs is preferred.

MODULE 39 REFERENCES

Allsup, R. E. 2010. "Philosophical perspectives of music education." In H. F. Abeles & L. A. Custodero (Eds.), *Critical issues in music education: Contemporary theory and practice*. New York, NY: Oxford University Press.
Broackes, J. 2014. *Iris Murdoch, philosopher*. New York, NY: Oxford University Press.

SUGGESTED READING

Tutt, K., & Townley, M. (2011). Philosophy + advocacy = success. *Music Educators Journal*, 97(4), 60–63.

Verbal and Nonverbal Elements in a Speech—Defining Artistry—Cutoff Gestures in Various Meters—A Successful Music Education Career

I n this module, you will focus on:

- Personal awareness: The continuation of combining verbal and nonverbal elements in a two-minute speech.
- Personal musicianship: The definition of artistry.
- Pre-conducting: Performing cutoff gestures while conducting the 3/4 and 2/4 patterns.
- Professional knowledge: Formulating a recipe for a successful music education career.

PERSONAL AWARENESS: COMBINING VERBAL AND NONVERBAL—THE TWO-MINUTE SPEECH

Continue working on the personal awareness component in module 39, where you had the opportunity to combine all the elements of the verbal and nonverbal exercises you've experienced.

PERSONAL MUSICIANSHIP: MOVING TOWARD ARTISTRY II

For this component, the focus is to:

- Review the definition of artistry.
- Sing a melody with limited pitches (t,-d-r-m-f-s-l-t-d') in stick notation.
- Perform chordal accompaniments to a melody using Roman numerals and solfège syllables.

In module 39, the definition of *artistry* was provided. Turn to a partner or neighbor, define the term, and explain how one can incorporate artistry into basic vocal warm-ups and folk melodies. Using the group activity from module 39 as a starting point, you will now combine the artistic suggestions of your classmates into a final performance.

Small-Group Activity

1. Divide the class into groups of four or five students.
2. Each group determines one suggestion for performing the melody in figure 40.1 with "artistry." (Refer to module 39 for possible options.)
3. Write each suggestion on the board for easy reference.
4. As a class, determine how to combine *all* suggestions into a final performance. Perhaps you will repeat the melody and incorporate a dynamic contrast during the repeat. Perhaps you will create an introduction and/or coda using your knowledge of triads and chordal accompaniments. And so on.
5. Perform, and embrace your musicianship and artistry.

Figure 40.1 "Galway Piper," standard notation.

PRE-CONDUCTING: PERFORMING CUTOFF GESTURES A, B, AND C WHILE CONDUCTING THE 3/4 AND 2/4 PATTERNS

This exercise is an extension of the ones in modules 8 and 9 where you developed cutoff indications in the left hand/arm using gestures A, B, and C. However, in those components, you did not conduct a 3/4 or 2/4 pattern while completing the cutoff gestures. You will now conduct the 3/4 and 2/4 patterns while performing all three cutoff patterns. You should carefully monitor the movements suggested through self-observation and feedback from other individuals.

Classroom Setup

All class members can complete exercise simultaneously. Students should stand and allow one arm's length of space around them. An instructor should initiate each exercise and each step so the class practices as a unit.

Exercise

1. Gesture A begins at the right shoulder, gesture B begins at the waist and extends forward to shoulder height and back, and gesture C begins at the waist and then moves horizontally.
2. Establish your conducting posture, and begin conducting a 3/4 pattern using a tempo of mm = 52.
3. Perform a cutoff on the downbeat in the 3/4 pattern using gesture A, then B, then C.
4. Perform a cutoff on the second beat in the 3/4 pattern using gesture A, then B, then C.
5. Perform a cutoff on the third beat in the 3/4 pattern using gesture A, then B, then C.
6. Begin conducting a 2/4 pattern using a tempo of mm = 52.
7. Perform a cutoff on the downbeat in the 2/4 pattern using gesture A, then B, then C.
8. Perform a cutoff on the second beat in the 2/4 pattern using gesture A, then B, then C.

Assignment

Once you feel secure completing the cutoff on different beats, try performing the cutoff using different tempi.

Observation

Notice the movements your directors and conductors use when indicating cutoffs.

PROFESSIONAL KNOWLEDGE: RECIPE FOR A SUCCESSFUL MUSIC EDUCATION CAREER

For this component, the focus is to:

- Begin formulating your individual recipe for a successful music education career.

> This is my invariable advice to people: Learn how to cook—try new recipes, learn from your mistakes, be fearless, and above all have fun! (Child, 2007)

Within this book, you have spent time reading about aspects of music education, enhancing your own personal musicianship, reflecting on effective classroom teaching, and heightening your awareness of messages conveyed through facial expressions and nonverbal gestures. Every classroom of children and teachers is unique; teachers will organize their classrooms in a variety of ways and will make personal choices regarding warm-ups and repertoire selections. "Good teaching comes not from following a recipe, but from consistently putting student needs first" (Christenbury, 2011, p. 47).

Think of two of your favorite restaurants. If you ordered the same dish from both eating establishments, would they taste identical? In all likelihood, there would be similarities but also some small twists in recipes that set them apart from each other. It is now your opportunity to formulate your recipe for a successful music education career. What ingredients do you need to bring to the kitchen? What ingredients do your students need to bring? What do you need from colleagues and community members? What are the appropriate measurements for the ingredients? What is the order for mixing the ingredients? How long should the ingredients cook? How should the recipe be served to appeal to all members of the music community?

Assignment

Use the recipe card template in figure 40.2 to help you prepare your dish. As Julia Child suggests, "try new recipes, learn from your mistakes, be fearless, and above all [definitely] have fun!" Happy cooking and *bon appétit*.

Recipe for Successful Music Education	
1 Tb	1Tb.
1 c.	1 c.
1 tsp.	4 c.
½ tsp.	2-4 years
Mix together:	
Add:	
Bake	Temperature:
Serve:	

Figure 40.2 Recipe card template.

MODULE 40 REFERENCES

Child, J. (2007). *My life in France* (reprint). New York, NY: Anchor.
Christenbury, L. (2011). The flexible teacher. *Educational Leadership, 68*(4), 46–50.

INDEX

CPSIA information can be obtained
at www.ICGtesting.com
Printed in the USA
BVHW032028271119
564848BV00005B/178/P

9 780190 245085